DEATH TO JUSTICE

THE SHOOTING OF LEE HARVEY OSWALD

Paul Abbott

Copyright © 2025 by Paul Abbott. All rights reserved.

No part of this book may be reproduced
in any form without permission from the publisher or author,
except as permitted by international copyright law.

Book Cover by: Peter Andrews

Hardback Edition 2025

To Sara, Charlotte & Sophie… always.

And to those who never stopped for truth's sake.

Contents

FOREWORD BY PAUL BLEAU..i
PREFACE iv
INTRODUCTION vi
CHAPTER ONE - ON THE SURFACE...1
CHAPTER TWO - LEE HARVEY OSWALD......................................11
CHAPTER THREE - DID HE? OR DIDN'T HE? 28
INTERLUDE - INMATE 54018 45
CHAPTER FOUR - THE FIRST SHOOTING ON LIVE TELEVISION 48
CHAPTER FIVE - AFTERMATH 60
CHAPTER SIX - PREPARATIONS..79
CHAPTER SEVEN - CIVILIIANS OVERLOOKED 94
CHAPTER EIGHT - MEDIA... 107
CHAPTER NINE - POLICE 150
CHAPTER TEN - COUNTDOWN...171
CHAPTER ELEVEN - SHOOTING 187
CHAPTER TWELVE- SHOOTER..220
CHAPTER THIRTEEN - RUBY ON TRIAL.....................................263
CHAPTER FOURTEEN - CONSOLIDATION 281
CHAPTER FIFTEEN - SUSTAINED SPECULATION 297
CHAPTER SIXTEEN - CONCLUSION..332
ACKNOWLEDGEMENTS..338
REFERENCES 341
APPENDICES..350
INDEX..390

FOREWORD

By Paul Bleau

Paul Abbott and I live at opposite ends of the world - he in Australia and I in Canada. We got to know one another because of the Garrison Files. After reading some ten thousand pages of these, I knew that hidden away in this collection, there were gems that were not on the radar when it came to analyzing the JFK assassination. Just one example is how Garrison was on the trail of Latinos, with likely links to Guy Banister, who frequently escorted Oswald.

I knew that if others went through these, they could pick up on clues I may have missed. Paul reached out and provided the community with a research booster that is an archive asset of great value: the Garrison Files Master Index. Garrison's unfairly dismissed primary research can now be referenced with ease digitally by info ferrets. It took Paul over a year to build the index, and he deserves our thanks.

So, when Paul asked me to write a foreword for his book, I felt an obligation to do so. This was risky, in a way, as I refuse to plug material of mediocre quality. What if I did not like it?

You have guessed by now that I like this book... a lot. Thousands of books have been written about the Kennedy assassination. A few classics have been written about the Tippit murder, which is often covered in more JFK-focused writings. Question to the reader: What do you know about the other murder of that weekend? In my case, it was not much. Yet it, as much as the JFK murder, has all the fingerprints of a conspiracy. It matches the

JFK assassination when it comes to poor security. The elimination of Oswald sealed the lips of the most important witness. The shooter likely had assistance to get to the victim and was clearly mob-linked.

There are many ways one can zero in on the leaders of the JFK assassination conspiracy; Work your way up the ladder around the equally suspicious prior plots to kill JFK; Find out who pulled strings with the media ineptness and the botched autopsy or the Warren Commission charade; Solve the Rosselli, Giancana murders; Figure out who Cubanized Oswald and organized his impersonations… There is a good chance that we will draw vectors pointing in the same direction to the string pullers.

Ask yourself who organized the removal of the witness who, with his life on the line, could have revealed everything we have painstakingly come to know, suspect about him and his associations and obviously those who conspired to kill Kennedy would be the prime suspects. Yet what do we really know about this crime. Certainly, the Warren Commission's lame explanation around a series of unfortunate mishaps that led to his unfortunate death should carry even less weight than their impeached whitewash of the JFK assassination. I mean really, two misguided lone nuts… Give me a break!

Who were the witnesses? What did they say? What was the series of events that led this obvious ruse to obstruct justice? How could this murder have been carried out? Who are the persons of interest? This book delves into all of this and a lot more. Factually, brilliantly and clearly!

It is amazing how one Australian on the opposite end of the planet from Dallas can say ten times more about this murder than the FBI, CIA, Warren Commission and Dallas Police Department combined.

The man who gave us the master index to the Garrison files has now provided us with the all-defining book around the unsolved murder of the most important witness of the twentieth century, which will stand as the go-to reference on the most ignored murder of that infamous weekend in November 1963 in Dallas and shed light coming from an ignored source on the mother of all conspiracies.

Paul Bleau holds an MBA from McGill University, Montreal, Canada. With over 25 years' experience as a strategic planner on national accounts, Paul eventually took ownership of and presided over Bleau Marketing Communications. He co-founded Harmonia in 2006 which has grown to become a leading commemorative services provider in the Quebec Market. Paul has also sat on many boards. He now is in his eighteenth year as a teacher in the P. W. Sims Business Program at Champlain St. Lawrence College. Presently a CAPA member, he has a long track record of research and writing about the JFK assassination which includes appearing in Oliver Stone's documentary JFK Revisited: Through the Looking Glass, writing numerous articles for KennedysandKing.com, and speaking regularly as a guest on BlackOp Radio and on other podcasts.

PREFACE

A note to the reader - the assassination of President John F. Kennedy has been the subject of hundreds of books. In most, there is minimal reference to the murder of his alleged killer, Lee Harvey Oswald. Therefore, it is the purpose of this book to flip this ratio by mostly focusing on Oswald's shooting and referring to the Kennedy assassination for context. In this book, we will go into a greater level of detail regarding the events surrounding and during Oswald's murder than ever before.

The journey started in April 2022, whether I knew it then or not, when I undertook the simple, yet mammoth, task of organising and creating an index of names and topics contained within a batch of folders that belonged to former New Orleans District Attorney, Jim Garrison. They are accessible on the internet but I had sourced them from Len Osanic of BlackOp Radio. From them, in October 2023 I published an index as an excel spreadsheet that consists of approximately 40,000 lines of names with columns to sort them by date and broad context to assist any researcher. This is available at blackopradio.net[1] and kennedysandking.com.[2]

The story goes that the folders had been saved from being destroyed by Garrison's successor, Harry Connick. Yet they were too important to be lost to history because Jim Garrison remains as the only person responsible for bringing a person to trial for the assassination of President John F. Kennedy. The man was CIA-linked New Orleans businessman Clay Shaw and history shows that he would be acquitted of all charges. Scholars of the JFK assassination case will be familiar with the fact that Garrison's case had become increasingly weakened the closer it got to trial in early 1969. Some key witnesses died suddenly, some refused to testify and the investigation itself had been infiltrated by saboteurs on behalf of entities such as the mainstream media and the federal government. While Shaw was found not guilty of any involvement in the Kennedy assassination, what the Garrison case did was cast a light on the topic that has remained ever since. Consequently, there is a wealth of information on the summer of 1963 in New Orleans and how it relates to President Kennedy's eventual assassination in Dallas that November.

Contained within the Garrison folders is a vast number of clippings, book excerpts and reports on many other topics not just related to the Kennedy assassination so, in the end, there were 180 folders and approximately 13,000 pages to manually scan and collect names for the index. However, it was the file that contained the Dallas Police Department's (DPD) investigation into the transfer and subsequent shooting of alleged Kennedy assassin, Lee Harvey Oswald that I really stopped to scrutinise. In short, the DPD investigation was tokenistic and cursory so reading through it made it very clear to me how little has been focused on the death of Oswald, therefore uncovered.

With the same level of open-mindedness, patience, and painstaking attention to detail that I used to index the Garrison folders; I began an intensive investigation into of one of the most under-focused aspects of President Kennedy's assassination – the shooting of his alleged assassin Lee Oswald. My findings are laid out in this book.

INTRODUCTION

The assassination of United States President John F. Kennedy on November 22nd, 1963, in Dallas, Texas is a defining moment in modern world history. The leader of the most powerful country in the world shot and killed in public while riding with his wife, Jacqueline, in a motorcade on home soil in broad daylight.

President Kennedy was the symbol of a new era of progress and prosperity that was extinguished in the most sudden, brutal, and shocking manner. Kennedy's death and its implications on world events continue to fuel rigorous debate. From a global and domestic standpoint, what would or would not have happened had he'd not been killed and therefore, in all probability, served a second term as U.S. President. For example:

- Would the conflict in Vietnam have continued to escalate?
- What would have come from Kennedy's support of emerging Third World countries including Congo, Ghana, and Indonesia?
- Would the Middle East have stabilised because of Kennedy's overall stance of respecting other countries' sovereignty?
- And would détente with Cuba have been the first step to ending the Cold War?

These questions and so many more from a domestic policy viewpoint, particularly civil rights, for which Kennedy was also impactful on, are important because all still have clear ramifications on the world we live in today. Detailed insight and contentions on these topics and more have been thoroughly presented by historians and researchers such as Peter Dale Scott, James Douglass, John Newman, Larry Hancock, Aaron Good and James DiEugenio to name a few.

More immediately, the weekend of Kennedy's assassination was filled with historic and defining images and moments that few alive at the time could forget. For instance:
- The non-stop television coverage of the events in Dallas that started with panicked interruption to regular programming and included Walter Cronkite's stoic announcement of the president's death.
- The murder of Dallas Police Officer J.D. Tippit barely an hour after that of the president.
- The image of Jacqueline Kennedy, stained with the blood of her husband, standing next to Lyndon Johnson as he was being sworn in as U.S. President on Air Force One.
- Robert F. Kennedy helping Jacqueline off Air Force One at Andrews Air Force Base later that evening.
- Witness testimony from those in Dealey Plaza about the assassination.

Amongst the chaos of that weekend was the arrest and incarceration of local man, Lee Harvey Oswald, in connection to the Kennedy and Tippit killings. With the gravity of the event, the advent of news media and a close relationship with the police, members of the press were permitted to fill the halls of Dallas' City Hall to capture every single public movement and utterance made by and about Oswald. Photographs and footage of a scuffed-up Oswald being led between offices through the throng of media helped fill the tapestry of chaos, shock, and unprecedented nature of the weekend. Adding to this was perhaps one of the most surprising aspects of Oswald's period in Dallas Police custody – his being brought before the media and having questions barked at him to answer, essentially, in the format of a press conference. It typifies how life was distorted beyond all recognition during the weekend of President Kennedy's assassination particularly when also considering how Oswald himself would be shot on live television before fifty million viewers that Sunday morning.

'Death to Justice – The Shooting of Lee Harvey Oswald' provides a careful and evidence-based analysis of all aspects of the shooting of Lee Oswald including the investigations into it. Because at any other time, the killing of a person while handcuffed and defenseless in police custody would shock the public and demand attention and scrutiny for answers on how and why it could happen – let alone on live television. One only need recall the 2020 death of George Floyd while he was detained by police in handcuffs and the uproar it rightly caused.

But given the significance and shock of President Kennedy's murder barely forty-eight hours earlier and the subsequent distraction and numbing of the public's senses from its round-the-clock coverage, the shooting of Lee Oswald became an alarming but macabrely apt bookend for the horror of that weekend. There was no discernable consequence for the Dallas Police Department letting it happen on their watch either. Yet it is still largely regarded as one of the more 'open and shut' aspects of that weekend and indeed the assassination of President Kennedy. But as this book will prove, the case is anything but.

It is true that the shooting of Oswald was captured by still photography and film and took place in front of dozens of witnesses. However, when all visual records are examined alongside each other and with the testimony of those present, there are alarming inconsistencies and discrepancies which have lain largely overlooked ever since but clearly present some startling possibilities.

On the weight of its significance, the killing of Oswald should be considered as suspicious and unresolved as those of Officer J.D. Tippit and President Kennedy. Each remains so open for speculation due to clear anomalies between what was established as happening by investigative authorities and the obliging media of the day verses witness testimony, available evidence and proof.* And with the effective sealing of remaining classified records regarding the Kennedy assassination, all three cases remain vulnerable to eternally languishing in the middle of a veritable 'Bermuda Triangle' of evidence, discrepancies, and the official narrative. However, sensible, and fact-based scholars of the assassination of John F. Kennedy will know that to understand the *how* and *why* his murder took place is to consider it as though it were an onion - something with multiple layers that is far from being linear and is not as it seems at first glance.

---

*Evidence is defined as anything that asserts or demonstrates a possibility or conclusion. Proof is defined as something that uses evidence and facts to prove something is true.

With that perspective, the high-stakes nature of silencing Oswald in such a drastic fashion could lend a new and important glimpse into the desperation, ruthlessness, and resourcefulness of those ultimately responsible for the carnage of that weekend.

Why else is uncovering the murder of Lee Oswald important some sixty years after the event? Perhaps the people most overlooked in the entire Kennedy assassination cannon are Oswald's family. He no doubt allowed himself to be mixed up in some very complex business and nefarious people so he was far from a saint but with his life cut so short, they never had closure for him for anything related to the Kennedy and Tippit killings. Do they not deserve to have as much of the truth as possible?

Lee Oswald's murder is a unique case for many reasons but particularly due to how little was done to properly investigate it at the time. And compared to other aspects of the Kennedy assassination, little has been done since.

So, because there is such limited source material to scrutinise it with, the opportunity is there to really drill down into the minutiae of the case and bring it all out into the light in a logical and sensible fashion. This means it need not remain relegated as a subject worthy of only a few pages in even the most exhaustive of works focused on the assassination of President Kennedy anymore. There is and always has been so much more to it than meets the eye. Therefore, it should not just be fodder that only fringe elements of the JFK Assassination research community dare focus on. It should be given its own regard as another key element of the assassination of President Kennedy worthy of its own field of research.

In writing this book, my intent is to elevate the murder of Lee Harvey Oswald to a subject warranting its own field of interest. To ensure it is accessible to people of all knowledge levels regarding President Kennedy's assassination, I have structured it with layers of context so those who have only ever had a passing interest in the topic can gain as much from it as the most ardent of scholars. And with that, another aspect of the Kennedy assassination that has largely been underestimated and seen as a haven of at least some clear-cut understanding in the case can actually be brought out into the light and be given its due scrutiny.

Because as long as questions continue to be asked, evidence is sensibly analysed and answers sought, scrutiny of the events that weekend in Dallas will remain alive and ensure the responsible perpetrators somehow remain on the hook of the truth.

PART ONE

INFAMY

CHAPTER ONE

ON THE SURFACE

November 20th, 1963 marked the one-year anniversary for two actions of President Kennedy that perhaps best contribute overall to his legacy. On that day in 1962, Kennedy provided a significant win for the civil rights movement by signing Executive Order 11063 into effect to prohibit racial discrimination against current and future tenants of federally funded buildings.[1] That same day, Kennedy also declared that there would be peace in the Caribbean 'if all offensive weapons are removed from Cuba and kept out of the hemisphere in the future' and that Cuba is not used for 'furthering Communist purposes.'[2]

1963 was arguably the most productive and successful year of the Kennedy presidency. Having adroitly avoided direct confrontation with the Soviets over their housing of intercontinental ballistic missiles in neighbouring Cuba in October '62, President Kennedy's status as a true statesman had only continued to surge domestically and globally. His re-election prospects, against the looming hard-hitting conservative Barry Goldwater, were growing stronger.

November 20th, 1963, now saw Kennedy preparing to make a political 'fence-mending' trip to Texas. Too early to be considered part of his '64 re-election campaign, the trip would still be made with that in mind while addressing the 'Texas political situation' that consisted of bitter in-fighting between key Texan Democrat party members, Texas Governor John B. Connally and Senator Ralph Yarborough. Texas was far from a secure state that Kennedy could rely on to re-elect him so, with no help from his Vice President and Texan-native, Lyndon B. Johnson and his inability to handle the matter himself, the decision was made - Kennedy would need to take a tour of Texas to symbolise Democratic party unity. It was still not something he was looking forward to. But when dining with leaders of the congress on the morning of November 20th, according to William Manchester's 'Death of a President', Kennedy said that 'things always look so much better away from Washington'. Having his wife, Jacqueline, accompanying him would also provide a silver lining to the trip.[3]

The next day, the presidential party flew to Texas to, firstly, attend a dedication ceremony at the Aerospace Medical Center in San Antonio and, later, a testimonial dinner for Representative Albert Thomas in Houston. Kennedy was warmly received by large crowds at all events and during motorcades in both cities. The question was, how would he be received in the increasingly more volatile and right-wing city of Dallas* the next day?

---

*Despite being completely landlocked and devoid of any geographical features or advantages such as mountain ranges or expansive rivers that most cities are formed around, Dallas endured years of hardship through devastating floods to become incorporated in 1856. To overcome its disadvantages, Dallas fully committed to establishing rail infrastructure that would link it to the rest of the state and country. This, with the emergence of the oil industry, boosted the local economy with investment and activity that would see it expand to road infrastructure with the advent of the automobile. Overcoming the ever-present risk of becoming yet another ghost town in its infancy through resilience and *(continued next page)*

That leg of the trip had raised the most questions for all involved. After all, it had only been a month since U.S. Ambassador to the United Nations, Adlai Stevenson, was physically accosted by local citizens accusing him of being a communist traitor after a speech he had delivered there.

Having flown to Fort Worth from Houston the night before, President Kennedy emerged from the Hotel Texas on the rainy morning of Friday November 22nd to another friendly crowd. On the back of a truck, he declared that there were no faint hearts in Texas along with other locally relevant platitudes. After that, back inside the hotel, he attended a breakfast held in his honour by the local chamber of commerce, even making light of Jacqueline upstaging him with her late entrance. Soon the presidential party set off from Fort Worth on Air Force One for the fifteen minute flight east to Dallas.

Ambush

It was another scene complete with a friendly crowd on hand to greet President Kennedy and Jacqueline. Having been received by dignitaries as they stepped off Air Force One at Dallas' Love Field Airport, the president and his wife went to shake hands with the large crowd that had gathered.

The presidential party set out on the hour long motorcade that would take them on a near loop from the North of Dallas down through the CBD and back northwards to Market Hall to attend a luncheon. Virtually the entire route was lined by waving onlookers, but the crowd was at its most dense in the city along Harwood and Main Streets.

-innovation instilled a proud and hardened exterior that continues to run through the Dallas lineage. In subsequent years it would become a bedrock of both prosperity and far-right political movements and activity that would further sharpen the hard edge of Dallas.

Only occasionally was there a sign held up in protest. And if there were any jeers or slurs for Kennedy, they would have been dimmed out by friendly clapping and cheers. Just before emerging from the canyon of cheers on Main Street, Governor John Connally's wife, Nellie, turned back to President Kennedy in the limousine and said, 'You sure can't say Dallas doesn't love you, Mr President.' Kennedy smiled and replied, 'No, you can't.' They were the last words he would ever speak.

The motorcade made a right from Main onto Houston Street. It was now driving directly towards the Texas School Book Depository. On the left was Dealey Plaza. At the next junction, the President's limousine made a sharp left onto Elm Street under the Book Depository and a large, leafy Texas Oak. President John F. Kennedy had entered the ambush awaiting him.*

Much has been speculated about how the assault on President Kennedy took place. But what has been credibly established is that:
- There were approximately six hundred people in Dealey Plaza that day. Either lined along Houston and Elm Streets or scattered throughout the plaza on either side of Elm and on the railway overpass ahead.
- President Kennedy sustained three gunshot wounds – one in the neck, one in the back and one in the head.

---

*Dealey Plaza is an expanse of lawn that is intersected by Elm, Main and Commerce Streets. It's bordered by large trees, gardens, a railway overpass bridge, and Houston Street. Commemorating the site of the first home built in Dallas, it has pergolas on the northern, eastern, and southern perimeters. Elm, Main and Commerce Streets run inward at a downward angle through the plaza to converge under the overpass. Most of the crowd were on the northern and eastern sides of Dealey Plaza to watch the presidential motorcade travel along Houston then Elm Street. As of 2024, it is still in the form that it was in 1963.

- Governor Connally, seated in front of Kennedy, sustained wounds in the chest, left wrist, and inner right thigh.
- Onlooker, James Tague, who was standing directly ahead of the presidential limousine on Commerce Street below the railway overpass was nicked on the cheek by a piece of concrete that flew up from a ricocheting bullet.
- Witnesses at the scene (including Secret Service agents) testified to seeing the back right of the president's head being blasted out.

Some forty witnesses testified to either hearing gunshots or smelling gunpowder from an area to the front right of the president, soon to be termed the 'Grassy Knoll.'[4] All of which ran counter to the Warren Commission* narrative that all shots were fired by a lone assassin using a manual bolt-action rifle from high up behind and to the left of the presidential limousine.

It could be debated that there isn't another slice of ten seconds in history that has been so scrutinised as the assassination of President Kennedy. After all, films and photographs taken by members of the crowd serve as records of the shooting. Names like Zapruder, Wills, Muchmore, Moorman, Altgens and Nix are synonymous with the event.

---

*The Warren Commission, officially the 'President's Commission on the Assassination of President Kennedy' but so nicknamed after its chairperson, Chief Justice Earl Warren, was established on November 29, 1963, by President Lyndon Johnson. Consisting of a panel including Warren, four current senators plus former CIA Director, Allen Dulles and World Bank President, John J. McCloy to oversee and convene witness testimony and examination of evidence relating to the assassination, it produced a report, the 'Warren Report', nine months later finding that Lee Harvey Oswald was solely responsible for the shootings of Kennedy, Governor Connally and Officer Tippit.

Their films and photographs continue to be scrutinised for what they did and did not capture of the ambush.

The terms 'Grassy Knoll,' 'Badgeman,' 'Single Bullet Theory,' 'Magic Bullet Theory,' 'Conspiracy Theory,' 'Jet-effect' and 'Zapruder film' all entered the world's vocabulary in the wake of Kennedy's assassination. An entire industry on the event was hatched – one where countless books and publications, documentaries and films have focused on that single event, yet the case remains an unsolved mystery for it has never been definitively proven who shot the president and on the orders of whom. It is not the intention of this book to delve into the minutiae of the assassination of Kennedy. Others have put forth much more extensive and credible works on this.

President Kennedy and Governor Connally were rushed to Parkland Hospital for emergency treatment. Connally, though critically wounded, was stabilised and would recover. However, President Kennedy, was pronounced dead at 1:00pm local time – approximately twenty-five minutes after the shooting.

Like the ambush in Dealey Plaza, accounts of what transpired during the frantic moments to save President Kennedy's life have been the focus of much interest and speculation. Speaking to the media gathered at Parkland soon after the announcement of Kennedy's death, Doctor Malcolm Perry recalled a baseball-sized wound in the back of the president's head but would not be drawn on its point of entry. He also noted a bullet entry wound in Kennedy's neck, just below the Adam's apple. The inference being that it was from another gunshot from the front. Despite this, Perry would soon be pressured to recant his statement on Kennedy being shot in the throat from the front. However, other attending doctors and personnel would say that they saw the same head and throat wounds that Perry described. Acting-Presidential Press Secretary, Malcolm Kilduff even told the press at Parkland Hospital that day, while pointing to his right temple, that Kennedy had been shot through the head.

Back in Dealey Plaza, it was a state of chaos, shock, and confusion. Immediately after the motorcade had rushed out of there, onlookers began to race to where they suspected shots had been fired from the right along the top of the Grassy Knoll at the northern side of Dealey Plaza - and even as far down as where it met the railway overpass. The rest of the crowd milled around in a wake of disbelief and shock of what they had just witnessed.

Police and Sheriff personnel also followed the crowds up to the top of the Grassy Knoll where there was a parking lot between it, the railway tracks, and the Texas School Book Depository. Police Officer Joe M. Smith, with his pistol drawn, was among the first to arrive there. He testified that he could smell gunpowder and told of seeing a man who was already in the area.[5] When Smith approached him, he noted that the man was wearing plain clothes including a sports jacket and that he had dirty hands. Despite not wearing the customary black suit, the man was quick to produce Secret Service credentials, so Smith let him be. While it was true that there were twenty eight members of the Secret Service in the presidential motorcade that day, none were ever away from the procession and on the ground in Dealey Plaza. Interestingly, another police officer, D.V. Harkness would also testify to encountering several 'well armed' men dressed in suits behind the Book Depository who also told him they were Secret Service.[6] Speaking of which, the Book Depository had a large crowd that began to mill outside that consisted of onlookers as well as employees. It was from there where shots were also suspected as having been fired from. The building was searched by members of the Dallas Police and Sheriff's departments but would not be sealed until between twenty to thirty minutes after the shooting. However, Dallas Police would soon be alerted to another shooting – that of Police Officer J.D. Tippit.

Manhunt

In the half hour following the shooting in Dealey Plaza, Officer Tippit, alone in his patrol car and miles from his designated patrol area, was witnessed at several locations around the nearby suburb of Oak Cliff acting frantically as if waiting for or trying to find someone:

- At 12:45pm, he was seen sitting in his parked patrol car at the Gloco Gas Station at the other end of the Houston Road viaduct watching the flow of traffic leaving downtown Dallas. He left within ten minutes by speeding out of there and west along Lancaster Street.[7]
- A minute or two before 1:00pm, Tippit rushed into the Top Ten Record Store on Jefferson Boulevard, still in Oak Cliff, stating he needed to use the phone. He dialled a number but didn't speak for the minute or so that he was on the phone. He then hung up and rushed back out the store.[8]
- Immediately after 1:00pm, Tippit frantically pulled over a man driving a couple blocks away from the Top Ten Record Store. Without saying a word, he ran back to the car and looked in through its windows at the

rear and front seats. Seeing nothing and still having not said a word, he returned to his car and rushed off.$^{(9)}$

Officer Tippit would be next seen nearby slowly driving down East 10th Street just past where it intersected with Patton Street. He brought his patrol car to a stop in front of a driveway that ran between the houses addressed 404 and 408 E. 10th Street and close to where a man was walking toward him on the sidewalk. The man walked over to the passenger window and leant down to speak to Tippit. After approximately a minute, Tippit got out and walked around to the front of his car. The other man drew a handgun and shot Tippit three times in the abdomen causing Tippit to fall back onto the road. The man walked closer and shot him in the head, killing him.

The murder of Officer J.D. Tippit and his actions leading up to it remain unsolved. Was he just caught in the wrong place at the wrong time? Or was he somehow part of the plot and his death was an intended, or unintended outcome? Witness accounts of his shooting differ from each other – some described the shooter as being heavy set, others said he was slim. Some testified to there being two shooters that fled in separate directions and that there was even another police car at the scene parked further back in the driveway Tippit had stopped in front of. The time that the shooting of Officer Tippit happened ranges from between 1.06pm to 1.16pm depending on who is asked. It all made for yet another aspect of November 22nd that continues to remain shrouded in mystery. I recommend Joseph McBride's 'Into the Nightmare' for the most comprehensive and reasoned examination of the Tippit shooting.

Only a few blocks west of E 10th Street, back on Jefferson Boulevard, sat the Texas Theater. At 1.50pm, nearly two dozen Dallas Police personnel consisting of uniformed and plain clothed officers descended there following a report that a man seen acting suspiciously had entered the theater without paying. Within minutes, a man was apprehended inside, brought out through the front doors of the theatre in front of a crowd, then bundled into a police car, and was driven away. He was Lee Harvey Oswald.

CHAPTER TWO

LEE HARVEY OSWALD

Lee Oswald no doubt was a fascinating figure across all phases of his life. Yet you will not find a bestseller mainstream biography that dares apply any objectivity to the question of if he had any involvement with the Kennedy and Tippit murders or even his confirmed status as an FBI informant. This runs consistent with the Oswald-did-it orthodoxy that is the most lucrative for the authors who espouse as much. Norman Mailer's 'Oswald's Tale' is a good example of a voluminous take on Oswald's life complete with detailed and extensive coverage of events at most stages that all but gave up on applying any critical thinking when it came to Oswald in Dealey Plaza. Reasons why there isn't a credible biographical source on Lee Oswald are bolstered by the simple facts that he only lived to the age of twenty four and his entire adult life is virtually shrouded in official and unofficial secrecy. This book does not seek to devote too much focus on Lee Oswald's background – but it is important to provide some context.

Lee Oswald was employed as an order filler at the Texas School Book Depository at the time of President Kennedy's assassination. He started working there on October 16th 1963, two days before his twenty forth birthday, with the help of Ruth Paine - the woman with whom his wife, Marina, was friends and living with at the time. Paine, according to her

Orleans Grand Jury testimony,[1] contacted the Book Depository's superintendent, Roy Truly, herself to canvas for any work there on Lee's behalf. She secured an interview for him the next day and as a result, Oswald was asked by Truly to start the following day. However, like most things in the Lee Oswald narrative, it wasn't quite as simple as that.

To begin with, Linnie Mae Randle, who was a neighbour of Ruth Paine's and whose brother, Buell Frazier worked at the Book Depository, testified to the Warren Commission,[2] that she told Paine there were not any job vacancies at the time she was focused on helping Oswald get a job. Yet, with the help of a cold call from Ruth Paine to the superintendent at the Book Depository, Lee was secured an interview. Add to this the fact that Ruth Paine had clear connections on both sides of her family with U.S. Intelligence, namely the CIA, which led all the way up to former Director Allen Dulles, and she quickly became a very compelling figure of interest. Furthermore, Robert Adams of the Texas Employment Commission (TEC) testified to the Warren Commission that he telephoned the Paine residence, where Oswald had all correspondence directed to despite living in a nearby rooming house, on October 15 to notify him about a better paying job than the one at the Book Depository as a baggage handler at Love Field Airport.[3] The fact that Oswald in all probability didn't receive the message from Paine adds to the question of whether her helping him find work at the Book Depository was her participating (wittingly or unwittingly) in a plot to frame him as part of the overall assassination plan. This episode just typifies the myriads of questions and rabbit-hole-esque nature of just who Lee Harvey Oswald was and how he came to be thrust forward as the alleged killer of President Kennedy and Dallas Police Officer J.D. Tippit.

Lee Harvey Oswald was born on October 18, 1939, in New Orleans. His mother was Marguerite Oswald (nee Claverie), and his father was Robert Edward Lee Oswald Sr., who died of a heart attack just two months prior to Lee's birth. Lee had one brother, Robert, and a half-brother, John Edward Pic who were both older than he. Oswald's youth was spent moving between New Orleans and the Dallas-Fort Worth area depending on his mother's current situation. Combinations of troubles of his mother's with jobs, family friends and men all made for a turbulent and chaotic upbringing for Lee that included a stint in a New Orleans orphanage when he was four years old. He came close to some normalcy when Marguerite married John Ekdahl. He was the closest to a father figure young Lee had until John and Marguerite divorced. The instability of living and schooling arrangements continued for Lee right the way through his childhood and teen years. So much so that he and his mother travelled as far to New York's Upper East Side, without notice, showing up on John Pic's doorstep and in need of a place to stay. The entire time they stayed with him and his wife, Margaret (Margy) in their cramped apartment, was mired in tension - Marguerite's pernicious and irrational ways no doubt a lead contributor. After a fight between Marguerite and Margy, during which Lee hit Marguerite and pulled out a pocketknife, Oswald and his mother moved out and into their own apartment.[4] Lee was sent to two schools, but he barely attended either, preferring to roam the streets and subways of New York City. He was soon declared truant and referred to Youth House for psychiatric evaluation. The social worker there,

Evelyn Siegel, declared Lee to be pleasant and that he had an 'appealing quality about his emotionally starved, affectionless self which grows as one speaks to him.'[5]

If Oswald was lonely and rudderless as a child, his inherent curiosity would lead him to an interest in Marxism and Socialism. Both gave him a newfound sense of guidance and structure that he so badly lacked with to look at and understand the world that seemed so against him. Moving back to New Orleans from New York with his mother didn't improve his schooling but he would immerse himself in any socialist literature he could find. He would later write in his diary that 'I had to dig for my books in the back of dusty shelves of libraries.'[6] His interest gave him a sense of purpose which, combined with a likely lust to break away from his domineering mother, saw him follow his brother, Robert by enlisting in the U.S. Marines at the age of seventeen. There he maintained his interests in Marxism and Socialism to the point that he earned the nickname 'Oswaldovich' from his fellow marines.

We come to yet another chapter of Lee Oswald's life that has been subject to much conjecture over the years. What's established is that he was a mediocre shot at best with a rifle having scored just over the 'sharpshooter' requirement after intensive training but dropped down to the lowest grading of 'marksman' when tested six months later. Beyond his time in the Marines, Oswald was only seen using firearms a couple of times. According to his brother, Robert, in his testimony for the Warren Commission,[7] he recalled he and Lee using rifles when they took a hunting trip in 1959. The next time was in the Soviet Union when Oswald was also taken on some hunting trips in the countryside there by friends. In March of '57, Oswald commenced training as a radar controller, an opportunity that only Marines with an above-average IQ could gain. He was soon promoted to Private First Class, but it was also around this time that he is alleged to have first publicly expressed interest in communist literature despite having received a promotion and higher level of security clearance. By that September, Oswald would ship out to Japan and serve as a radar operator at Atsugi Naval Air Station. It was from there that the highly classified U-2 surveillance spy planes were based to make flights over the region and as far as the Soviet Union.

By this point you may already know, or be beginning to understand, that the more that is written about Lee Oswald during the years of his service in the U.S. Marines, predominantly in East Asia, the more enigmatic he appears. To further the point, the next two years would see Oswald:

- undergo intelligence work in nearby Tokyo to pass on fake intelligence to KGB agents.
- learn to understand and speak Russian
- accidentally shoot himself only to have the bullet graze his left elbow and be court-martialled for possessing an unregistered weapon (a Derringer pistol)
- be promoted to Corporal
- assault a fellow marine and be sentenced for up to forty five days in the brig (the equivalent of jail on a military base)
- continue in his classified radar operator duties
- enrol into the Albert Schweitzer College in Switzerland (but never attend) and,
- apply for a passport stating he intended on visiting Cuba and Russia.

In August of '59, Oswald applied for a discharge from the Marines to support his mother. It was granted the next month, but he only stayed with her in Fort Worth for two days before leaving for New Orleans. From there, he would sail to England. By the time he turned twenty that October, Oswald had already arrived in Moscow having travelled through England and Finland – where he obtained a six day holiday Soviet visa. During that time, he expressed his desire to local authorities to apply for citizenship. When his six day visa was about to lapse and having not heard back about his bid for Soviet citizenship, Oswald cut his left wrist and was admitted to a local hospital for eleven days. His request for citizenship remained open for consideration so he visited the local American Embassy and stated that he wished to revoke his U.S. citizenship. This was never actioned. Instead, his passport was retained by the American Embassy and in the following January, he was given 'residency' status by the Soviets.

Lee Oswald's time in the Soviet Union remains a mystery. It was never conclusively established if he had been recruited whilst there by Soviet intelligence or that they did or did not act on the, most likely, conclusion that he was sent there on a U.S. intelligence objective. Both the United States and Soviet governments denied both scenarios then and do so until this day. What is clear is that Oswald was transported to Minsk and provided free accommodation in an upmarket apartment and provided a job in a local radio factory. From a U.S. perspective, it is suspicious that a 201 file wasn't opened by the CIA the moment Oswald arrived in the Soviet Union. Per the CIA's Clandestine Services Handbook,[8] 201s are opened to collect all records and documents relating to 'subjects of extensive reporting and CI (Counterintelligence) investigation, prospective agents and sources, and members of groups and organisations of continuing interest.' Therefore, in the case of Oswald, a former marine who worked in a classified position that was nestled within operations aimed squarely at the Soviet Union, it ought to have been standard operating procedure that a 201 folder be opened on him the moment it was known that he had arrived in the Soviet Union. Yet it was not done until December 1960, fourteen months after his arrival there, which compels the conclusion that Lee Oswald was sent to the Soviet Union for a reason, or reasons, by U.S. intelligence.

But one episode during 1960 that has so fuelled this speculation is the crash of the United States' U-2 spy plane piloted by Gary Powers over the Soviet Union. Effectively destroying the foundations for President Eisenhower and Soviet Premier Khrushchev's scheduled peace talks in Paris within a matter of weeks, the incident is more mysterious given the fact that Lee Oswald was in the Soviet Union at the time. Having worked in radar operations monitoring U-2 spy planes, the question continues to linger if the downing of Powers' plane was helped through intelligence that Oswald provided Soviet intelligence or not? Reasons Oswald could have been sent to the Soviet Union by U.S. intelligence have been speculated as everything from feeding false or accurate information on the soon to be decommissioned U-2 spy plane to the Soviets, to help weed out Soviet infiltrators within U.S. intelligence to simply being a dangle for whatever Soviet intelligence interest is shown in him. Or a combination of all the above. The evidence suggests that the Soviets were suspicious of Oswald from the very beginning so it is likely that they would not have regarded anything he would have been willing to tell them because they had him pegged as some kind of plant, whom they codenamed the Russian word for reckless, 'Likhoi'.⁽⁹⁾

Aside from the Oswald – U.S. intelligence angle, conjecture continues that Powers' U-2 plane was sabotaged or had simply experienced engine faults that meant it lost enough altitude to be detected by Soviet radar and therefore in missile range to be shot down. Another interesting and similar case to Oswald is Robert Webster, a U.S. citizen whose story of defecting to the Soviet Union only to return 2 years later, almost overlaps Oswald's as he arrived in the Soviet Union two weeks prior to Oswald and left to return to the United States - two weeks before Oswald would do so as well. See Gary Hill's 'The Other Oswald' for more. ⁽¹⁰⁾

Despite the tensions that arose between the Soviet Union and the United States over the U-2 affair, life continued as normal for Oswald in Minsk. There is relatively little on record for Oswald's time in the Soviet Union in general. His known movements are mundane and routine. For all intents and purposes, he appeared to be living the life of any regular man barely in his twenties. He formed friendships, worked a full time job, took vacations, and had romantic interests including a local woman, Marina Nikolayevna Prusakova, who he married in April of '61, only six weeks after meeting her. In fact, before she met Lee Oswald, Marina had a relationship with Robert Webster, as detailed in Gary Hill's 'The Other Oswald'.⁽¹¹⁾ Either she had a particular fondness for American men who happened to be in town or her attraction was something more nefarious e.g. as a plant or as a spy. Curiously but perhaps not coincidentally, Marina had an uncle who was employed by the KGB at the time.

Later that year, Oswald began to make it known that he wished to return to the United States, providing he not be prosecuted for any crimes. With Marina in the picture, he intended on bringing her with him. In February of '62, Lee and Marina would welcome their first child, a girl named June Lee, and make the long journey to the United States the following June. However, it has never been adequately addressed how Marina could ever have been allowed into the U.S at all given she was had a relation in the KGB and how close in time she had relations with two U.S. citizens in the Soviet Union given the current climate of the Cold War. Lee Oswald, former-Marine turned wannabe-Soviet defector, returned to the U.S. aboard the 'S.S. Massadam' with Marina and their daughter. There they were met with no fanfare and only a representative from the 'Traveller's Aid Society,' an organisation with CIA and right-wing linkages, before flying to Dallas, via Atlanta. Reunited with family, the Oswald's stayed with his mother in Fort Worth however the local FBI would not interview Lee until two weeks after his return. The coming home of a self-declared defector to the Soviet Union back in the United States, with a Soviet-born wife, was, publicly, strangely, and suspiciously low-key. When Robert Webster had returned, two weeks earlier than Oswald, there were news articles reporting on it but in Oswald's case there was no coverage at all. The only time he had made the newspapers was when he first arrived in the Soviet Union three years prior – and even then, he was named in the article.[12]

Oswald started a job a month after his return to Texas at the Leslie Welding Company assembling doors and windows, but it would be his next job which was more interesting. It was as an assistant at Jaggars-Chiles-Stovall, a company on contract to the United States government to produce typeface for U-2 surveillance photographs and maps, among other documents. That Oswald was able to acquire this job, having lived in the Soviet Union for most of the previous three years and the timing of when he started, just prior to the Cuban Missile Crisis, is another 'beyond coincidence' type of event in the Oswald lexicon.

It was around this time that a mysterious figure would come to prominence in the Oswald story. was a Russian-born man of nobility who fled with his family from there during the outset of the Russian Revolution. A journeyman through various business interests, de Mohrenschildt would zero in on geology and come to be based in Dallas. He soon became a doyen of the local White Russian community who were staunch anti-communists. The fact that de Mohrenschildt became friends with Oswald, who appeared to be, broadly speaking, a student of the very left wing principles and systems that White Russians like de Mohrenschildt vehemently opposed, sounds like yet another curiosity. However, de Mohrenschildt had long been linked to the CIA, who would use him to gather and report local intelligence on his travels around the world since at least the late 50's. According to Greg Poulgrain's 'JFK vs. Allen Dulles',[13] de Mohrenschildt's connections included CIA Director, Allen Dulles. And, unlike Ruth Paine – with her own intelligence ties, George de Mohrenschildt would confess to being contacted by local Dallas CIA agent, J. Walton Moore, to making contact with Lee Oswald. In 1977, soon after admitting his assignment from the CIA to effectively 'mind' Oswald, George de Mohrenschildt was found dead from a self-inflicted shotgun blast to the head. His death joined the long list of suspicious deaths relating to the Kennedy assassination. Ruth Paine, who was still alive at the time of the writing of this book, has never admitted to any actions on her part in regard to 'minding' Lee or Marina Oswald on behalf of U.S. Intelligence.

Lee and Marina would remain in Dallas until April of 1963 before he would relocate to New Orleans in search of work. Two weeks prior to his leaving Dallas, an event would take place that would be linked to Lee Oswald only after his death.

The General Walker Shooting

On the evening of April 10, 1963, former U.S. Army Major General and right wing figurehead, Edwin A. Walker was sitting in his study in a back room of his home in the affluent Dallas suburb of Turtle Creek when a steel jacketed 30.06 calibre bullet was fired through the window and narrowly missed his head. Fifteen year old Kirk Coleman, who lived nearby, told the police that he had heard the shot fired so he ran outside from his house and looked over the fence. He saw one male running toward a car parked in the back laneway that was idling and had its headlights on. There was another car parked further ahead in a church carpark with a man inside. The DPD investigated but could not bring charges to anyone. Come that November, the case was still unsolved, but it would make the headlines again when Lee Oswald was speculated as being the person who shot at Walker. It is not clear what exactly prompted authorities to reignite the investigation to factor in Oswald as a suspect but when Kirk Coleman was shown photographs of Oswald by the FBI, he could not identify him as being either of the men he saw near Walker's home straight after the shooting that night back in April.

However, shortly after his death, Oswald's wife, Marina, would implicate him with statements that included his confessing to carrying out the shooting at Walker. The inconsistencies in her statements and the circumstances of stress and pressure she would have presumably been under automatically brings what she said into question. There was also a note found in books, that had already searched through by authorities at the Paine residence, which was allegedly written to Marina by Lee in Russian telling her what to do if he were to suddenly disappear. However, Oswald's fingerprints could not be found on the letter.

Add to this the fact that no one ever saw Oswald travel by public transport to the scene and back, that he did not have a drivers licence or a car to drive nor did anyone testify to seeing him carrying out the shooting and the case against Oswald was incredibly flimsy. In later years, General Walker himself would dispute the bullet that was held in government records as the one that Oswald allegedly fired from his Mannlicher-Carcano rifle as being completely different to the one that was pulled out of his wall just after the shooting. This was proven to the be the case as the Mannlicher-Carcano could only fire copper jacketed 6.5 calibre bullets. The FBI merely ruled it 'inconclusive' that the Walker shooting bullet was fired from the Mannlicher-Carcano. [14] But like the proverbial mud, the inference stuck to the mainstream legend of Lee Oswald - that the shooting at Walker was some kind of tragic precursor to the assassination of President Kennedy. The above is only a very broad overview of the Walker shooting but we can conclude that it is another topic worthy of its own field of research.

Next, Oswald moved back to New Orleans from Dallas on his own. The time he was there from April to September 1963 has also been the subject of much interest and speculation in relation to the Kennedy assassination. Largely regarded as the period that 'formed' Oswald the eventual assassin of President Kennedy, that summer of 1963 in New Orleans saw Oswald in the company of people of both sides of the political spectrum because, like Dallas, it was a hotbed of political extremism. Based there were among the largest and active chapters of far-right wing groups such as the Ku Klux Klan, John Birch Society and Minutemen. Laced in with these elements were among the most rabid anti-Castro Cubans.

The United States had received a flood of Cubans who had fled Cuba in the wake of Fidel Castro's revolution in 1959. With the southernmost tip of Florida only ninety miles from the northernmost point of Cuba, the concentration of Cubans who fled their homeland settled in Miami and greater Florida. As time passed and the tension of the Cuban situation continued, Cuban emigrants would disperse across the United States. New Orleans, naturally due to its location, would soon accumulate a large community of anti-Castro Cubans and a much smaller pro-Castro community. Fuelling the anti-Castro sentiment was the 'would there or wouldn't there be' question of another attempt by the United States to invade Cuba and overthrow Fidel Castro once and for all. In the Florida Keys, CIA backed training camps had been set up to train combat and warfare tactics to volunteers before the Bay of Pigs in April of '61. And the same would soon be done in New Orleans, with training camps built on the other northern side of Lake Pontchartrain in preparation for the next opportunity to invade Castro's Cuba.

When Lee Oswald arrived in New Orleans, he stayed with family on his mother's side. He got a job as a machine assistant at the Reilly Coffee Company but would soon be handing out flyers titled 'Hands Off Cuba!'

across the city as the one, and only, local member of the Fair Play for Cuba Committee (FPCC).

The FPCC was based in New York and formed to consolidate support for Fidel Castro across the United States and was rumoured to have actually been set up by the CIA to attract, monitor, control and interfere with U.S.-based support for Castro as part of an overall operation against communist subversion. In the meantime, the FBI's COINTELPRO focused on domestic communist activity, was heavily targeted on the FPCC making for a fascinating, yet convenient, convergence that Lee Oswald was no doubt deeply immersed in. The FPCC had a large membership on the west and east coast of the country but, in a city where pro-Castro supporters were entirely outnumbered by anti-Castro Cubans, before Oswald, it was sitting at zero. In the months leading up to the Kennedy assassination, the FPCC was becoming more and absorbed with other left wing elements such as the Socialist party. But when it was made public that alleged-assassin Oswald was an FPCC member, the organisation soon disbanded completely.

On the face of it, it may have run true to form that a man interested in Marxism and who had returned from living in the Soviet Union would be seen handing out flyers in support of a communist leader such as Fidel Castro. But what skews the picture is that the address stamped on the flyers as the location of the local FPCC was that of Guy Banister – a notorious right wing anti-communist in New Orleans. Such an anomaly raised eyebrows even at the time because that August, Oswald, when handing out FPCC flyers, got into a fight on the streets of New Orleans with some anti-Castro Cubans he had supposedly approached to assist them with their cause only the day before.

His actions were clearly those of a provocateur working to some ulterior motive. Even more so when, it had since been revealed that Oswald was urging his attackers to punch him during the scuffle and that an FBI Agent would speak with him while he was in custody after the incident.

The entire New Orleans episode brought forth a host of characters that, alongside Oswald, have been the focus of researchers ever since. Banister, Clay Shaw, David Ferrie, Carlos Bringuier, 'Leon' Oswald, Frank Bartes, Orestes Pena, Richard Case Nagell, Loran Hall, Billy Seymour, Thomas Beckham, 'Angel' & 'Leopoldo' all continue to orbit around the enduring narrative of Lee Oswald because all had clear ties to him that summer. In fact, in the cases of Ferrie and Nagell, their associations with Oswald even pre-dates his time in the Soviet Union. But with this cast of characters, and more, it too is difficult to pinpoint just what was going on with and around New Orleans that summer. District Attorney Jim Garrison fought doggedly to shed light on it all during the mid to late 60's. In doing so he charged Clay Shaw for his involvement in a conspiracy to kill President Kennedy, but he would be acquitted as the evidence to convict was not enough. In the very least, Garrison had pulled on a thread that showed how complex the atmosphere was around Lee Oswald that summer in 1963. The numerous instances of interference and sabotage from elements within the federal government, intelligence agencies and mainstream media validates that Garrison must have been onto something. But just how connected the New Orleans episode was to what took place in Dallas also still lingers as a mystery. Perhaps the one vital piece of evidence that links Lee Oswald and his anti-Castro infiltration manoeuvres in New Orleans and thereafter is the fact someone named 'Lee' contacted the FBI in Chicago just prior to President Kennedy's visit there in early November of '63 to warn of an assassination plot being hatched there by anti-Castro Cubans. Interested readers would do well to read the works of researchers such as James DiEugenio, Joan Mellen, Anthony Summers, Dick Russell, and Paul Bleau.

The road back to Dallas from New Orleans for Lee Oswald in 1963 also remains paved in mystery. The story went that Oswald travelled from New Orleans to Mexico City and tried to gain a visa to travel to the Soviet Union by way of Cuba in late September of '63. However, there has not been any solid evidence to prove that Oswald even stepped foot in Mexico. To add to all the murkiness, it was at this time that he, and at times even his wife and daughter, were impersonated. This is evidenced by witness accounts placing him (and at times his family) in places and times when he (and they) was provably elsewhere. Accounts of Oswald springing up around Dallas continued throughout September, October, and early November. My work creating the Garrison folders uncovered a document stating that Oswald was seen in the company of a short, stocky Hispanic man around Dallas in the weeks leading up to Dealey Plaza. Also, since his return to Dallas from New Orleans, Oswald stayed in rooming houses away from his daughter, June, and wife Marina, who was expecting their second child. Why he lived apart from his family remains open to conjecture but in the scheme of things, is just another curious aspect to Oswald that could mean something sinister or could be perfectly innocent.

At this point, I recommend John Armstrong's book 'Harvey and Lee' and the work he continues to produce regarding the theory of there being two Lee Oswald's since their respective childhoods and how they were manipulated separately to ultimately converge in Dallas on November 22nd. [15] It is a contention that is extensively researched and incredibly compelling. This brings the backstory of Lee Oswald full circle back to the assassination of President Kennedy. His life has been so scrutinised and interpreted to gain a better understanding of who he was and what clues there are to his association with the assassination of John F. Kennedy. To the purpose of this book, it is also important to provide some analysis of the evidence for and against Lee Oswald regarding the Kennedy and Tippit shootings as it makes his own death more compelling and tragic.

CHAPTER THREE

DID HE? OR DIDN'T HE?

One thing that is incontrovertible about Lee Harvey Oswald was that he did not live to stand trial for the murders of President Kennedy and Officer Tippit. Therefore, the narrative set at the time by an apparatus consisting of the government, intelligence agencies and an abiding mainstream media ensured that the dye was set throughout the wool – Oswald was *presumed* responsible and anything counter to that would be, and still is, labelled 'conspiracy theory.' And, again, tempting as it is to delve into that rabbit hole, it is not the purpose of this book. However, examining the matter of his innocence regarding the Kennedy and Tippit shootings lends context to the elaborate framing of Oswald and his own murder.

Did Oswald fire any shots at President Kennedy and Governor Connally?

Firstly, nobody testified that Oswald made any utterance or declaration that he did not like President Kennedy or that he wished him harm. While he was in the Soviet Union, Oswald did write a letter to the then Secretary of the Navy, John Connally to protest his dishonourable discharge status from the Marines. But revenge against Connally, who, as Governor was riding with Kennedy and also wounded, could rank among the flimsiest of reasons for Oswald to carry out the carnage in Dealey Plaza. In fact, everyone who knew Oswald and was asked about this expressed that he never spoke of violence and only spoke favourably of President Kennedy. This is important in the scheme of things but has largely been glossed over by the convenient Oswald-angry-loner myth. To add, if Oswald were as left leaning as he was purported to be by so many, therefore closer to the side of Castro, Khrushchev, and communism, it makes no sense that he would want to kill Kennedy, the most liberal U.S. President since Franklin Roosevelt.

On the morning of November 22nd, Oswald was given a ride to work by fellow Book Depository employee, Buell Frazier. This wasn't anything too far out of the norm as Oswald would often stay the night with Marina and his children and go from there to work the next morning. However, Frazier, nor anyone at the TSBD saw Oswald carrying a rifle, fully assembled or in a package large enough to carry it in parts, either on November the 22nd or prior. Nor was one recovered from the TSBD after President Kennedy's shooting. The only thing Oswald was carrying with him into work on November 22nd was a small paper bag containing a cheese sandwich and an apple.

That morning, in the lead up to the arrival of President Kennedy's motorcade, no one could attest to seeing Oswald acting suspiciously whilst at work in the Book Depository either. He carried out his normal duties of filling book orders from cartons across the upper floors of the building. At the time that the motorcade was scheduled to arrive in Dealey Plaza, 12:25pm, Book Depository employee Carolyn Arnold saw Oswald seated in the second floor lunchroom on her way out to see the motorcade.[1] This is hardly where any kind of assassin would place themselves if they were about to commit, arguably, the murder of the century from the upper floors of the same building. Consider also, the fact that when President Kennedy's limousine was being driven along Houston Street, it was doing so directly toward the Book Depository, presenting the easiest of shots for a lone shooter perched within. Yet the volley of shots did not start until the limousine was in Dealey Plaza. This could only be because the intent was to strike down Kennedy from multiple directions.

To this day, a single witness is yet to come forward who conclusively saw Lee Oswald on the sixth floor at the window in the Book Depository just prior to, during and after the shots were fired. People standing on the street below and looking up at the Book Depository gave varied accounts of seeing one or a couple of men at the time of the assassination in either the easternmost window, where rifle shells were found close together on the floor and immediately linked to the shooting, or in the westernmost window on the same floor. The descriptions of these men include those of dark-complexions, heavy set and with receding hairlines. Some thought they were Secret Service, but none bore any resemblance to Lee Oswald. When in police custody in the afternoon of the assassination, Oswald was given a paraffin test to detect any traces of barium and antimony – core ingredients of gunpowder – deep in the pores of his hands and cheeks. The test came back negative for traces on his cheeks indicating he had at least not fired a rifle that day. And any traces that were detected on his hands would have easily been ruled inadmissible on a court of law as barium, in particular, is also found in common items such as grease, printing ink, paper, rubber – all items that Oswald and any other labourer in the TSBD would have handled during their normal course of work. And regarding Lee Oswald's fingerprints, they would only be detected on the rifle when it was tested again, two days after his own murder.

More recently, researchers Sean Murphy, Ed LeDoux, Stan Dane and Bart Kamp have brought the concept of 'Prayer Man' closer to the forefront of JFK assassination research. Prayer Man is a figure, resembling someone with their hands together, as if in prayer, which is visible in footage of the front entrance doorway of the Book Depository barely thirty seconds after the last shot was fired at Kennedy. Because of the midday sun, the figure is completely in shadow and somewhat blurry as they were only briefly filmed by cameramen, Dave Wiegman and Jimmy Darnell, as they were riding past in the motorcade. Being presented unclear images to interpret outlines and figures within has been part and parcel of the price of admission for JFK assassination researchers. However, the contention that Prayer Man is Lee Oswald is bolstered by the testimony of TSBD employees present that day. Through a process of deduction, these researchers contend that Prayer Man could only be Lee Oswald, or at the very least, a person not employed in the TSBD. However, none of the TSBD employees testified to seeing a person in the vicinity that they did not know or recognise to be a fellow employee. This is evidence gathering and analysis at its finest. Add to this that that Oswald himself stated to police that he was standing outside with his supervisor, Bill Shelley, who actually was located there, as the motorcade passed, and it blows apart the notion that he was five storeys above at the time and shooting out of the window.

Further to the contention that Prayer Man was Oswald standing at the entrance of the Book Depository as the motorcade passed, it could be speculated that perhaps he was never to have left the Book Depository alive.

With him inside the building – as intended and / or presumed by the plotters - while most were outside watching the motorcade, it would have been easy for a quick-thinking police officer to shoot and kill the fleeing suspected assassin in Oswald. That said, it is interesting to view the Darnell footage and see Police Officer Marrion Baker veer sharply away from the Book Depository steps to the right while the Prayer Man figure resembling Oswald was still standing there. Is this evidence of a foiled first attempt to kill Oswald? And did this then mandate the need to initiate back up plans by the plotters to implicate Oswald, i.e. the Tippit murder and subsequent Texas Theater arrest?

But leave the scene alive Oswald did and how is still very much open for debate as there are two vastly different scenarios laid out, each with witnesses in separate locations at the same time who testified to encountering Oswald just after the shooting in Dealey Plaza:

#1 - Public Transport Getaway:

At approximately 12:40pm, Oswald was identified by Mary Bledsoe as boarding a bus (that would not take him anywhere near his rooming house) between seven and eight blocks east along Elm Street.[2] Coincidentally, or not, Oswald rented a room from Bledsoe for a few days the month prior. With the bus mired in traffic and only slowly crawling back toward the source of the congestion, Dealey Plaza, Oswald is alleged to have asked the bus driver, Cecil McWatters, for a transfer and to be let off.[3] Having left the bus, Oswald walked a few blocks south towards the Greyhound Bus Station. He went to get into a taxicab at the stand there only to offer it to a lady who was already waiting. She refused so Oswald did get in and asked the driver, William Whaley, to be taken to near his rooming house - southeast of Dallas in nearby Oak Cliff.[4] This was how Dallas Police claimed Oswald told them he left work that day but there was no recording or transcript of what Oswald said during any of his interrogations so we can only take their word for it. The DPD allegedly also found the transfer ticket he got from McWatters in his pocket in pristine condition later that day.

However, William Whaley kept a timecard that indicated when he picked up each fare. And in the instance of driving Oswald, it had him starting his journey at 12:30pm – some twenty minutes earlier and at the same time President Kennedy was being shot at in Dealey Plaza.

Mary Bledsoe's alleged recognition of Oswald on the bus is far from conclusive And McWatters, and passenger, Roy Milton O.A[5] would not be able to identify the man as Oswald in police line-ups that weekend either.

#2 - Ride with an Accomplice:

However, also at 12:40pm, Marvin Robinson and his employee, Roy Cooper were driving in separate cars on Elm Street in Dealey Plaza. As they passed the Book Depository, a station wagon in front of Robinson stopped suddenly. This caused Robinson and Cooper to slam on their brakes. Alerted to what could have caused the sudden stop, Robinson[6] and Cooper[7] recalled seeing a man run down the grass from the Book Depository and get into the station wagon which then rejoined the flow of traffic and continue on down Elm Street and under the railway overpass. Both would testify to the man as being between twenty to thirty years old. While not a conclusive identification of Oswald, there were others who witnessed the same scene take place, only they got a better look at the man who ran down to the station wagon. Helen Forrest and James Pennington were standing, separately, in Dealey Plaza on the side of the Book Depository, and they would identify the man as Lee Oswald.[8] Deputy Sheriff Roger Craig also witnessed a man running down through Dealey Plaza from the western side of the Book Depository and get into a station wagon. According to his WC testimony,[9] it came to light for him very quickly because he mentioned what he saw to Dallas Police that afternoon, so Homicide Captain J.W. Fritz then let him look at Oswald as he was sitting in an interrogation room. When Craig laid eyes on Oswald, he immediately identified him as the man he saw getting into the station wagon on Elm Street.

Roger Craig was a decorated United States Army veteran and long-time member of the Dallas Sheriff's Department. He never veered from his account that the man he saw rushing down from the Book Depository and into a waiting station wagon at 12:40pm was Lee Oswald. Craig was called before the Warren Commission to testify and he recalled the above episode as well. However, as detailed in his book 'When They Kill a President',[10] he suffered for his stance having been disgraced into leaving the Sheriff's Department and surviving attempts on his life. Ultimately, his life would be tragically cut short when, in 1973, he is alleged to have committed suicide with a self-inflicted gunshot.

There is one key point that orbits both 'Oswald-getaway' scenarios. Assuming that he was set up as the only person to fire shots in Dealey Plaza that day, the scenario of him fleeing by public transport fits and suits the Warren Commission's conclusions. But if Oswald left Dealey Plaza in a waiting car instead, or someone doubling for him did, why would the plotters let that happen out in the open for many to see and recall if the plan was hinged on framing him as a lone assassin? It's been a point of contention in the lone assassin vs. patsy dichotomy ever since and has perhaps clouded thinking around how multi-faceted the plotters were with their planning. So, without wanting to wander too far off topic, perhaps the original plan for those behind the assassination was to make it seem as though 'pro-Castro' communist Oswald had confederates in the shooting of Kennedy. And in the event that he left the scene alive, they would hedge their bets either way, and muddy the waters of confusion, by letting him be seen being driven away or taking public transport on his own. There was more than one shooter in Dealey Plaza that day – Kennedy, Connally and Tague's wounds plus witness reports corroborate that. So, it is plausible that Oswald (or a double, if the bus scenario is to be believed) was seen getting in a car with another man who had a dark complexion that could be portrayed as Hispanic / Cuban. From that point, if circumstances permitted in terms of the fallout to the shooting, it would not have been too much of a stretch to blame Kennedy's murder on Fidel Castro-supporting Cubans. This would generate justification for the United States to take action against Castro and his Cuba once and for all. To an extent, this logic could extend to holding Soviet Premier Nikita Khrushchev and the soviets to blame for murdering President Kennedy. After all, Oswald lived for three years, and it would be impossible to prove or disprove if he had been recruited in some shape or form to return to the United States as an asset of theirs. However, history shows that Castro, or the Soviets, were not roundly blamed for the assassination of Kennedy therefore there was no direct fallout between the United States and Cuba or the Soviet Union.

Perhaps this was part of the plotters reckoning – to railroad the U.S. government to not thoroughly investigate the assassination by using the threat of a confrontation with Cuba or worse, the Soviets. Instead, Oswald was conveniently blamed completely as a disillusioned loner who killed the president, and it was made all the easier by the fact that he was killed within forty eight hours and silenced forever. The threat of nuclear warfare costing the lives of millions was averted and the plotters surely leveraged off this to evade investigation and capture. If this was the case, the level of their ingenuity and cunning is something beyond a level most could comprehend.

Oswalds, Oswalds, Oswalds

What cannot be disputed is that there were numerous proven instances of Lee Oswald being impersonated leading up to and including November 22nd:

- In the summer of '63 in New Orleans, a man named Leon Oswald, who was not Lee Oswald, was present during conversations among others about assassinating Kennedy.
    - Richard Nagell testified to this as he knew the real Lee Oswald (having served in U.S. intelligence in East Asia at the same time as Oswald) and had encountered and described this other man named 'Leon Oswald.'[11]
- In Dallas, on the night of September 26th, when Lee Oswald was still reported as being back in New Orleans, three men knocked on Silvia Odio's door. Two of them, Angel and Leopoldo, were described as Latin American and the third, Caucasian, was introduced to Odio as 'Oswald.' They appeared to be looking for her uncle. A few days later,

Leopoldo called Odio at her house and referred to the other night. He asked her what she thought of 'the American Leon Oswald.' When Silvia offered him no opinion either way, Leopoldo would also say that Leon Oswald was an ex-marine, 'kind of nuts' and that President Kennedy should have been assassinated right after the Bay of Pigs by Cubans.

- o When Oswald's image was broadcast after President Kennedy's assassination, Silvia Odio instantly recognised him as the man who was introduced to her as 'Leon Oswald.' [12]
- In Mexico City, also in late September, a man described as having dirty light brown hair identifying himself as Oswald, and barely able to speak legible Russian, unlike Oswald who could, entered the Soviet Embassy to enquire about a visa.
  - o Another man, much older and huskier than Oswald ever was, was photographed outside the Soviet Embassy and referred to by local U.S. intelligence as the man who called himself Oswald.
- On October 3rd, a man referring to himself as Oswald walked into a printing agency in Alice, Texas saying he was returning from Mexico and needed work. A young woman and an infant girl were seated in the car he had parked outside. [13]
  - o Marina never corroborated this story, and Oswald was not licenced to drive.
- On November 2nd, a man referring to himself as Lee Oswald test drove a car, at high speeds on a Dallas freeway, and was comparing the car to ones in the Soviet Union, espousing to the car dealer right wing rhetoric and bragging that he would be coming into money soon. [14]

- o   Again, Oswald never had his licence to drive, and he was far from a confident learner driver.
- While the real Lee Oswald was at work in the TSBD on the morning of November 22nd, another man buying bottles of beer in a nearby convenience store produced identification with the name Lee H. Oswald and a birth year of 1939.[15]
- The fact that there are two separate documented versions of Oswald leaving Dealey Plaza by car and on foot before boarding a bus several blocks away and being seen doing so at the same time, it makes sense that one of the men was a double for Oswald.

So, like many aspects of the Kennedy assassination, Oswald impersonators and doubles aside, how Oswald left Dealey Plaza remains a hotly debated subject. The mystery continues with what transpired between the shots in Dealey Plaza and his arrest at the Texas Theater just over one hour later.

Did Oswald shoot and kill Officer Tippit?

It is still useful to use the Warren Commission to highlight the many lingering anomalies between the purported account and what transpired on November 22nd. Regarding Oswald's movements after leaving the Book Depository, the Warren Report posited that he asked the cabdriver, who had driven him from the Greyhound Station, to drop him off a few blocks along from his rooming house on N. Beckley Street in Oak Cliff. [16] Having walked back there, he entered without saying a word to landlady, Earlene Roberts and went into his room. She would testify to hearing the honk of a car horn coming from the street out the front very soon after he arrived.[17]

When she looked out the window, she described seeing a police patrol car that had stopped at the kerb out front. Within a few minutes, Oswald left his room and the house, still without saying a word. When Roberts looked out the window once more, she saw Oswald standing across the road as if he were waiting. A few minutes later when she looked out the window again, he was gone. This all took place over a matter of minutes prior to and just after 1:00pm. Yet again, what happens next remains hotly debated:

- The scene of Officer Tippit's shooting was an eighth of a mile (1.2 kilometres) from Oswald's rooming house. To have made it there by foot in time to have encountered Tippit and shot him, even at the time that the Warren Commission stated he did, Oswald would have had to have run non-stop, up a gradual incline, or be driven there, from his rooming house in no more than 12 minutes.
- Two cartridges found discarded at the scene were from an automatic pistol yet the revolver (which, by design, did not automatically eject spent rounds) that was 'found' in Oswald's possession during his arrest, was fully loaded with six live rounds.
- The discrepancy of when exactly the Tippit shooting took place has already been mentioned in Chapter One but something that firmly counters Oswald shooting Tippit is the fact that Texas Theater employee, Butch Burroughs, testified to his entering the Theater, having paid for a ticket, at around 1.08pm – almost thirty minutes before he was alleged to have snuck in and entered the theater, according to the Warren Commission.[18]
    - 1.08pm is also the earliest reported time of Tippit's shooting.

The impersonations of Oswald did not end with his 'getaway' out of Dealey Plaza or at 10th and Patton either. Bernard Haire, who owned a hobby store next to the Texas Theater, witnessed a man being brought out its side door into the alley and loaded into a police car at the same time Lee Oswald was being taken out through the front doors and being bundled into a police car before a crowd of onlookers. For years, until he saw the infamous photographs of Oswald being put into a police car at the *front* of the theater, Haire thought that what he witnessed was how Lee Oswald was taken out of the theater and away by police.[19] What is almost certain is the person that Haire saw was another Oswald double. Could he have been the same person that impersonated Oswald to help lead the police from the Tippit scene to the Texas Theater as well as either the man witnesses saw get into a wagon in Elm Street or take the bus and cab? What backs this up is the fact that a man was arrested on the balcony of the Texas Theater at the time Oswald was being apprehended on the ground floor. There even exists a report within Dallas Police records that names the man as Lee Oswald *(see this report in the appendices)*.

Barely thirty minutes later, and when Lee Oswald was in Dallas Police custody, mechanic T.F. White saw a man sitting in a parked car near the Texas Theater. As television news reports broadcast images and footage of the actual Lee Oswald, White swore it was Oswald he saw sitting in the parked car. For more interesting reading on the final alleged sighting of an Oswald double that day, refer to James Douglass' 'JFK & the Unspeakable'[20] and James P. Johnston's 'Flight from Dallas.'[21]

There was a concerted effort to assassinate President Kennedy and ensure Lee Oswald either took all or part of the blame. The fact that Governor Connally was seriously wounded and that local police officer, J.D. Tippit was killed would have been immaterial to the plotter's primary objective. Illustrating the evidence to support this contention, and the lack of evidence and proof against Oswald firing any weapons that day, demonstrates how contrived the carnage on November 22nd was allowed to become by an all-points cover up.

So, on the face of it, it is almost incredulous to think that the person on whose shoulders it was all being loaded upon could be killed in such a neat and straightforward manner by comparison. Like most things related to that weekend, so much has been shown to not line up including how poorly Lee Oswald was treated and handled by Dallas Police while in their custody. So why should his execution have been any different?

By the 1970's, the subsequent murders of Malcolm X, Martin Luther King Jr., and Robert F. Kennedy meant that President Kennedy's assassination was no longer such a unique event. And with those, criticism, and speculation of the official narratives of all four cases accumulated, alongside a rising distrust of the U.S. government no doubt helped by the Watergate scandal. This sparked several investigative committees and bodies formed in the U.S. Senate in the early to mid-1970's.

The **United States President's Commission on CIA Activities within the United States** (otherwise known as **'The Rockefeller Commission'**) [22] was established in the wake of a damning report in the New York Times in 1974 that highlighted acts committed by the CIA on U.S. home soil – illegally and in contravention of its charter of only operating outside of the United States.

The Rockefeller Commission exposed CIA operations such as MKULTRA and illegal citizen surveillance including mail opening. While the commission shed light on the CIA in these, and other instances, its focus on President Kennedy's assassination was very narrow and culminated in concluding that only three shots were fired from behind the motorcade in Dealey Plaza. The fact that Warren Commission alumni, David Belin and future U.S. President, Gerald Ford, was on the Rockefeller Commission did not go unnoticed.

The **United States Select Committee to Study Governmental Operations with Respect to Intelligence Activities** (otherwise known as **'The Church Committee'**),[23] formed in 1975, sought to expand on the Rockefeller Commission's work by focusing on assassination plots against foreign leaders hatched by U.S. intelligence. What this led to was the revealing of how deficient the initial investigations by the FBI and the Warren Commission in the aftermath of the JFK assassination were in terms of information they did not have available at the time. However, the Church Committee revealed, not only more on domestic and foreign surveillance operations, but the level of control and resources the CIA had across the media under Operation Mockingbird. While there was no standalone report or conclusion from the Church Committee on its findings related to the JFK assassination, it did give rise to valuable output from contributing senators Gary Hart, Walter Mondale, and Richard Schweiker on crucial aspects of the case that had been officially overlooked until that point such as organised crime involvement and Lee Oswald's ties to U.S. intelligence. These strands, and many more, would dovetail into the HSCA.

The **U.S. House of Representatives Select Committee on Assassinations (HSCA),**[24] established in 1976, focused on the assassinations of John F. Kennedy and Martin Luther King Jr. but was fraught by sabotage, politics & in-fighting that reduced it to being a toothless tiger. Much like the case of Jim Garrison's investigation being marred by sabotage and slander to derail it. But thanks to the persistence of noted journalist and JFK assassination researcher, Jefferson Morley, it has since been proven that the former agent that the CIA provided the HSCA as its liaison, George Joannides, did have direct ties to CIA-backed anti-Castro groups in Miami and New Orleans in the early 60's - the same groups that Oswald orbited around during that summer in New Orleans. Joannides' background and clear conflict of interest was never disclosed to the HSCA; therefore, he was able to control and stem the input from the CIA meaning a full investigation could never have been carried out. Nonetheless, the HSCA concluded that Oswald fired three shots, that there was one more shooter in Dealey Plaza firing at the president from the front right but missed, and that organised crime had some involvement. Fortunately, the HSCA did provide a more critical and insightful overview of Lee Oswald's shooting within its final report, but it is still far from a complete picture – hence the purpose of this book.

The release of the Oliver Stone movie, 'JFK' in 1992 would reinvigorate public interest in President Kennedy's assassination. So much so that, in response to the public outcry stirred by the film's case for conspiracy and its stated fact of thousands of documents related to the case still being withheld from the public, the U.S. congress at the time, including then-senator and future president Joe Biden, instituted the JFK Records Act that brought into law that all remaining records relating to the case would be reviewed to declassify or not. All documents that were declassified were to be made available to the public by 2017. The JFK Records Act also triggered the formation of the **Assassination Records Review Bureau (ARRB)**[25] in 1992 which, per its name, reviewed all accessible records of the JFK assassination and secured their release. However, as of 2024, there remain approximately 4,000 records sealed, and they are looking more likely to stay that way thanks to Presidents Trump and Biden's refusal to abide by the law of the act to release them. If it was a simple as Lee Oswald being a lone nut who killed President Kennedy, what do United States intelligence, and the government still have to hide?

What has been proven over and over again thanks to the work of many esteemed researchers is that the fingerprints of intelligence were all over Lee Harvey Oswald for most, if not all, of his adult life. He had been used, employed, manipulated, and manoeuvred by forces for ends that most find hard to comprehend. But the moment he was taken into police custody in Dallas on November 22nd 1963, his usefulness was over, and he was a liability that had to be mitigated.

INTERLUDE

INMATE 54018

Lee Harvey Oswald in Dallas Police Custody

Lee Oswald was brought into Dallas' City Hall just after 2:00pm, after his apprehension inside the Texas Theater. Aside from how grossly dramatic and heavy-handed his arrest was, to say that Oswald's basic human legal rights were violated in Dallas Police custody is a major understatement. Here are some examples of the treatment Oswald was subjected to during the last two days of his life:

- He would be paraded in line-ups next to other men that did not resemble him in looks or appearance – which counters the very purpose of suspect identity parades / lineups.
- He repeatedly asked for, but was never provided, access to legal counsel.

- He was led unprotected and in direct contact with hordes of news personnel through the halls of City Hall at all hours of the day and night. This included being put forward before a room full of reporters and directly asked questions.
- None of his interrogations were recorded on tape or by a stenographer. Only notes, either handwritten in short form or retrospectively by some of those present, chronicle what Oswald was supposedly asked and what he said.
- Directly implicated for both the Kennedy and Tippit shootings by members of the DPD and Attorney's office – making it impossible for a jury to have impartiality at a trial.
- and was arguably not charged for killing President Kennedy

All the while, Oswald appeared to have acquitted himself calmly behind closed doors and in front of the reporters even declaring himself to be a patsy and that he was taken in because he had lived in the Soviet Union. He was administered a paraffin test which he passed. And while Oswald was in custody, Dallas Police and the FBI could not recover his fingerprints on the suspected Kennedy murder weapon. They would only be found on the same rifle after he was killed.

The gross, yet incredibly suspicious, incompetence of the Dallas Police Department that weekend really is astounding. I recommend the recent works of Bart Kamp (Prayer-man.com and his book 'Prayer Man – More than a Fuzzy Picture'[11]) as excellent starting points for a detailed, black, and white account of the DPD's (mis)handling of the incarceration of Lee Oswald. So much so that the remainder of this book is able to focus entirely on how the shooting of Lee Oswald took place to further establish how incompetent and / or suspiciously the Dallas Police Department conducted themselves that weekend.

CHAPTER FOUR

THE FIRST SHOOTING ON LIVE TELEVISION

In 1963, the Dallas Police Department and City Hall was based in the Dallas Municipal Building. In 1956, the Annex Building, also called the 'Municipal Building' was built next door to accommodate the expansion of the Police Department and the city's need for jail and courtroom space. See a high level view below:

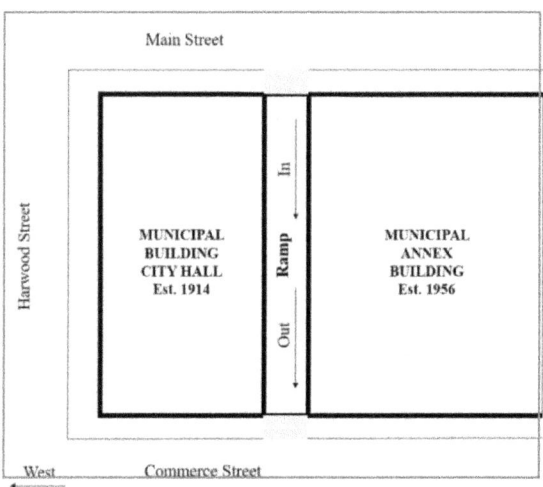

Copyright Paul Abbott

Under half of the Annex Building, that consisted of three floors above ground, was a basement in which police personnel cars parked. It was accessed by a ramp that cars would enter down from Main Street and exit from up to Commerce Street. The ramp sat under the point where the Annex Building connects to the Municipal Building (the old City Hall). On the other side of the basement carpark were a stairwell and elevators that provided access to the basement from the Annex Building above.

In the basement level of the Municipal Building was elevator and stair access from the floors above. There was also the jail office where prisoners were processed before or after being held in the cells above on the Fifth Floor. See the map below:

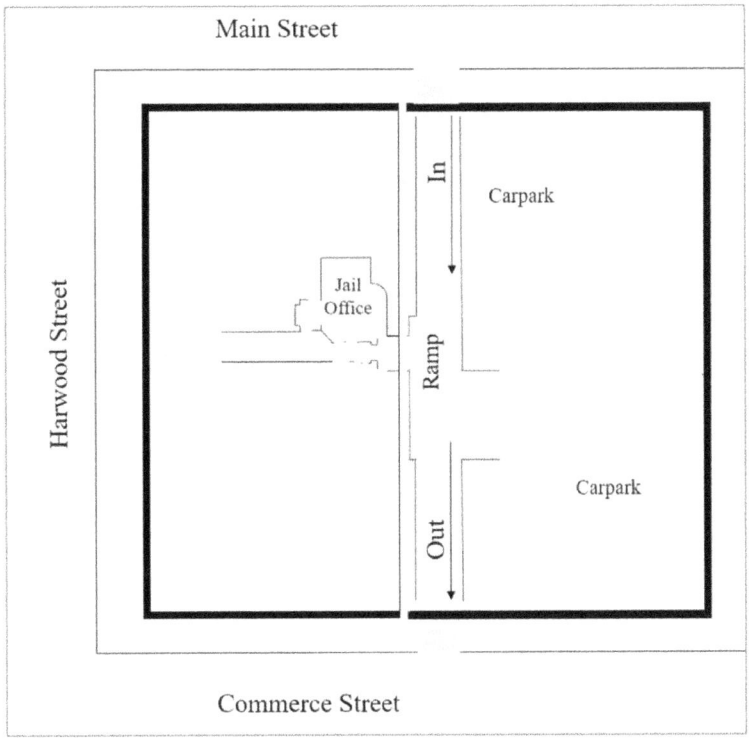

Copyright Paul Abbott

On Saturday November 23rd, the talk throughout City Hall turned to when Lee Oswald would be transferred to the Dallas County Jail – some twelve blocks west on Houston Street, ironically where it overlooked Dealey Plaza. That evening, Dallas Chief of Police, Jesse Curry told some members of the press that Oswald would not be transferred overnight but the next morning.[1]

However, there would be a string of alleged threats made to Oswald's life in the hours after midnight of Sunday morning. But despite details allegedly stated in the alleged threats, Dallas Police decided that Oswald would still be placed in the armoured truck for the transfer. It would be in a convoy with unmarked police cars to escort it with Oswald inside for the journey to the County Jail.

As the morning went on, more members of the press began to assemble in the corridors of City Hall and then down in the basement. Additional DPD personnel, namely volunteer reserve officers, had been called on to assist with preparations and security. The basement was sealed off by posting officers at entry points then it was searched from ceiling to floor at 9:15am. When the area was given the all-clear, members of the press were allowed to enter the basement. Most gathered outside the jail office but instructed by DPD to clear the area so most would ultimately end up on the carpark side of the ramp behind the railing. They would effectively form a wall of people and lights that Oswald would be led straight towards when he emerged out of the jail office. According to those present, estimates of how many people (police and media personnel) were in the basement prior to Oswald being brought out range from 50 – 150 people.

See the below diagram for how police and media personnel were generally concentrated around the point (X) where Oswald would be shot:

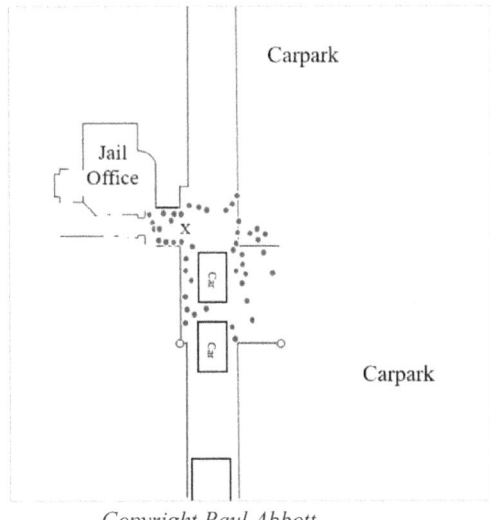

Copyright Paul Abbott

At the last minute, Fritz suggested that Oswald be transported in a car instead of the slow and cumbersome armoured truck. Detectives Beck, Brown and Dhority swung into action to ready all vehicles for the convoy. Lieutenant Pierce was also instructed to manoeuvre a car from the basement and out to the front of the armoured car on Commerce Street. At 11:21am Captain Fritz followed Lieutenant Swain out of the jail office and observed the scene. Deciding all was in place and ready, he gave the okay to Detectives Leavelle and Graves who were escorting Oswald to follow. As they did so, Detective Montgomery followed close behind. Leavelle, wearing a cream white suit and white Stetson hat, had his left wrist handcuffed to Oswald's right wrist. Graves, wearing a black suit and black fedora hat, was holding Oswald's right arm. They led him through the cordon of detectives towards the bottom of the ramps.

Fritz had gotten within touching distance of the unmarked car that Oswald was being led to as it was still reversing back. At that moment, a car horn sounded again and a man wearing a dark suit, and a fedora hat leapt forward from in between a police officer and a reporter to Oswald's front left and shot him with a revolver in the abdomen. The gunshot was a muffled but loud roaring sound. Oswald recoiled, threw his head back and let out a guttural cry instantaneously.

Photographer Bob Jackson's Pulitzer winning photograph capturing the moment Oswald had been shot.

Oswald slumped to the ground and the scene erupted into chaos. The man who had shot him was reached out to by both Leavelle and Graves to keep him back. The shooter even appeared to lunge again at Oswald as if attempting to shoot him again after he had collapsed to the ground. A swarm of detectives closed in, disarmed him and within seconds, both he and Oswald were taken away into the jail office. The media were kept back by police personnel, but they would continue to film and photograph the aftermath. Both ramps were sealed to ensure no one left or entered.

In the jail office, Oswald had been placed on the floor he had just walked on behind the counter. The medical intern on duty that morning was called to attend and when he couldn't detect Oswald's heartbeat, he carried out resuscitation on him. The shooter was pinned to the floor, handcuffed, searched, and then taken up to the Fifth Floor Jail by elevator. He had been identified as local nightclub owner, Jack Ruby. In the meantime, an ambulance had been called and it would arrive a few minutes later and take Oswald to hospital.

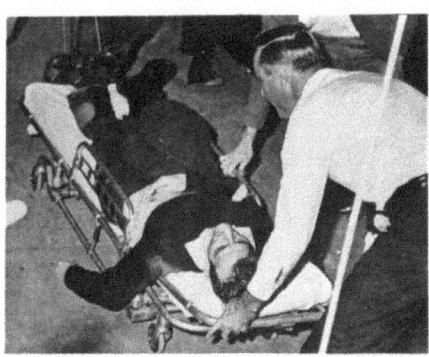

Oswald being brought out of the jail office on a stretcher (photograph by Jack Beers)

Once at Parkland Hospital, Oswald was rushed in through the same emergency department that President Kennedy and Governor Connally had been almost two days prior to the hour, although he was taken into Trauma Room 2 out of respect for the late president, who had been treated in Trauma Room 1. Doctors fought feverishly to save Oswald, who was bleeding internally throughout his abdomen. The bullet he had been shot with had torn through his spleen, stomach, kidney, liver, aorta, and vena cava. Despite it being fired into him at point blank range, it did not pass all the way through his body and out of his back. Lee Oswald was pronounced dead at 1.07pm – approximately ninety minutes after his arrival at Parkland. According to attending doctor, Charles Crenshaw,[2] Oswald died of haemorrhagic shock - the result of waste building up in his veins due to deprivation of blood and oxygen that effectively overloaded and poisoned his heart when circulation of his system was restored during the fight to save his life.

Visual Records

The killing of Lee Oswald was captured on film as there were at least six cameras documented as being in the basement that filmed the scene before, during and after Oswald's shooting. Another was non-operational as it was brought down from the third floor too late to be set up in time for Oswald's transfer. What is clear in all films of the incident are that Oswald was led out into a corridor of people and toward a wall of camera lights and waiting vehicles. When he was shot, each of the films captured the frenzy that immediately broke out.

It was as if Oswald and his assailant were both swarmed all over by people never to be seen again in an instant. Let's examine who and where the acknowledged camera operators were in proximity to the shooting:

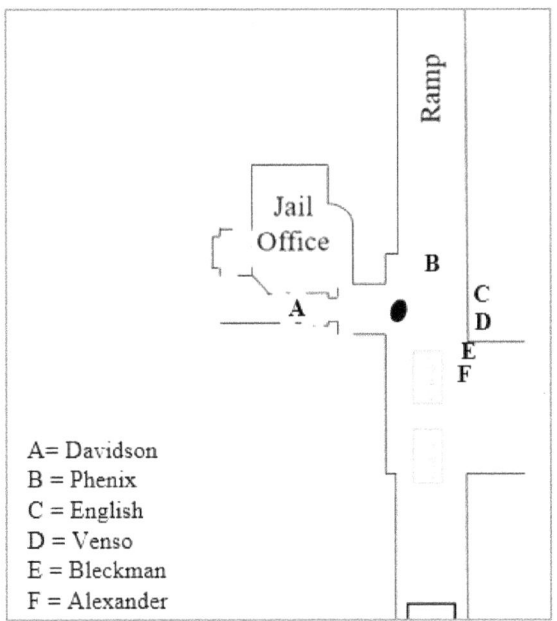

Copyright Paul Abbott

James Davidson (A) was present to record the transfer with colleague Warren Ferguson for the ABC. Contrary to widely held belief that all cameras in the basement were only filming Oswald from the front, Davidson stayed positioned next to the windows of the jail office window – therefore behind where Oswald would emerge out into the basement. Davidson's footage starts with filming through the jail office window as Oswald is being led out of the elevator into the jail office by Fritz, Swain, Leavelle, Graves and Montgomery. It then follows him being escorted through the office before cutting to him being led through the basement and being shot. The footage then resumes with capturing the movements of police personnel handling Oswald and Ruby. It ends with Ruby being led to the elevator by a police officer.[3]

George Phenix (B) was a camera operator for local, CBS-affiliated TV station – KRLD. He was positioned out to the left of where Oswald would be led out to the ramp. Virtually behind Ruby as he squeezed past Officer William J. 'Blackie' Harrison, Phenix was using a handheld camera that was using 16mm film (common for media use of the day as it could be used and viewed by individual frames), connected to a microphone and mounted on a unipod. Phenix's footage provides a continuous record of the shooting and chaos immediately following.[4]

J.B English (C), a camera operator for Channel 4, was positioned behind the railing directly across the path that Oswald was led to the ramp along. English was also shooting with 16mm film.[5]

Homer Venso (D), the camera operator for local NBC affiliate, WBAP-TV, was positioned next to English across the ramp, only what he was filming was broadcast on live television. He captured Oswald being led out and then Ruby shooting him from directly front on. Venso's camera captured both Oswald and Ruby being closed in on by DPD personnel but, unfortunately, Venso apparently changed a lens a split second prior to Ruby advancing at Oswald, resulting in a jump in the footage. Standing to the direct left of the camera on the other side of the railing was his news director, Jimmie Turner.[6]

Isadore 'Izzy' Bleckman (E) was to the left of Venso and was present for United Press International (UPI). Bleckman's footage of Oswald appearing, being shot and the ensuing melee is continuous. It is also taken from a lower angle as he was crouching at the time. He was not acknowledged by the DPD in their investigation.[7]

Steven Alexander (F), a freelance videographer, was able to position himself at a position in line to where Detective Dhority was backing the car to meet the detectives and Oswald. He also captured uninterrupted footage of the shooting. Like Bleckman, Alexander was only interviewed by the FBI. And even in the Dallas Police investigation, he is merely acknowledged as being present at the scene of the shooting.[8]

There were three photographers in the basement who had prime position to also capture the before, during and aftermath of the shooting. Their most widely circulated photographs can be easily found on the internet.

Frank B. Johnston, with United Press International, was standing across the driveway and directly in front of Oswald as he was brought out through the cordon of police and media personnel. He captured Oswald glancing over to his left a second before Ruby lunged forward to shoot him.[9]

Photograph by Jack Beers.

Jack Beers was a freelance photographer who took the above photograph by standing up on the railing where the TV cameras were to photograph the scene over the heads of the numerous reporters in front. His photograph shows Ruby lunging towards Oswald, about .3 of a second before shooting him. Also visible in the Beers' photograph, is cameraman, George Phenix's microphone hanging from the ceiling.

Bob Jackson, who's photograph is displayed earlier in this chapter, was with the Dallas Times Herald and was standing between camera operators Bleckman and Alexander on the other side of the ramp. He captured perhaps the most prolific image of the event, the moment that

Oswald reacted to being shot. Jackson would on to win a Pulitzer Prize for his perfectly timed and dramatic photograph.

Most worryingly, there were more camera operators and photographers in the basement that morning, but most would not be interviewed or even acknowledged as part of any of the investigations. Nor would most, if not all of the footage and photographs that they took ever surface.

What has been laid out in this chapter is the mainstream narrative of how Lee Oswald came to be shot in the abdomen by Jack Ruby in front of dozens of DPD personnel and members of the media. And Ruby was only able to do so by accessing the basement and get into position in the very moments before Oswald emerged.

Despite an overwhelming perception and evidence of incompetence, no heads rolled at the Dallas Police Department for the death of Lee Oswald in their custody. Business was seemingly allowed to carry on as per usual and the focus turned quickly from an obligatory internal investigation to the incarceration of Oswald's alleged killer, Jack Ruby.

To summarise, the briefness of this chapter is symbolic of how limited the coverage and scrutiny of this event is and largely remains. Footage and photographs largely form the sum of what has been understood and attributed to how President Kennedy and Police Officer Tippit's alleged killer, Lee Harvey Oswald came to be murdered. And as such, it has been treated as an open and shut aspect of that weekend. But we will now delve to the next layer of the 'onion' and uncover how brittle this narrative is when held up to further inspection and questioning.

CHAPTER FIVE

AFTERMATH

Reactions to Lee Oswald's killing were far ranging. According to Manchester's 'Death of a President'[1] in Washington, those among the closest to the late president received the news of Oswald's killing as if it were an intrusion or of barely any interest at the most. From a foreign policy perspective, officials were shocked and fearful of how the United States would be perceived. At least with the president's alleged assassin in custody, order, fairness, and justice – among the highest of democratic virtues – could be demonstrated. That changed with the untried Oswald's death. Newspaper outlets across the country instantly wound back up again to cover yet another shocking killing. Understandably, criticism levelled at the Dallas Police Department came thick and fast. The Omaha World Herald laid the blame for Oswald's death squarely at their feet because 'officials undertook to turn the transfer of a suspected murderer into a Roman circus.'[2] The New York Times referenced the old frontier of vigilante justice being allowed to take place at 'high noon and with the widest possible advance announcement… and it was an outrageous breach of responsibility'.[3]

In the face of criticism of the Dallas Police, its two highest officers were belligerent. Chief Jesse Curry told the press 'If I hadn't promised you people, I would not take Oswald until this morning, we would have taken him during the night. I told you I wouldn't back down on my pledge'. His ability to somehow blame the press for his own choices yet defend his commitment to a promise is astounding. When questioned about the criticism of him and his police force, Curry said 'We've done our best and it's easy to criticise.' Rumours soon began to circulate that Curry had resigned as Chief of Police but his superior, City Manager, Elgin Crull went into bat for Curry saying he had not resigned and if he did, he would not have accepted it. Mayor Earle Cabell, who Chief Curry was on the phone to in his office at the time of Oswald's shooting, called for hysteria to be resisted and said that he was proud of Chief Curry and his department and how they performed under the most difficult circumstances. Homicide Captain J.W. Fritz told the Sun Telegraph that Oswald's killing meant the investigation into President Kennedy's murder had ended because they had their man in Oswald. There was probably little telling back then how arrogant, inappropriate and off the mark such a statement would turn out to be. He also dared say that he did not think the shooting could have been avoided given 'he (Ruby) didn't have to move more than a few feet to shoot the man'. This statement is more galling when it is clear in photographs and film of the shooting that it was Fritz who left the front wide open for Ruby to shoot Oswald in the first place.

The shock of Oswald's killing was quickly accompanied by the news that the Dallas Police Department and FBI would investigate the shooting. The Warren Commission, the formation of which was announced a few days later on November the 29th, would also devote a portion of itself to the events of November 24.

Dallas Police Department's 'Investigation of the Operational Security Involving the Transfer of Lee Harvey Oswald'

It is a small detail but it is worth noting the above title of the DPD's investigation as it infers an emphasis on the security regarding Oswald's transfer. However, if the investigation just focused entirely on security plans and measures that the DPD implemented, frankly, for many reasons that are laid out in this book, it would not be a very long or detailed document. Regardless, the DPD concluded ('to a reasonable certainty') that Jack Ruby entered the basement from the Main Street ramp without any collusion between him and any Dallas police officer or member of the press. And that he was only able to enter due to a series of 'unfortunate coincidences' which resulted in a 'momentary breakdown' of security.

To come to this conclusion, a panel was formed on behalf of the DPD consisting of Inspector J.H. Sawyer, Captain W.R. Westbrook and Captain O.A. Jones. They enlisted Lieutenants F.I. Cornwall, Jack Revill, P.G. McGaghren and Detective H.M. Hart to interview Dallas Police personnel, citizens and members of the media that had some interaction with the events surrounding or directly related to the shooting.

That said, as the DPD conceded, there were witnesses from interstate and even other countries but they did not have the resources or time to interview people that they determined wouldn't be able to 'throw additional light on this matter' anyway. Lack of resources and time and mounting pressure aside, perhaps the best way to aptly symbolise the hasty and inconclusive nature of the DPD investigation is to refer to a schematic map that Captain M.W. Stevenson had drawn up of the City Hall basement, jail office, ramps, and surrounding streets at the time of the shooting:

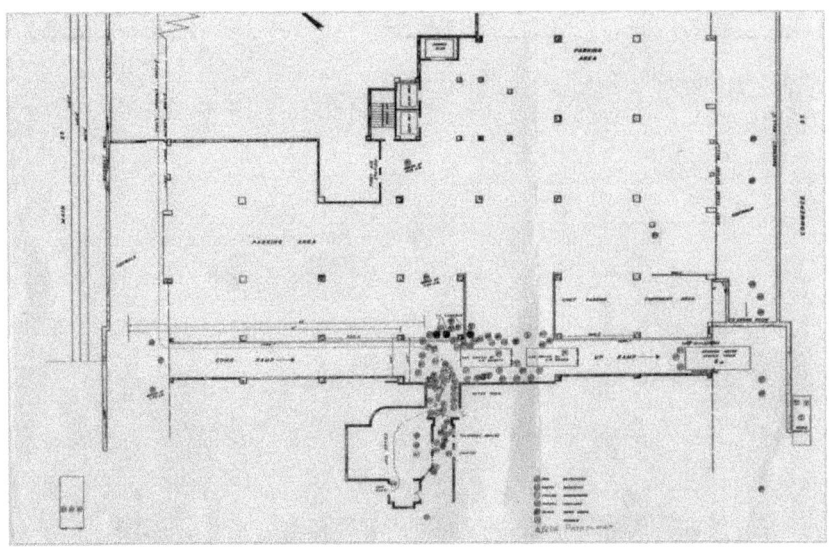

This diagram displays where Dallas police (including reserve officers & clerks) and media personnel were in proximity to the shooting. Confined to a single page and requiring a magnifying glass to identify the hand drawn circled numbers, that have since been coloured per category of people (i.e. detectives in purple, media in grey etc..), to correspond with an index of names, it is both confusing and misleading in a few ways.

Unfortunately, the map neglects to account for others who were confirmed by the DPD as being there at the time of the shooting. As part of my investigation, I have recreated this schematic map to contain more accurate references of where people were located based on theirs, and where applicable, other testimonies confirm. This mainly applies to the dozens of media personnel present who, until now, have largely been unaccounted for at the scene of the shooting. We will explore this in a later chapter.

The schematic map has been provided in the appendices in sections that include clear numbers for easy identification.

The DPD investigation commenced straightaway with personnel being ordered to submit statements to Chief Curry about their whereabouts during the shooting and whether they knew Jack Ruby. They were then interviewed to give more detail or change anything in their initial statements and in a couple of instances, lie detector tests were administered. In total, there were 121 people interviewed consisting of:

- 70 Dallas Police personnel - 21 Dallas Police reserves
- 23 members of the media - 7 civilians (including Jack Ruby)

Of the **70** Dallas Police personnel interviewed for the investigation, *22* were not in the basement at the time of the shooting and neither were *12* of the **21** reserve officers interviewed. The presence of reserves in the basement at the time of the shooting is yet another curious facet to the morning of November 24 that has escaped scrutiny.

Essentially volunteering members of the community, they were clearly relied upon, in the circumstances, to take part in the lead up to the transfer of Lee Oswald. We will touch on this aspect in a later chapter. But in the meantime, below is a list of the reserve officers led by Reserve Captain Arnett who presented to City Hall on the morning of the shooting:

Charles O. Arnett	Alvis R. Brock	James D. Brockway
Arthur W. Capps	Roland A. Cox	A.B. Craig
Kenneth Croy	Robert T. Davis	Oliver W. Harrison
Harold J. Holly	J.R. Hopkins	J.C. Hunt
Jerome Kasten	Harry M. Kriss	Logan W. Mayo
J.C. McCain	Ben McCoy	Barney Merrell
*D.J. McDonald	*(FNU) Montgomery	William J. Newman
Donald Suits	Gano E. Worley	

The investigation report contained an introductory summary from Captain J.W. Fritz titled 'Interrogation of Lee Harvey Oswald'.[4] It starts with recounting the DPD's search of the Texas School Book Depository that includes word of Roy Truly telling police around 1pm that Lee Oswald had left the building. This is false because if Oswald was named to police as missing from the Book Depository (and he was one of a few employees that did not return that day but, predictably, that is omitted from Fritz's report), his name and a more accurate description would have been broadcast as an all-points bulletin – potentially preventing the shooting of Officer Tippit, per the official version of events.

---

*Reserve officers 'Montgomery' and 'McDonald' in this list are only speculative as they were only ever referred to by other reserve officer's statements for the DPD investigation – (Montgomery – O.W. Harrison & McDonald – Robert T. Davis). Montgomery and McDonald were never interviewed regarding the events related to the Oswald shooting.

Instead, an incredibly general description of an 'unknown white male, approximately 30, 165 pounds, slender build, armed with what is thought to be a 30-30 rifle, - repeat...' was broadcast pointing the finger of suspicion at a large section of the Dallas male population. The proven distortion by Fritz in the first page of his report makes it difficult to hold too much faith for the rest of his accounts regarding anything related to that weekend particularly as, he even conceded, he was writing it from memory and 'rough notes'. Captain J.W. Fritz's reputation as the case-breaking captain of the Homicide and Robbery Bureau preceded him.

But it was widely acknowledged that he was not the greatest administrator of paperwork and records. More on this interesting and important aspect can be found in Bart Kamp's 'Prayer Man – More Than a Fuzzy Picture'.[5]

It also talks to a point prevalent in so many aspects of the Kennedy assassination case. That, either purposefully or not, specks and items of truth are dotted with distortions and untruth throughout the records making it hard to distinguish truth from fiction (as in the instance highlighted in the above). If done so by design, it is one hell of a tactic to ensure as much of the truth remains covered up as possible.

Bookending the investigation report is an overview of the security measures implemented by the DPD prior to the shooting and factors they determined to have contributed to Jack Ruby being able to shoot Lee Oswald to death. The below points summarise what the DPD concluded:

Security was set up throughout the basement parking area on the morning of the shooting. This consisted of clearing the area of any unauthorised personnel (including media and City Hall workers such as porters and maintenance engineers) and then a search being carried out across the parking area by police and reserve officers. When the search was completed, officers were placed at all entrances and were instructed to not let anyone in except police and media personnel with the proper credentials.

To transport Oswald, an armoured truck was ordered to City Hall. However, the plans were then changed at the last minute from transporting Oswald in the armoured truck to moving him in a police car as part of a convoy that the armoured truck would still drive in as a decoy.

Members of the press assembled outside the jail office which included setting television cameras to film the moment Oswald emerged. When the area became too congested for anyone to move freely, all media were ordered to take their positions on the other side of the railing in the parking area.

When Oswald was to be brought down, he was to be escorted by two detectives on either side and one directly behind. Captain Fritz would be walking at the front and leading them to a waiting squad car for Oswald and his detective escorts to be loaded into and driven out of the basement. So, with the above measures in place, how did the DPD conclude that Jack Ruby was able to enter the basement and be in position at precisely the right time to shoot Oswald?

Coincidence / happenstance: The DPD verified that Ruby sent a money order to employee, Karen Carlin from the neighbouring Western Union at 11:17am that day. They measured the distance from there to both the top of the Main St. ramp and down to the basement where he shot Oswald (339.6 feet and 99 feet respectively) and timed it as taking 1 minute and 13 seconds to cover the distance to the ramp from the Western Union office and then 22 seconds to walk down the ramp to the point where Oswald was shot.

The DPD further pushed the coincidence point by saying that no officer interviewed knew the time that Oswald would be brought to the basement and transferred out. Therefore, Jack Ruby couldn't have had foreknowledge from any confederates within City Hall to time his entrance into the basement precisely before Oswald emerged. This implies that it could only be down to the element of chance and coincidence that Ruby could gain access to the City Hall basement with perfect timing.

Lights, camera... : The bright lights of the assembled media's cameras were a factor as they were positioned to directly shine onto the route that Oswald would be escorted along after being brought out of the jail office. This apparently made it difficult for the officers facing the lights to observe any sudden movements from where Ruby emerged from. The DPD concluded that many of the detectives in the direct vicinity of where Oswald was shot were looking at him and not looking around for any threats.

All told, the above points were conveyed as fact and without barely any acknowledgement of wrongdoing. Perhaps even more frustrating is the fact that the Dallas Police Department provided no detail on what more or else they could have done to avoid such an inexcusable thing as a defenseless prisoner being killed while in their custody in the first place and therefore, again. In all, they excused themselves of any blame for Oswald's shooting and put it down to an ambiguous combination of extraordinary circumstances and coincidence.

The **FBI** probe into the investigation swung into effect immediately as well. According to the Mary Ferrell Foundation, it took over from the DPD and would launch its investigation before being rendered an investigative body for the Warren Commission.[6] In total, 103 people were interviewed consisting of:

46 Dallas Police personnel   11 Dallas Police reserves

35 members of the media   9 civilians (not including Jack Ruby)

1 Secret Service & 1 Sheriff official

While the FBI interviewed fewer people than the DPD did, they interviewed a higher percentage of media and civilians including many people that the DPD did not. This provides additional perspective to what happened surrounding the Oswald shooting. The fact that the FBI's investigation kicked off while the DPD's was running meant most statements given to the FBI and DPD were done within a short period of time of each other. This aspect is particularly interesting because, very quickly, inconsistencies began to emerge between what one person told the DPD and the FBI. A good example of this is in the accounts that Sgt. James A. Putnam gave. He was in the front passenger's seat of a squad car that drove up the ramp to Main St. and exited there just prior to Oswald being shot. He detailed all aspects of the short ride around the block from there to the Commerce St. ramp to both the DPD and FBI but he only told the FBI of an incident where he helped stop a man running down the corridors of

City Hall in the minutes after the shooting and when he arrived at the Commerce St. side of City Hall. Why omit such an important detail?

Reserve Captain Charles Arnett is another good example. In his statements to Dallas Police on November 27th and December 9,[7] Arnett seemingly gave the bare minimum of how he helped coordinate the search of the basement with Sergeants Dean and Putnam just after 9am on the morning of the shooting and who he recalled seeing in the basement that morning. Whereas to the FBI, on December 5,[8] he provided extensive detail about which of his reserve officers he assigned to who and where, descriptions of members of media and recalling the moments before and after Oswald's shooting. Detective Wilbur J. Cutchshaw also appears to have been selective with what he told to whom. He was standing near the door from which Oswald was escorted out into the basement from. He provided a minimal account for the DPD investigation of seeing three men wheeling a camera down to the ramp from the elevator just prior to Oswald emerging but only seeing two of the men after the shooting.[9] Yet to the FBI, he goes into great detail about instructions he and his colleagues were given by Captain O.A. Jones with regards to where to stand, the instance of the camera being wheeled out and that it was he who told Detective Leavelle, who was handcuffed to Oswald, to come out to the basement.[10]

What Putnam, Arnett and Cutchshaw said and didn't say may or may not mean anything in the scheme of things regarding the happenings of the shooting, but they are just a few examples of gaping inconsistencies between statements made for different investigations – no doubt sowing seeds of confusion around what actually took place ever since.

The line of questioning by the FBI for members of the DPD is pretty evident. Questions most commonly asked were along the lines of:
- Where and when were they on duty,
- What were their duties and in what location/s,
- Were they aware of security measures for Oswald's transfer,
- Did they see any unauthorised people in the basement prior to the shooting,
- Did they know Jack Ruby, see him in the basement prior to the shooting, work for him or know of any other DPD officer that did.
- Were they aware of any relationship between Ruby and Lee Oswald.

It is interesting to note that as early as the days after Oswald's shooting, the FBI were so focused on a possible connection between he and Ruby. For interviews with members of the media and civilians, they mainly consisted of accounts of why they were where they were that morning, timings, and recollections of events before and after the shooting.

Jack Ruby's trial took place across a week in early March of 1964 and he would be convicted of murder with malice and receive a death sentence. Ruby would successfully appeal this on the grounds that he never could have received a fair trial in Dallas because of all the publicity around the case. A new trial was scheduled for February 1967 but Jack Ruby died the month prior. The trial is useful to factor into this examination of Oswald's shooting as a total of 15 people who, also gave statements across the DPD, FBI, and, later, the Warren Commission, took to the witness stand at Jack Ruby's trial. Particularly when we consider that their sworn testimonies were given under threat of perjury. We will scrutinise these statements in their various contexts throughout this book.

The **Warren Commission** interviewed witnesses to the events before, during and after the shooting of Oswald between the months of March and July in 1964, mainly in Dallas. With only a few exceptions, the Warren Commission interviewed people that had already been interviewed by both the DPD and FBI or by one or the other. It would devote a portion of its time with each person to clarify anything that was previously stated to the FBI. Along with the findings of the FBI, the Warren Commission would provide a mere thirty-five-page summary and conclusion on the handling of Oswald's transfer and subsequent shooting within its 900-odd page report released in August of 1964.[11]

While the Warren Commission would provide some due criticism of the Dallas Police for Oswald's death, its level of detail and focus was lacking overall. Like the DPD conclusion, the Warren Commission provided a broad context conclusion that summarised that Jack Ruby was able to slip into the City Hall basement unaided and shoot Lee Oswald thanks to the mass-presence of media and the confusion it caused to the otherwise 'meticulous' plans of Dallas Police. The report did at least acknowledge key failings that the DPD did not. For example:

- not transferring Oswald during the night before, considering the threats that allegedly had been received against Oswald's life that same night and the fact that the approximate time for his transfer was commented on by Chief Curry to the media the evening before,
- that there was not one single person who took overall responsibility for the handling of the transfer,
- and with the last-minute decision to change the method of transport for Oswald in the armoured truck to an unmarked police car, the expected car was not in place when it was decided to bring Oswald out into the basement.

The Warren Commission is legendary for misrepresenting what people stated and what appeared in the final report but there is one troubling example that relates to the Oswald shooting.

Jimmie Turner was positioned with most of the press personnel in the basement facing the corridor Oswald would come out into from the jail office. In the final Warren Report, it states that he saw 'a man he is confident was Jack Ruby moving slowly down the Main Street ramp about 10 feet from the bottom.' However, in his actual, statement to Warren Commission Counsel Leon Hubert,[12] what he said he saw was quite different:

> **Turner:** I happened to glance up and this was at the same time the car drove out *(car driven by Pierce up to Main Street)* of the - - I'm not sure. I couldn't - - that right down where the ramp it hit - - the - -
> **Hubert:** Level part?

Turner: Level part. I saw Mr. Ruby coming in.

Hubert: Now, had you ever seen him before?

Turner: No, sir, I certainly hadn't. Let me mark "10" as the point where I actually saw Mr. Ruby *(at a point of a map that is at the bottom of the ramp up to Main Street as indicated below)*

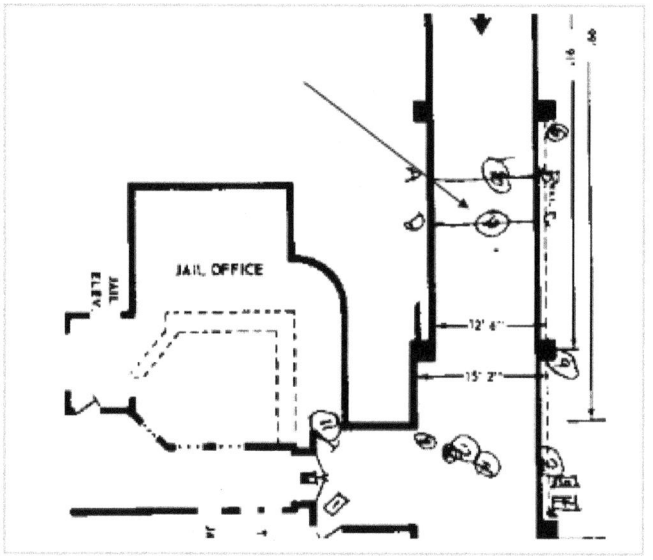

'Turner (Jimmy) Exhibit No. 5080' (Courtesy of the Warren Commission)

At no point in his statement to the Warren Commission did Turner say he saw Jack Ruby walk down the ramp from Main Street. He clearly clarified that the first time he saw him, and he did not know Jack Ruby to recognise him, was at the bottom of the ramp where it met the driveway. This meant Ruby could have come to that position from somewhere else and within the basement. It does not just mean that he could have only entered down the Main Street ramp. Yet in the absence of anyone else testifying to seeing Ruby, or anyone resembling him, entering down the ramp, what

Turner said was used to contend just that. However, Turner would describe the hat he saw Ruby wearing as one with a larger brim than the dark fedora Ruby actually wore. Interestingly, in his statement to the DPD, Jimmie Turner explicitly said that he did not see Jack Ruby until 'a split second before the shot was fired' and that he did not recall seeing him in the basement.

Thanks to the tireless work of early critics such as Sylvia Meagher, Harold Weisberg and Mark Lane, the Warren Report was almost instantly discredited for finding Oswald solely guilty of the Kennedy and Tippit murders despite the gross lack of evidence. Furthermore, panel members Hale Boggs [13] and Richard Russell [14] did not agree with the findings either. Whether it was to avert any geopolitical fallout at the time or assure Lyndon Johnson's presidential re-election in '64, it does not change the fact that the report was a pure 'whitewash'. This included how the committee conducted itself such as deciding on the witnesses that would and would not testify, the line of questioning that was pursued and, as per the case of Jimmie Turner and many others, how accounts differed between what was said during the hearings and how it was purported in the final report. When it was published, the Warren Report was done so without a comprehensive subject index making it all the less appealing and accessible to read and comprehend by the average layman. In fact, panel member Allen Dulles declared that only the most ardent researcher or academic will read it because most people 'don't read as much these days.'

To pick at the many holes in the Warren Commission is among the lowest of low-hanging fruit when it comes to the case for conspiracy and cover up of the JFK Assassination as it was clearly always geared to accounting all blame on Oswald. However, for all of its clear faults, there are instances of pragmatism and truth seeking within the Warren Commission, which we will acknowledge later in this book. Sylvia Meagher's 'Accessories After the Fact',[15] Gerald McKnight's book 'Breach of Trust'[16] and Walt Brown's 'The Warren Omission' [17] are the most comprehensive works on the Warren Commission.

Perhaps this photograph *(below)* of Warren Commission Exhibit 881, from the Warren Report, of a model of the scene of Oswald's shooting demonstrates best how the Dallas Police department projected where the media were situated at the time of Oswald's shooting – out of the way and contained at the bottom of the Main Street ramp. As we will see, this is a far from accurate representation of where most of the media personnel actually were.

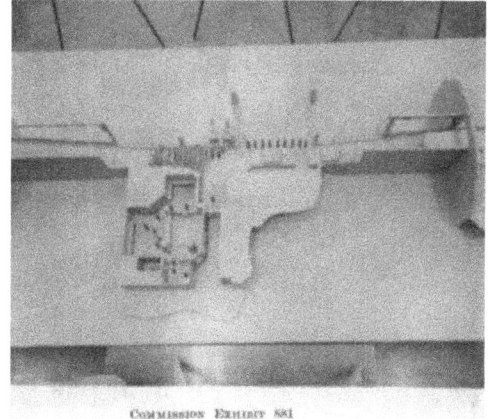

COMMISSION EXHIBIT 881

The **HSCA,** as introduced in Chapter Three, however did focus some attention to the shooting of Lee Oswald and as such, had seventeen pages within its final report devoted to the topic.[18] Using the perspective of fifteen years since the event, the HSCA reviewed the DPD, FBI and Warren Commission findings and carried out its own questioning of some witnesses to the Oswald shooting. In doing so, it was able to highlight glaring deficiencies not just in the security measures at Dallas City Hall on November 24 1963 but of the subsequent investigations. The HSCA even hypothesised a number of ways that Jack Ruby could have entered the basement that morning - which was more than the DPD, FBI and Warren Commission ever did. As already stated, the HSCA was not immune from its own controversy and compromise and perhaps that is because it did venture into territory within the JFK and Martin Luther King assassinations that no government body had up until that point.

PART TWO

PREPARATIONS AND PEOPLE

CHAPTER SIX

PREPARATIONS

In the case of Lee Oswald's shooting, we have the benefit of hundreds of statements given by people that witnessed events leading up to, during and after it. What these provide is an opportunity to form as complete a picture as possible to reveal the most accurate account of what took place. To do this properly, it will be useful to scrutinise witness statements and testimonies in comparison with each other. This will mean that information that most have either found too confusing or confounding regarding Oswald's shooting will now be distilled and enable us to pose sensible questions about what really happened on November 24, 1963.

Let's start with the preparations as discussed by the Dallas Police for Oswald's transfer from the City Hall Jail to the County Jail. Per protocol,[1] prisoners could be transferred over to the custody of the local Sheriff within hours of a complaint being filed i.e. charges laid for a crime within the county the alleged crime took place in. The process thereafter was a simple one that consisted of either a Dallas County Sheriff or Constable presenting Dallas Police with a warrant for the prisoner who had been charged. For Dallas County, this was typically done at the jail office in the basement of City Hall. The prisoner was then retrieved from the jail on the Fifth Floor by DPD personnel, brought down to the jail office, signed out and loaded into a vehicle for transport to the County Jail. Only very occasionally was this process subverted when extraordinary circumstances, which Oswald clearly presented, dictated that the DPD took a prisoner to the County Jail instead. In Oswald's case that weekend, he *technically* could have been transferred to the County Jail as early as the evening of Friday November 22nd as that is when he was charged with the murder of Officer Tippit.

This brings us to an interesting point – just when was Lee Oswald charged for the murder of President Kennedy? In 'Prayer Man – More than a Fuzzy Picture', Bart Kamp focuses on this aspect and seriously questions whether Oswald was in fact charged at all by analysing testimonies and Oswald's movements at the stroke of midnight that Friday and Saturday night when his arraignment was purported as taking place.[2] Interestingly, during the time Oswald was paraded in front of the press a few minutes after midnight, Saturday November 23, he was asked about and then told by reporter, Bill Mercer, that he had been charged with killing President Kennedy. Oswald's clear reaction of surprise and then resignation at hearing this is very telling.[3]

Either way, he would be kept at City Hall in the custody of the Homicide and Robbery Bureau whilst he was being interrogated because Fritz admitted after the fact that it would have been too awkward to do so at the County Jail. Also, according to Fritz's statement for the DPD investigation, Chief Curry first broached the question with him of transferring Oswald to the County Jail early in the afternoon of Saturday November 23rd. Fritz told Curry that he was still questioning Oswald so Curry asked if this would be completed by 4pm that afternoon. Fritz said he didn't think he could have it all finished by then so Curry asked if it would all be finished by 10am the next morning – Sunday November 24. Fritz said that it could. In his statements to the FBI[4] and Warren Commission,[5] Curry did not give as much detail about this exchange. He merely said that Fritz recommended that Oswald not be transferred that night because the darkness would 'make it harder for them to see anyone wanting to cause trouble.'

We are now faced with the first of many dilemmas to this story in terms of deciding what is the most plausible of accounts between two people regarding a particular aspect of the case.

Fritz's account of Curry asking him when Oswald would be ready for transfer and his not being sure given, he, his detectives, and others such as representatives from Secret Service, FBI and U.S. Postal Service were still questioning Oswald, is plausible.

Curry's explanation that Fritz was worried about the cloak of darkness being used by would-be attackers, however, does not sound plausible given the most serious threats to Oswald's life would not allegedly materialise until that night. So, we can deduce that Curry's assertion that Fritz was worried about darkness as a reason to keep him overnight was most likely Curry deflecting any pressure that he could have been perceived as applying regarding moving Oswald, therefore culpability on his part for the shooting.

Beyond Curry and Fritz, the only other person whose perspective we can draw on for talk on Saturday about Oswald's transfer is Sheriff Bill Decker. He testified to the FBI of first hearing from reports on Saturday afternoon that Oswald would be brought to the County Jail on Sunday.[6] Upon hearing this he called Dallas Police and spoke to either Chief Curry or Captain Fritz who confirmed that Oswald would be transferred the next day. Worryingly, he was still none the wiser about whether his department would be carrying out the transfer or if it would be Dallas Police.

Threat/s in the Night

As Oswald slept in his cell on the Fifth Floor of City Hall, at the other end of town at the County Jail, Deputy Sheriff C.C. McCoy, was fielding calls (drunken, in one instance), some long distance even, that ranged from ones of sympathy for the people of Texas to word from a leader of '14,000 negroes that were coming to town to get this bunch straightened out.' According to his report to Sheriff Decker the next day, McCoy also received a call at 2:15am from a man who was well spoken and a member of a group of one hundred men and that he 'wanted the Sheriff's office to know that they had voted one hundred percent to kill Oswald while he was in the process of being transferred to the County Jail' and that he wanted this department to 'have the information so than none of the deputies would get hurt.'

Still according to McCoy's report, [7] a short time later, FBI Agent Milt Newsom called and asked if he had received any calls threatening Oswald's life. McCoy said he had so Newsom asked him to contact Dallas Police to alert them to it. McCoy did and spoke with someone in Captain Fritz's office, but he didn't get a name. Whoever McCoy said he spoke to, they told him that they, at the DPD, hadn't received any threatening calls.

McCoy would soon answer another inbound call from a man who asked if it was the Sheriff's Department. When McCoy said it was, the man told him to wait a minute. Another man came on the line and said that Oswald would 'never make the trip to the County Jail.' McCoy could not tell if the voice was of the same man that rang earlier.

Per his testimony to the Warren Commission,[8] it was actually Captain William Frazier at the DPD that McCoy spoke with to relay news of the threat as he said he spoke to someone with the surname of or similar to 'Coy' from the Sheriff's Department that night. Regarding the call with McCoy, Frazier said that Oswald's scheduled transfer was discussed between them. Then, Frazier said, McCoy told him Sheriff Decker recommended that the transfer be brought forward and that if it were, there could be two supervisors on hand at the County Jail to assist with receiving Oswald. Frazier said that he told McCoy that he would try to reach his superiors and see what could be done.

Just before McCoy's call, Frazier testified that Agent Newsom called to tell him of a threat on Oswald's life as well. In a memo by FBI Director, J. Edgar Hoover the next day, during the afternoon after the shooting, he ruefully referred to the threat to Oswald and that, in response to their calls for heightened security, the 'Chief of Police' (Curry, presumably much later that morning) assured the local FBI that 'adequate protection would be given'. Of course, in the myriads of communications and chaos of that weekend, the calls for heightened security could have been in a few different methods and levels.

The Billy Grammer Call:

However, Dallas Police Officer Billy Grammer, of the Patrol Division, also allegedly received a call at City Hall that night from a man who did not identify himself but warned that Oswald would be killed in the basement if he was not transferred in secret. Curiously, according to Grammer, the caller also referred to an armoured car being used as a decoy by the DPD. Grammer said he told his supervisor about the call and later signed an affidavit about it. He also said that he only recognised the caller as being Ruby, who he was friends with and allegedly met for coffee on Saturday November 23rd, after Lee Oswald's shooting.

I believe that these claims by Billy Grammer are highly dubious to the point of being completely false for a variety of reasons:

1. Over the years, the times that Grammer said he took the call have varied from 9pm Saturday night through until 3am Sunday morning.[9]
2. There is no corroborating testimony from anyone else that any such call came into City Hall, particularly those who were either there at the time or referenced by Grammer including:
    - Captain Frazier, who as we have seen, actively responded to word of the threat from the FBI and Sheriff's Department only by trying to reach his superiors.
    - Sergeant Putnam, Grammer's superior officer.
    - Chief Curry, who Grammer said he gave a copy of the notes he wrote during the call and submitted the affidavit to,
    - and Jack Ruby, who never mentioned meeting Grammer for coffee or calling him later to warn of a threat on Oswald's life in any statements he gave after the Oswald shooting.
        - To be fair, if it did happen, admitting it would have likely scuppered Ruby's defense, the following year, that his shooting Oswald was not premeditated.

3. There is no trace of the affidavit Grammer wrote up and submitted to Chief Curry.
4. Whenever Grammer said he received the call, it had not yet been determined how Oswald's transfer would take place let alone whether the DPD or Sheriff's Department would carry it out, until the middle of the next morning. So how could something that there is no record or evidence of being discussed have already been leaked?
5. Grammer only recognised Jack Ruby as the person who called him *after* Oswald's shooting, not during the alleged call itself. If he had only just met with Ruby on Saturday November 23, wouldn't his voice have still been fresh in his memory?
6. It is drawing a very long bow to contend that, despite hearing that those plotting to kill Oswald knew of an armoured car to be used as a decoy in the transfer, the DPD would *still* ultimately decide to use an armoured car as a decoy in the actual transfer.
7. During their investigation, the FBI asked all DPD personnel about any associations that police personnel had with Jack Ruby. If the call was real and known to them, the FBI would have interviewed Grammer to probe his connection with Ruby. But they, the DPD and the Warren Commission did not ever interview Grammer.

In the absence of *any* supporting evidence, the instance of Grammer saying he took a call from Jack Ruby warning of an attack on Oswald appears to be yet another case in the JFK assassination universe of a tenuous tale being spun for which only one person's word can be relied upon. And further to this, Grammer has been referred to by many researchers and it has become lore that Jack Ruby either had foreknowledge of a plot to kill Lee Oswald or indeed was trying to scuttle some kind of assignment or order he had been given by 'calling' in a threat and giving them cause to alter whatever transfer plans they had.

So, if the Grammer call did not take place, this presents the very startling possibility that the Dallas Police Department did not directly receive any threats on behalf of a 'committee' of people wanting to kill Oswald that night. And if the 'threats' phoned into the FBI and Sheriff's Department were truly made out of concern for the safety of Sheriff *and* Police personnel, why was the DPD not contacted directly by the 'committee' as a warning as well?

We know they weren't because, Grammer's account aside, Captain Frazier only testified to receiving word of the threat from the FBI and Sheriff's Department. Deputy Sheriff McCoy's report to Sheriff Decker corroborates this. It would seem that no one else at City Hall would testify to any threats from a 'committee' coming in either.

What are we to deduce from all of this? Having factored out the Grammer call and given the consistency of detail in the threats phoned into both the FBI and Sheriff's Department, what has been attributed to as a 'series of threats' on Lee Oswald's life in the early hours of the day of his eventual shooting, if they took place at all, could have actually only been one threat made *twice*. And thanks to a lack of any statements from FBI Agents Milt Newsom and Vernon Glossup to give any further insight, McCoy's report to Sheriff Decker and another statement he gave to the FBI (both on the same day) really is all we have ever had to go on. Perhaps what is most suspicious and casts a question of doubt over the entire 'Committee Threats to Oswald' episode is who from the FBI took McCoy's one and only statement:

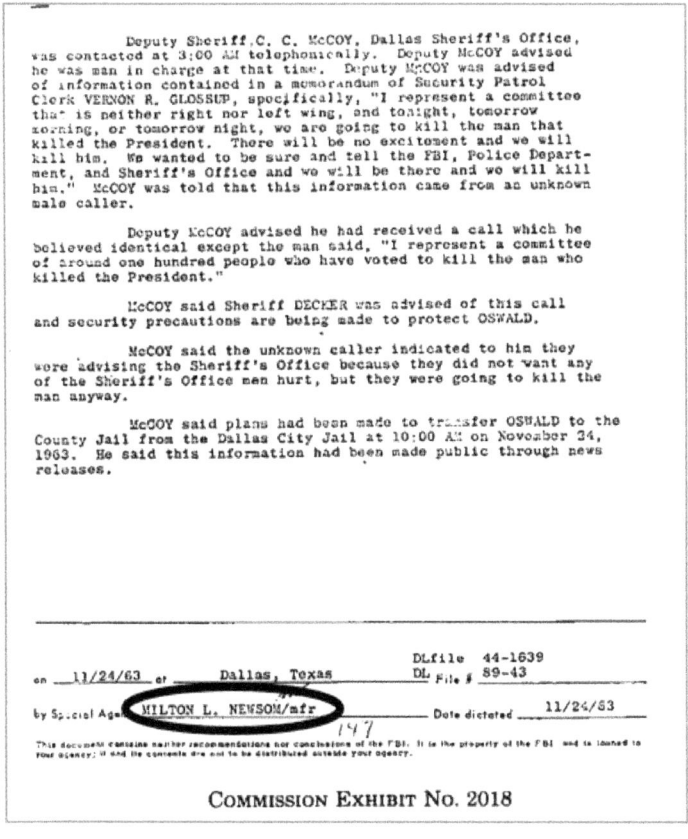

COMMISSION EXHIBIT NO. 2018

Reading this statement that Agent Newsom took from McCoy in comparison to the report McCoy submitted to Sheriff Decker is like reading the accounts of two separate events. McCoy's report to Decker is detailed, and logical at three pages long *(provided in the appendices)*. Whereas the Newsom statement is brief and does not line up with McCoy and Decker's version of events. To add, Newsom neglects to include in his report the statement he took that it was he who rang McCoy to enquire initially about whether any threats on Oswald's life had been phoned into the Sheriff's Department. This ought to have been an easy detail to remember and a hard one to forget. The statement of Capt. Frazier that Agent Newsom took *(also provided in the appendices)* is also questionable because when he was asked to read and confirm it was correct by the WC Counsel Hubert, Frazier said that he did not say what Newsom attributed to him as saying in paragraphs three and four, because he never knew what the transfer plans were.

What we have are the potential makings of a convenient 'closing of the circle' when it comes to the threats to Oswald for the FBI. That is to say that the Dallas FBI office was all across the receiving of them and the final word on them by censuring both key persons in the McCoy and Frazier about them! Furthermore, is it not too far away within the realms of possibility that someone at the FBI phoned the Sheriff's Department posing to Deputy McCoy as the representative of the a 'committee' making a bold threat on Oswald's life? We'll never know for sure so this is purely speculative on our part but Newsom's actions are suspicious. No further investigation or inquiries were made into just who this 'committee' was that voted to avenge President Kennedy and kill his alleged assassin because, like most things with this case, what was the point once Oswald was dead? No committee or a member of one ever came out and testified to being responsible for such threats either. So, what would the FBI have to gain from manufacturing the 'Committee-Threats'? Regardless of how the DPD would respond to the threats, could it all have been part of some kind of exercise in deflection by them onto the DPD to shield themselves from any current and future blowback regarding Lee Oswald? With the benefit of hindsight, we know that the FBI did come under scrutiny for both its handling of and association with Oswald so it is something worth considering.

Regardless, DPD Captain Frazier said that he first reached Captain Fritz by phone at his home to tell him of the threats that had come in. He then said to Fritz that Oswald would have to be transferred straightaway but Fritz suggested he call Chief Curry as it was he who wanted Oswald transferred in the morning. But when Frazier attempted to reach Curry, he could not get through as the phone line was... out of order. After a few attempts to contact Curry by phone, Frazier sent an officer to Curry's house to tell him of the threats and get any further instructions. How unfortunate, unlucky or something worse was it that the Chief of Police could not be reached at such a crucial time to make a call either way about whether to enact Oswald's transfer earlier considering the threats. In all likelihood, if Curry were reached straightaway by phone, for reasons that will become clear later in this book, he never would have agreed to bring Oswald's transfer forward and go against his original pledge to the press of when it would be carried out.

According to Warren Commission testimony of Patrol Division Captain Cecil Talbert, who had clocked on to relieve Frazier by the time Curry would be reached, he said that Curry's only instruction from home was to tell FBI Agent Newsom and Sheriff Decker that he would arrive at City Hall between 8:00am and 9:00am that morning.[10] Upon Curry's arrival at City Hall later that morning, it had still not been made clear if the Sheriff's Department would carry out Oswald's transfer to the County Jail or if the DPD would. To this point, Assistant Chief of Police Charles Batchelor recalled overhearing a conversation Curry was having with Sheriff Decker over the phone that morning at around 9am about the transfer that culminated in Curry saying, 'If you want us to, we will.'[11]

A Basement in Parts

At around the same time as the call between Curry and Decker on the Sunday morning, the basement would be subjected to a search by regular and reserve officers in preparation for Oswald's transfer. As part of the process, officers were assigned at three entries into the basement and that is where they would stay until after Oswald had been shot. However, there were other points of entry that had been overlooked.

As has already been demonstrated in diagrams provided in this book, in the basement, there were ramps from street level that led into the car park, elevators and stair access up into the Annex Building, a First Aid Office, the jail office from where Oswald was brought through and emerged from prior to being shot, telephone booths and utility spaces such as a Janitor's Closet and Meter Room. However, there was also the Assembly Room which, across that weekend, was where Oswald participated in line-ups for witnesses, was where he was brought before the press and where Reserve Officers were assigned from ahead of his planned transfer.

Adjacent to the Assembly Room was the Records Room. Unfortunately, it is hard to be precise about where exactly the Assembly and Records Rooms were situated as there is no record to be found of the layout of that part of the building.

The basement also extended to under the sidewalks of Main and Commerce Streets and it was under each street that were doors to access the sub-basement. Refer to the black rectangles below for their locations:

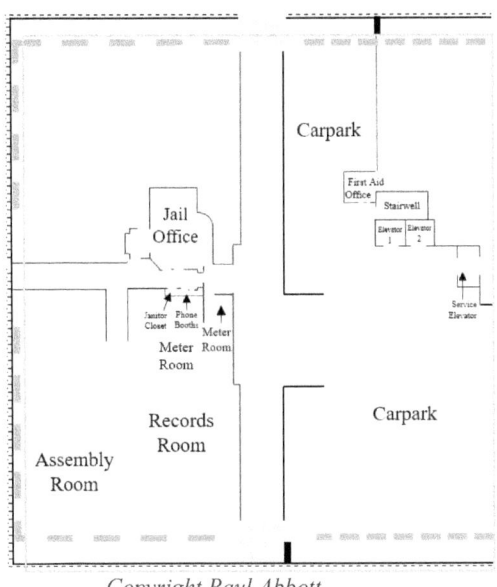

Copyright Paul Abbott

Essentially a level below the basement, the sub-basement was part of the Municipal Building's original construction so it spanned under City Hall and the basement car park. Across it were Engine Rooms, a Locker Room and apparently at one stage, without any irony intended, a shooting range.

Aside from the doors under the Commerce and Main Street sidewalk, there were other ways to access the sub-basement. For instance, there was a service elevator that ran from the top of the Annex Building all the way down to the sub-basement. On the back of it was another door which opened out to the fire escape stairs when the elevator was on the First (Ground) and Second Floor. On the First Floor there was an outer door opened out to a vacant lot. This enabled service workers to have access to the service elevator without having to walk all the way through the Annex Building.

On the morning of the shooting, the service elevator would be left locked on the First Floor from 10am. And the two general purpose elevators (labelled 1 & 2 in the above diagram) adjacent to the service elevator already had their power cut to ensure they too could not be used that morning.

Still in the sub-basement level but under the City Hall building was a Locker Room. It was accessible by a stairway down from the hallway that intersected the Assembly Room and Records Room on the above basement level. A large space which accommodated lockers for personnel, across it was a television, four payphones, a bathroom, recreation room and vending machines to purchase food, drink, cigarettes and cigars. It will become apparent that the Locker Room had both civilian and police personnel come and go from it in the minutes leading up to the shooting. And like the rest of the sub-basement level, there is also no record of the Locker Room being searched and sealed either. However, we can use investigation statements to gather how it could be accessed. To this point, the City Hall building had, and still does have, three large sets of stairs as main entries from Main, Harwood and Commerce Streets. Flanking each set of stairs were steps that would descend below ground level to access the basement and, in the case of the ones leading down from Commerce Street, the sub-basement Locker Room. This was for a functional purpose to allow personnel ease of access when starting or finishing their shifts. While it was true that all entrances at the top of the steps from street level were locked, we will soon discover instances of people being able to walk down the side steps of the Harwood Street entrance without being checked and get all the way down to the jail office in the minutes leading up to Oswald's shooting.

Moving back up to the basement car park, let us focus on the stairwell that led from there all the way to the Third Floor of the Annex Building. We've already touched on how a fire escape could be accessed through the back of the service elevator on the First and Second Floor levels. However, there is no evidence that this point, or any other point of the stairwell up to the Third Floor was guarded or locked so as to prevent people entering or exiting through this way either. The basement was secured by a lock on the basement side of the stairwell door – as well as the reserve officers standing guard.

Up in the Annex Building, there were corridors on the First, Second and Third Floors that linked it to the Municipal / old City Hall Building. At the points where the two buildings joined, there was a lockable gate. However, Captain Stevenson testified that he did not know if the First Floor gate was locked that morning.[12] And there is no record of any other officers in the building to ensure the elevators and stairwell were not breached. At least City Hall maintenance worker, Edward Pierce, testified that the gate that Stevenson was referring to was locked.[13] But this does not alter the fact that the Annex Building was not fully sealed and guarded to prevent the stairway and elevators from becoming used that morning.

So, contrary to the findings of the Dallas PD and Warren Commission, all possible points of exit and entry were *not* guarded therefore secured that morning so we are presented with the conclusion that there was only the most minimal of security perimeters set up that encompassed the immediate area that Oswald's transfer took place within.

CHAPTER SEVEN

CIVILIIANS OVERLOOKED

Having laid out the geography of City Hall and the Annex Building basement levels and examining the many points not guarded, therefore could be accessed through, it is now important to focus on the accounts of those present in and around the basement prior to and during Lee Oswald's shooting. Given there were just under three hundred statements made regarding the Oswald shooting, it will be useful to group as many present as possible into categories: citizens, law enforcement, and media. And beyond those, specific instances and locations of events. With this approach, we can focus in depth on the many narratives that took place across City Hall during the hours leading up to Oswald's shooting.

The most under-represented cohort of witnesses that day were the civilian employees of both City Hall and the Dallas Police Department. While it is true that none were present to directly witness Jack Ruby shooting Oswald, their testimonies regarding the preparations for the transfer and the aftermath provide important pieces to the overall picture of the puzzle, as it were. However, other than in records of the DPD investigation and the Warren Commission, there is little to no reference to be found regarding these people and their stories – until now.

Below is the list of non-Police and media personnel that were at or outside City Hall that morning and who provided at least one statement to the subsequent investigations:

Fred Bieberdorf – *First Aid Attendant*
Frances Cason - *Dispatcher*
Napoleon Daniels – *Former police officer*
Nolan Dement - *Bystander*
Doyle Lane – *Western Union Supervisor*
Harold Fuqua – *Parking Attendant*
Michael Hardin – *Ambulance Driver*

Wilford Ray Jones - *Bystander*
Edward Kelly - *Maintenance*
Louis McKinzie - *Porter*
Johnny F. Newton – *Jail Clerk*
Edward Pierce – *Engineer*
Alfreadia Riggs – *Porter*
John Servance – *Head Porter*
Jerry D. Slocum – *Jail Clerk*

Any reasons behind the seemingly random nature of who was and was not interviewed by which investigation remains anybody's guess particularly when it came to who the DPD did not interview. Consider, for instance, how crucial the testimonies of Dallas locals Fred Bieberdorf, who provided Oswald with first aid after he had been shot, and Michael Hardin, who drove the ambulance that rushed Oswald to Parkland Hospital, ought to have been considered but were not taken.

That aside, we will first focus on a group of workers who were employed to ensure the smooth running of all infrastructure across both buildings of the City Hall complex including the basement car park. They were:

Harold 'Hal' Fuqua
Edward Kelly Louis
McKinzie

Alfreadia Riggs
John Servance
Edward Pierce

For the porter and parking workers, their base of work was clearly the car park in the City Hall basement. Their jobs were focused on keeping the area in order, getting police personnel cars parked or ready for use and keeping the general public from parking down there – which was most prevalent when it came to jail inmate arrivals and departures. For the maintenance and engineer workers, their work would take them to all parts of both buildings including the utilities spaces across the sub-basement level. There was also a female standing with the workers who was identified as a telephone operator by the name of Ruth – surname unknown – and it is not evident what her movements were after that point.

Once the search of the basement began, all media personnel were apparently cleared out but the City Hall workers remained in the far eastern end of the basement where the stairs and elevators went up to the Annex Building, having already stopped work to watch the comings and goings in preparation for the transfer. To this point, Harold Fuqua even testified to the FBI of observing car trunks being opened and searched.[1]

Edward Pierce also thought they could stay and watch the proceedings that morning up to and including Oswald's transfer if they kept out of the way. On the face of it, this was a fair assumption given where they were all positioned: nowhere near the transfer route and out of sight of the television cameras. But they were ordered to clear out of the basement and not just for the time it took police personnel to search it. In his own testimony to the DPD, it was Reserve Officer Brock who gave these orders.[2] And presumably this was done a few minutes after he arrived in the basement for assignment at around 9:30am.

Collectively, it is clear that the workers followed this directive by taking the service elevator up to the First Floor of the Annex Building. This was because the two public elevators had their power cut and were not functioning. Porter, Louis McKinzie, who was responsible that day for running the service elevator took the group up that way to the First Floor. From there the group would walk across to the City Hall Building to find a place to watch the transfer. Soon, Brock called for McKinzie to bring the service elevator back down so he (McKinzie) could escort, according to Brock's own testimony to the Warren Commission, 'one of the TV men over there, (who) wanted to go up the fourth – fifth floor to do some kind of work with the equipment there.' Both Brock and McKinzie would corroborate that the repair man only spent a few minutes doing whatever it was he was doing up in the upper floors of the Annex Building before being brought back down by McKinzie. There is no testimony from any of the media personnel present that day to explain who this person was and what it was they were doing. After that, Brock told McKinzie to leave the service elevator locked on the First Floor and not bring it back down to the basement. McKinzie did so by locking it in place with a key, then hung it on a hook within as was common practice. In his testimony to the Warren Commission, the time was 10:00am.[3] He then walked along the hallway on the First Floor of the Annex Building toward the City Hall Building. McKinzie confirmed in his testimony to the Warren Commission that there were three 'passageways' that connected the two buildings. They were on the First (Ground), Second and Third Floor and each could be locked with a metal, accordion-style expanding gate. Over nights and on the weekends, these gates were routinely locked so it is easy to imagine that they were in all probability locked on that day too. In fact, Edward Pierce testified as much when before the Warren Commission.

The workers, not wanting to miss any of the happenings surrounding Oswald's transfer, stayed on the First Floor, and walked to the Commerce Street entrance of the Annex Building. From there, behind the locked glass doors they stood and watched the activity outside and waited to watch Lee Oswald be driven away. This is where Louis McKinzie would rejoin them.

It appears that the group stayed together in this location for up to one hour. At which point, Harold Fuqua[4] and Alfreadia Riggs[5] decided to leave to find a television to watch the coverage of the transfer instead.

A Circuitous Journey

Having decided to leave the other workers at the Commerce Street entrance, Harold Fuqua and Alfreadia Riggs set off to find a television. Having both been long-serving employees of City Hall (Fuqua – 6 years, Riggs – 7 years) they would have known that the nearest television was down in the Locker Room in the sub-basement level next door.

However, given they had been ordered out of the basement as a security measure, and Oswald had still not been transferred, it is understandable that they chose to avoid taking a direct route to the Locker Room as it would have likely resulted in them being turned away or worse, in trouble.

Instead, they retraced the way they had come with the other workers through the Annex Building. From there, they continued along the First Floor to the far eastern end where the elevators and stairwell were.

As McKinzie had left the service elevator locked on the First Floor, it was in position for them to walk through it and exit through the rear door and out to the fire escape and passage that led directly to the outer door. According to both Riggs and Fuqua in their testimonies to the Warren Commission, it was Riggs who used the keys that McKinzie had left hung up in the elevator to unlock the outer door. He kept them with him but said that he made sure the alleyway door was locked by shaking on the door handle. This is an important point that we will revisit later.

Riggs and Fuqua walked through an alleyway to Main Street and began to walk west – along the front of the Annex Building. They then came to the top of the ramp that led from the street down to the basement. This is where Officer Roy Vaughn had been standing guard for at least the last hour. And it was this point where Jack Ruby was most commonly purported as entering the basement in time to shoot Oswald. We will also revisit this location and the comings and goings of people there in more detail. However, Vaughn did confirm in his testimony that 'some city hall janitorial' staff approached on foot from the east [6] – which is the direction Riggs and Fuqua would have come from. And they said they stopped at the top of the ramp for only a few moments to look down into the basement before walking on. Vaughn also corroborated this.

Riggs and Fuqua rounded the corner of Main and Harwood Streets and stopped below the steps up to City Hall. According to Riggs, Fuqua asked him to go down the steps and check to see if 'it would be all right for us to go down because we (they) were under the impression they had the police – had a police officer on the door.' Riggs did so and discovered that there weren't any officers guarding the basement entrance from there into City

Hall so he turned around and told Fuqua to come down. This further reiterates the fact that *all* public entrances into City Hall that morning were not guarded and therefore secure. Riggs and Fuqua walked down the hallway and got as far as the door before the jail office. There they got close enough to see all of the media assembled. They turned right and headed down the corridor that led to the Records Room, Assembly Room, and the stairs down to the Locker Room. Once down there they encountered someone who was all alone. Let's pick it up with Riggs' recollection to the Warren Commission's counsel, Leon Hubert with what happened next:

> **Hubert:** You mean you went down into the locker room? That is where all the policemen have their lockers and there's a recreation room and television and ---
>
> **Riggs:** Yes, sir, and television and – and there was a jail attendant down there, actually he didn't work in the jail office, he's not a policeman, but he works in the jail office.
>
> **Hubert:** What is his name? Do you know?
>
> **Riggs:** No, sir. I really don't. He told us that he didn't think they were going to show it on television. He imagined they were going to run a tape and show it later on. Said, "Well, we should have stayed up there. Maybe we could have seen him when they brought him out—"

Riggs and Fuqua testified to the Warren Commission on the same day – April 1st 1964. This was no coincidence as witnesses were organised into categories, particularly when the WC lawyers travelled to take testimonies. Riggs gave his testimony at 10:30am that day and Fuqua, at 3:55pm. Yet Counsel Hubert, who interviewed both men, did not pursue the question of the unidentified man in the Locker Room with Fuqua. But thankfully, Fuqua corroborated the encounter with the man and that he said he thought the transfer would be shown as reruns only. Yet, Hubert did not ask Fuqua if he could identify him. It can only be chalked up as another thread of questioning that was cut frustratingly early at the quick. So, we are left with some clear questions to consider:

- Who was the man Riggs and Fuqua encountered in the Locker Room? Per Riggs' speculation it well could have been any kind of a police officer that he saw or associated with the jail office. And this could feasibly have been any officer from reserve to patrol officer to detective – as all had reason to be there during normal times of operation. But, as we will uncover in later chapters, there is a clear candidate for who the man was that Riggs and Fuqua encountered.
- Why would the man urge Riggs and Fuqua to go somewhere else to observe Oswald's transfer? The locker room was large enough for them all to sit and watch whatever coverage was broadcast so what was the big deal with redirecting Riggs and Fuqua away?

Riggs bought a can of chilli from a vending machine, and he ate from it as he and Fuqua left there to go back upstairs. According to both men, they stood in the Harwood Street hallway and were there when Oswald was shot. They both would testify to not seeing it take place, just to hearing and seeing the chaos that broke out. In terms of other people mentioned so far in this book, their position was approximately a couple of metres behind cameraman, James Davidson.

After the shooting, Riggs and Fuqua kept out of the way but were able to note that all entrances had been sealed. When things had calmed down, Fuqua testified to the WC that he asked Captain George Lumpkin to escort he and Riggs across the basement car park to the service elevator and stairwell. None of the seven City Hall workers listed earlier in this chapter were interviewed for the Dallas Police investigation, despite being among the most accessible of people to do so. Perhaps, it was because they were all presumed to have not been in the immediate vicinity of the shooting. But Riggs and Fuqua were mentioned in others' testimony to the DPD such as Roy Vaughn. And others in the basement hallway would have seen them to identify them if only for the uniforms Riggs and Fuqua were wearing. Yet they were still not noted and considered for interviewing. But this does not diminish the fact that their movements reinforce the point of how lax security was across multiple points of the City Hall complex.

The Attorney

Dallas Attorney, Tom Howard's law firm was situated in one of the buildings across Harwood Street from City Hall. On the morning of Oswald's transfer, as he would have done, no doubt, many times before, he walked over to the City Jail. On this occasion, he would tell the FBI, he did so because he had received a call from someone in the jail office on behalf of someone else, presumably an inmate.[7] He was able to enter down into the basement level of City Hall from Harwood Street – down the same steps that Harold Fuqua and Alfreadia Riggs had. He did so with the intention of taking the elevator up to the Fifth Floor from the jail office. The obvious inference being that the main entrance from Harwood Street would have been locked – like the ones on Commerce and Main Streets.

Having walked down to the jail office, Howard testified that he did get to the elevator there and punch the button to go to the Fifth Floor. He said that he then turned to someone he presumed was a detective and asked if they were 'fixing to take him (Oswald) out of here?' Oddly, Howard couldn't recall if the detective said anything in response.

In any event, Howard did not go up in the elevator. Instead, he found his way back out into the hallway. Soon he would notice a 'sudden jostling and shoving among the newsmen' and then he heard a shot. He did not see Lee Oswald or Jack Ruby or any of the shooting. Instead, according to his own words, he turned around and simply walked back along the corridor he had entered from, then out onto Harwood Street and stood on the sidewalk. There he would confer with his legal partner, Coley Sullivan, before returning over the road to their offices.

Using the testimony of others, we can apply some firm question marks to Howard's one and only account of his movements in the City Hall basement in the moments prior to Oswald emerging and being shot.

Detective Homer McGee told both the DPD[8] and FBI investigations[9] that he was standing inside the jail office. There was an information desk and window which was opposite the elevator that faced out into the hallway. He noticed Tom Howard walk up to the window out in the hallway from either the Commerce or Harwood Street doors. Recall the layout of the basement because, even at that junction, it really was possible to access the basement level from the steps that ran down under both the Commerce and Harwood Street steps. According to McGee, Oswald then emerged from the elevator to be led out for the transfer. As that was happening, McGee said that Howard waved through the window, said that he'd seen all he'd needed to see and walked back up the hallway. Moments later, Oswald was shot.

Detective H. Baron Reynolds was the only other person to positively identify Tom Howard in the 'lobby' outside of the jail office in the moments just prior to the shooting.[10] And all Reynolds could add was that Howard was standing behind two uniformed officers. Tom Howard is just another case that exemplifies how easy the basement in City Hall was to access, right up to when Oswald was shot. However, what is even more strange about the case of Howard is the fact that, in barely a matter of hours, he would be acting as Jack Ruby's lawyer.

If Detectives McGee, and to a lesser degree, Reynolds, are to be believed, they put massive holes in Howard's account of him being in the jail office, getting as far as the elevator, saying something to a 'detective' but not recalling what was said to him. So, if Howard was lying about his movements in the crucial moments prior to the shooting, the question must be asked, why? His stake in the events of the day would apparently only come into play *after* Ruby had shot Oswald. He and his movements were allegedly of no consequence before that point of time. He could have had genuine reason, as a defence attorney, for being at City Hall Jail. His offices were across the road and clients of his were in the jail. But the coincidence of him being there at that point in time and his saying that he had 'seen everything he had needed to see' before exiting certainly is curious.

We will revisit the matter of Tom Howard in a later chapter but while we are focusing on the vicinity of the jail office, let's account for the two civilian clerks that were working in there on the morning of Oswald's shooting.

The Rest

Johnny F. Newton[11] and Jerry D. Slocum[12] were not police officers - both were civilian clerks for the jail office. According to their testimonies, that morning was business as usual in terms of the processing of incoming and outgoing jail inmates. Neither testified to venturing away from their workstations, down to the Locker Room for instance, or that they had received any special instructions nor experienced any changes to their workplace. Only Newton would comment about the build-up of police officers and media and his impressions of the shooting aftermath. However, one of his and Slocum's colleagues, Information Desk clerk, Melba Espinosa, according to Detective Buford Beaty, was not allowed to enter the jail office, where she worked.[13] Frustratingly and confusingly, she would be turned away near the basement car park giving her claim as one of the few people on the receiving end of any kind of strict police guard work that morning.

Nolan Dement was one of many civilians who had stopped on Commerce Street across from the ramp opening. It appears that the DPD chose to interview him because he had a camera, and they wanted to ascertain if he had been in the basement and taken any pictures there. He testified that he had not entered the basement and that he did not take any pictures 'or have anything of worth for the investigation'.[14] He was one of only two bystanders who were interviewed. One can only wonder again why, if Dement was deemed important enough to interview, then why were a multitude of others who witnessed the before, during and aftermath of the shooting overlooked? The other bystander interviewed, Wilford Jones, wandered between the Main Street and Commerce Street ramp openings before and after the Oswald shooting. He was interviewed by the DPD and stated that he was near the Main Street ramp entrance before walking around City Hall to the Commerce Street entrance.[15] When the shooting took place, he walked to a nearby parking lot for no apparent reason before going back to the Main Street entrance where he saw former police officer, Napoleon Daniels, who we will focus on in a later chapter. Interestingly, he recalled then seeing Attorney Tom Howard telling reporters that he heard of the Oswald shooting while on his way home.

The remaining civilians listed in the table earlier in this chapter will be discussed in the context of what they were interviewed for by at least one of the subsequent investigations. However, as we have already touched on, there are numerous people that witnessed the events that enveloped the shooting of Lee Oswald but were not called on for any of the investigations. So, as we continue to peel back the layer of the onion by scrutinising the many narratives that took place across Dallas City Hall on the morning of November 24, those that have lain obscured will finally be focused on to help piece together more of the overall puzzle.

CHAPTER EIGHT

MEDIA

Picture the scene: it's approaching midnight of Friday 22nd November at Dallas City Hall. What had unfolded over the last twelve hours must have made the concept of a new day arriving completely intangible and almost foreign to those caught in the middle of the chaos of that day as it unfolded. And as the hours passed, more media personnel had flooded into the building to capture every development to do with Lee Oswald and report it out – ensuring the dial of intensity remained turning.

Up in a small anteroom up on the Third Floor, members of the media were told that District Attorney Henry Wade would provide them with an update on the charges against Oswald down in the basement Assembly Room / makeshift Press Conference Room. Then, as if it were a mere afterthought, Chief Curry turned to the media and said they could 'have Oswald brought down, if you like?' And with that, and without any regard for how long it would take the media to transport their large television cameras amongst the rush of people through the corridors and down an elevator, he said it would start in twenty minutes.

Evidently in footage and photographs, the room was packed, wall to wall with reporters standing in between cameras towards the front then on chairs and tables all the way to the back. Before Oswald was brought in, Chief

Curry warned the assembled press not to crowd or push forward on Oswald, according to Fort Worth Star-Telegram reporter, Thayer Waldo.[1] But as footage of the event demonstrates, Oswald was asked questions by reporters but was never crowded on or pushed upon. However, after barely a minute, it ended, just after Oswald was told that he had been charged with killing the president.

Perhaps this is a good time to remind ourselves how, at the time, in Dallas, the relationship between the local media and the police was remarkably close. In fact, it was systemic. As outlined in the Warren Report, Chief Curry set in place 'General Order No. 81'.[2] This decreed 'that members of this Department render every assistance, except such as obviously may seriously hinder or delay the proper functioning of the Department, to the accredited members of the official news-gathering agencies and this includes newspaper, television cameramen and news-reel photographers.' Further explaining this order in a letter to all police personnel, Curry wrote 'The General Order covering this subject is not merely permissive. It does not state that the Officer may, if he so chooses, assist the press. It rather places on him a responsibility to lend active assistance.'

So, in short, from the top down, the DPD were organised to operate as stewards of public affairs and had an obligation to the public to allow them to know about police matters through the print, radio, and television media. This policy, and the intense interest in the happenings at City Hall that weekend from the public, explains why the press were allowed into City Hall and given regular briefings that weekend – right up to and including Oswald's eventual planned transfer to the County Jail.

Chief Curry gave many interviews and statements to the media that weekend – too many as far as FBI Director J. Edgar Hoover was comfortable with because, according to one article at the time,[3] he despatched a personal message to Curry requesting he not 'go on the air anymore until this case is solved.'

But when it came to the question of when Oswald would be transferred to the County Jail, regardless of when or if he got that message from Hoover, Curry pressed Fritz about it Saturday afternoon / early evening by saying that he would 'need to tell these people (no doubt referring to the press) something definite.' So, he told a group of reporters, including Thayer Waldo and Channel 5's Jim Kerr, that evening, at approximately 6pm according to some, that Oswald would be transferred some time the next morning. When pressed further, Curry said, according to multiple reporters testimonies, that Oswald would be moved at 10am – not after 10am, as has been most commonly purported since. With that, the intent to move Oswald the next morning was widely reported – and any advantage in secrecy or surprise that the DPD or the Sheriff's Department could have used to safely conduct Oswald's transfer was lost.

Any footage and photograph of someone in the moments immediately before, during and after being killed is polarising and confronting - the imagery of Oswald's shooting is no different. But zoom out on the images taken in the Dallas City Hall's basement that morning and what we are presented with is mostly Dallas Police personnel bearing witness to the shooting. So, factoring in the media personnel that took these photographs and film, the only members of the media evident in most visual records are three reporters from New York – Tom Pettit (NBC) and Ike Pappas (CBS) in the Jackson photograph and, in addition to them, Maurice Carroll standing behind Pettit in the Beers photograph.

What is evident across the records of investigations related to the Oswald shooting is just how many members of the media were present, and actually interviewed. In fact, it is downright sobering to consider that the most comprehensive accounts of Lee Oswald's shooting from the perspective of the assembled media were given during the investigations in late '63 and early to mid-1964. Of all of the scrutiny that has been laid upon the assassination of President Kennedy ever since including multiple government organisations, the perspective of the media present to witness the Oswald shooting is almost non-existent, even in the HSCA report... hence the purpose of this book.

Listed in full on the next page, is the most comprehensive list ever produced of media personnel (sixty in total) who were either officially or unofficially acknowledged as being either present at Dallas City Hall or within the vicinity before, during or after Lee Oswald's shooting or interviewed regarding events leading up to or after (Glen Duncan, David Hughes, Darwin Payne and Tony Zoppi, for example).

Steven Alexander# - *Videographer*
Gene Barnes# - *Cameraman*
Jack Beers - *Photographer*
Nelson Benton* - *News Producer*
Gene Blake # - *Reporter*
Isadore Bleckman - *Cameraman*
Maurice Carroll - *Reporter*
James R. Davidson - *Cameraman*
Gary DeLaune # - *Reporter*
William 'Glen' Duncan* - *Reporter*
Lowell 'Jay' Duncan # - *Reporter*
Geoff Edwards# - *Reporter*
J.B. English - *Cameraman*
Bob Fenley - *Reporter*
Warren Ferguson - *Sound Engineer*
Curtis Gans* - *Reporter*
Ed Haddad# - *Reporter*
Robert L. Hankal - *Floor Director*
Gladwin Hill# - *Reporter*
Robert Huffaker - *Reporter*
David Hughes* - *Reporter*
Unknown Japanese man # - *Reporter*
Robert Jackson - *Photographer*
Frank B. Johnston – *Photographer*
Seth Kantor - *Reporter*
Otis H. 'Karl' King# - Reporter
Bill Lord# - *Reporter*
Hank Machariella # - *Reporter*
Ted Mann# - *Sound Technician*

Terence McGarry# - *Reporter*
Ben Molina* - *Floorman*
Jeremiah 'Jerry' O'Leary - *Reporter*
Oliver Oakes* - *Reporter*
Ike Pappas - *Reporter*
Gene Pasczalek* - *Cameraman*
Darwin Payne* - *Reporter*
Francois Pelou - *Reporter*
Tom Pettit # - *Reporter*
George Phenix - *Cameraman*
Henry Rabun# - *Reporter*
Fred Rheinstein* - *Producer*
Bert Rhinehart# - *Reporter*
Warren Richey* - *Sound Technician*
Anthony 'Tony' Ripley# - *Reporter*
Peggy Simpson # - *Reporter*
Paul Sisco# - *Reporter*
David F. Smith# - *Reporter*
Johnnie Smith* - *Remote Operator*
Milt Sosin# - *Reporter*
James N. Standard - *Reporter*
John Tankersley - *Cameraman*
Robert Thornton - *Reporter*
David Timmons - *Cameraman*
Jimmie Turner - *Director*
Homer Venso - *Cameraman*
Thayer Waldo# - *Reporter*
Ira N. Walker* - *Remote Operator*
Wes Wise * - *Broadcaster / Director*
Peter Worthington# - *Reporter*
Tony Zoppi* - *Reporter*

- Those that are marked with a * next to their name were situated either just outside City Hall or since left the scene by the time of the shooting.
- Those that are marked with an # next to their name were confirmed as being present at the scene of the shooting by either the DPD or other members of the media but were never formally interviewed for any of the investigations.

The rest were present at the scene of the shooting and interviewed for at least one of the investigations. We will break down the list in this chapter.

It seems from numerous statements that the majority of the media personnel went straight to the Third Floor of City Hall upon arriving that morning. It makes sense as that had been where most of their focus had been for the past forty hours or so. Being the base of the Homicide and Robbery Bureau, which Oswald was in the custody of, it stood to reason that that is where they would also go to find out when and how he would be transferred.

Like so many of his colleagues in the press, Washington Evening Star reporter Jeremiah 'Jerry' O'Leary had flown to Dallas on the afternoon of Friday November 22nd to cover the aftermath of the president's assassination. On the Sunday, he arrived back at City Hall at 10:00am via the Commerce Street entrance without being stopped or asked for identification. At least when he got to the Third Floor, he would be asked to identify himself, according to his testimony to the FBI.[4] O'Leary also testified that Chief Curry held yet another mini-press conference at 10:20am on Sunday morning to approximately fifteen reporters up in the Third Floor anteroom. Curry told the reporters that he could have had Oswald moved the night before but didn't because he 'didn't want to cross you people.' However, he stopped short of saying why an overnight transfer might have been on the cards in the first place. One of the other reporters must have sensed a lead and asked if any threats had been made against Oswald to which Curry said there had been and that it included words to the effect of, he (Oswald) 'not arriving at the County Jail alive'. O'Leary said he then asked Curry about the security measures being taken. Curry replied that they were using an armoured car and when O'Leary asked where it was being obtained from, Curry told him from a local commercial firm. Curry added that they had 'enough men to handle it'. O'Leary said that Curry was asked how they (the DPD) were getting Oswald down from the 'Fourth Floor' to the basement. Curry said, in the elevator.

O'Leary was not the only reporter who referred to Curry's statements to the press an hour prior to Oswald's shooting. Despite not testifying to anything about this aspect at the time, in his 2015 book 'Accidental Assassin: Jack Ruby and 4 Minutes in Dallas',[5] fellow reporter Maurice Carroll confirmed Curry's comments to the press that morning. Reporter Geoff Edwards would say in later years that Curry also told the media on the morning of Oswald's transfer that there would be police snipers on rooves along the transfer route. Here we have, the Chief of Police, publicly and pre-emptively commenting on the particulars of Oswald's transfer despite making reference to the reasons for implementing such measures in the first place. It is like Chief Curry was getting the threat-makers attention and laying out the blueprint of the plans for Oswald's transfer therefore empowering them with information to plot any contingencies. But, as covered in Chapter Six, I think there is a good case to be made for questioning if these particular threats ever actually took place.

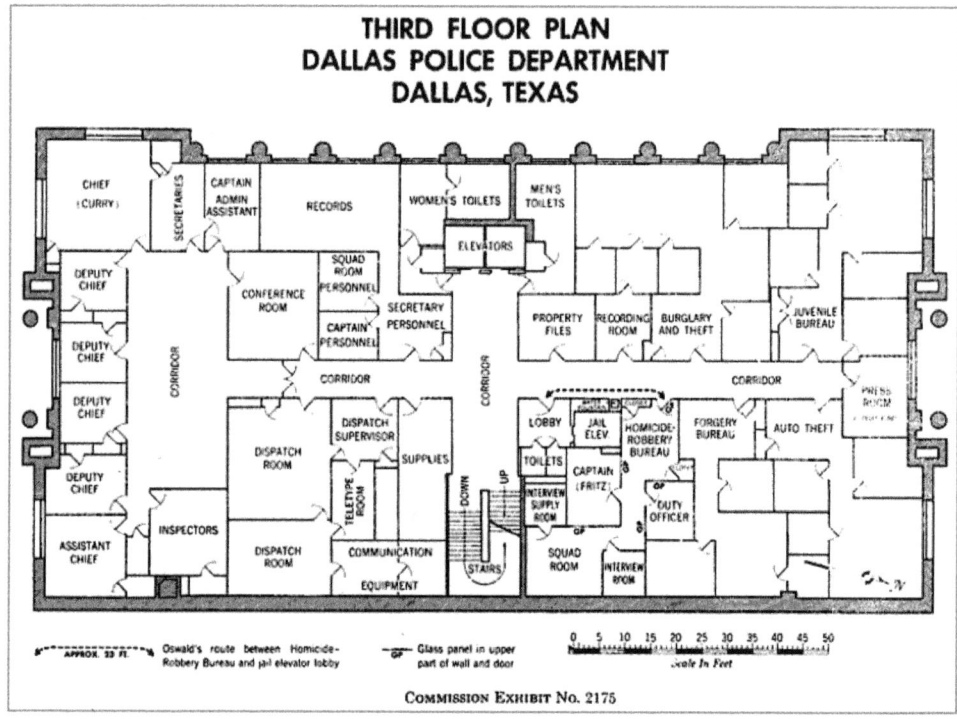

COMMISSION EXHIBIT No. 2175

From the Third Floor to the Basement:

Looking at this map of the Third Floor of Dallas City Hall, where the DPD's Homicide and Robbery Bureau were based and it is easy to gather how congested the corridors that intersected the numerous offices would have been across that weekend. Come the Sunday morning, it was a slightly different story. With it established that Oswald had also been charged with the president's murder in the early hours of Saturday November 23, it was expected by the media that he would be less accessible to them before he was transferred to the County Jail. Because of this, the number of media personnel on the Third Floor on the Sunday morning of the transfer had shrunk – particularly given, until 10:20am at least, it was not known to the media how Oswald's transfer would take place. This resulted in reporters basing themselves elsewhere such as at the County Jail to report on Oswald's arrival there and further afield, out at Parkland Hospital where Governor Connally's wife, Nellie, was expected to provide an update on his condition.

Reporter Maurice Carroll testified to the FBI that there were a number of fellow 'newsmen' on the Third Floor but most went down to the basement when it was made clear that Oswald would be taken out through the car park to the armoured truck.[6] Carroll said that he stayed on the Third Floor and saw that Ike Pappas and another reporter named 'Jerry' (O'Leary) had also. Confusingly, his statement then says that Oswald was led out of 'the room' by three or four DPD officers at *10am* and led to the elevator. This may be that Carroll simply got his time mixed up because he was not the only person who provided times in their statements that couldn't possibly line up with the official timeline of events.

In any event, Carroll said that Pappas, 'Jerry' and he ran down the stairway to the basement and once down there he was asked for his identification. Oswald had still not arrived and Carroll explained that this was 'probably due to the fact that the elevator was very slow moving.' To credit his consistency, he referenced the elevator again in 2015 in his book as being 'creaky and slow' as well. Carroll's statement continues with where he was in proximity to Oswald when he was shot but for the sake of clarity, it is important to now stop and unpack Carroll's version of events from the

Third Floor to the Basement compared to what Ike Pappas and Jerry O'Leary also recounted.

Firstly, in his statements to the FBI, Jerry O'Leary would give a similar account to Carroll in terms of racing down from the Third Floor to the basement using the stairs to get ahead of Oswald being brought down in the elevator.

Ike Pappas gave statements to the FBI on December 2nd and January 7$^{th.}$ In his Dec. 2nd statement, Pappas mentioned nothing of being up on the Third Floor.[7] In fact, it reads as if he was in the basement the whole time and that he was able to get there via a 'public stairway' without showing any identification. Yet, Pappas, unlike Carroll and O'Leary, also provided a statement to the DPD and he did so nine days after his first statement to the FBI.[8] He said that he was on the Third Floor to observe Captain Fritz and detectives as they were about to bring Oswald down. Only he caught the elevator first and got down to the basement a minute before Oswald arrived down there. He was then able to walk out and take his position for when Oswald was shot.

But in his second statement to the FBI on January 7th, Pappas said that he was on the Third Floor with two other reporters, Maurice Carroll and another whose name he didn't recall.[9] Presumably this was Jerry O'Leary as O'Leary himself referred to Pappas by name in his own statement. According to Pappas, as Oswald was led out of the offices of the Homicide and Robbery Bureau and being taken to the elevator, he, Pappas, said he asked him if he had anything to say. Oswald supposedly said something along the lines of wanting to see a representative of the American Civil Liberties Union (ACLU). Oswald was then placed in the elevator so Pappas ran down the stairs nearby to the basement. He was holding a tape recorder with a microphone connected to it and he testified to it being switched on and recording his interaction with Oswald. He also said that it stayed on and would record Oswald's shooting down in the basement. However, the only segment of Pappas' tape recording that was ever made public was from a few seconds prior to Oswald being shot and the immediate aftermath. Further to this, during his testimony at Jack Ruby's trial, Pappas would admit that when getting his tape ready to bring to the trial, he accidentally erased parts of his recording. He said that the parts effected were after Oswald's shooting and they caused short black spots in the tape.[10]

So, now we come back to the point where Carroll, Pappas and O'Leary's accounts to the FBI mainly start to line up. All testify to running down the stairs once Oswald was about to or was taken into the elevator. However, the stairway did not actually lead all the way down to the basement.

In the frustrating, yet non-surprising, absence of any publicly available floor maps for the sub-basement, basement, First and Second Floors of Dallas City Hall in 1963, I have taken a snippet of the Third Floor layout (already provided in full earlier in this chapter) and used the elevator that Oswald was led out of just prior to being shot as a reference point to then illustrate the path he was taken on once down in the basement:

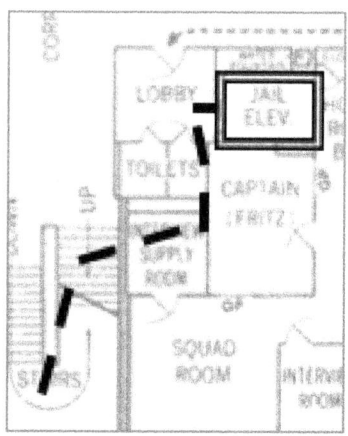

Evidently, the point where Oswald was shot in the basement is directly beneath where the stairway was situated on the floors above – and as you will recall in all footage and photographs of the shooting – there were no stairs visible. I can only deduce that there was a set of stairs closer to the Harwood Street entrance that Carroll, Pappas and O'Leary took to access the basement. This is because Pappas and Carroll, at least, would be seen in pre-shooting footage walking from the direction of the Harwood entrance in the basement fifteen seconds prior to Oswald's arrival in the jail office.

Contemplating the plausibility of Carroll, Pappas, and O'Leary racing down the stairs and across the First Floor to take the nearest stairs down to the basement brings to mind the classic 1957 movie, '12 Angry Men'. In a pivotal scene, Henry Fonda's 'Juror 8' character deftly sews the seeds of doubt in the minds of his fellow jurors, who were already convinced that the young boy in question killed his father, by sensibly questioning and disproving the movements of a key witness. The concept is not too dissimilar to the alleged journey Carroll, Pappas and O'Leary took at City Hall. In the movie, the accused boy is supposed to have stabbed his father in the bedroom of their apartment before fleeing. The boy is then allegedly seen running down the hallway by an elderly neighbour. However, Fonda's Juror 8 demonstrates that the witness, in his condition, could not have gotten to his front door quickly enough to open it and see the young boy run past. In modern terms, the scene was a 'mic drop' moment for Fonda's Juror 8 character and saw the turning of several of his fellow jurors.

Back to Dallas City Hall and consider how long the average elevator in a building takes to descend, or ascend, between three floors. In modern times, it is barely a handful of seconds. In 1963, could it have been so slow to take a minute, at best, to descend down three levels? If the stairs ran all the way from the Third Floor to the basement, there would be less reason to question the reporters' feat of beating the elevator by foot. A person in their 20's – 30's, per the ages of Pappas, Carroll and O'Leary in 1963, running down six flights of stairs with, say twelve steps on each flight could conceivably take thirty seconds. Add running towards the western end of the Dallas City Hall building to descend two more flights of steps before coming back the same in the basement with fifteen seconds to spare and the timeframe drastically increases. However long this route would take, it would still not be quicker than the elevator coming down from the Third Floor.

To help account for the three reporters being able to beat the elevator down to the basement by foot with time to spare, the elevator could have stopped on the Second and / or First Floor on the way down.

If it did, it certainly was not to collect anyone as the personnel that were filmed in cameraman, James Davidson's footage of them disembarking from the elevator in the basement with Oswald - Captain Fritz, Detectives

Leavelle, Graves, Montgomery and Lt. Swain, all testified to boarding it with him on the Third Floor – and none of them said there were any stops made either. Perhaps someone completely inconsequential to Oswald's transfer left the elevator after Oswald and his escorts got on it. In the realms of probability and considering how lax the DPD were in many ways regarding security, it is a possibility but still a stretch in terms of time. What did the DPD personnel that brought Oswald down have to say about the trip down in the elevator? Absolutely nothing. Fritz, Leavelle, Graves Montgomery and Swain did not mention anything about encountering any newsmen, any delays, stops or literally anything to do with the elevator in any of their statements for the investigations.

Without wanting to make things even more confusing, it must be noted that both Pappas and O'Leary did not mention that Carroll was running down the stairs with them in any of their statements. In fact, Pappas doesn't even mention O'Leary as running down the stairs with him either. In the context of the Third Floor alone, Pappas only refers to Carroll by name and O'Leary as another reporter in his January '64 statement to the FBI.

And Jerry O'Leary does not mention Maurice Carroll at all in his statements to the FBI. It is only Carroll that would say that he ran down the stairway to the basement with Pappas and O'Leary.

Jerry O'Leary, just like Ike Pappas, gave *two* statements to the FBI so he ought to bear further scrutiny at this point. In his first statement, given while he was still in Dallas, to FBI Agent Bardwell Odum on December 3, O'Leary recalled his movements ever since arriving in Dallas from Washington D.C. on November 22nd. It also covers his time at City Hall on the day of Oswald's shooting including Chief Curry's statements to the media at 10:20am and his racing down the stairs to the basement, with Ike Pappas, and where he would be and what he saw when Oswald was shot. In his second FBI statement, given on December 8 back in D.C. to Agent Richard Wood Kaiser, O'Leary largely sticks to what he provided in his first statement back in Dallas, only this time, it was more focused on the evening of November 23rd and the next morning.[11] Still, he makes no mention of Maurice Carroll but he did provide extra details of Pappas and he having an agreement with him to use the former's car to follow Oswald's convoy to the County Jail.

Why did recounting this episode have to be so complicated for three journalists... who's very profession relied on their ability to observe and report? Why did it take two statements to the FBI for Ike Pappas and Jerry O'Leary to account for their movements on the Third Floor and basement on the morning of Oswald's shooting? Why did neither testify that Maurice Carroll was with them? What happened between December 2 and 11 to make Pappas drastically change his version of events? The questions could go on.

But what about any other members of the media who testified to being on the Third Floor close to the time that Oswald was brought down from there? I speculate that they were at least Nelson Benton, Izzy Bleckman, Jimmie Turner, Tony Ripley, John Tankersley and David Timmons based on their accounts of their movements up on the Third Floor and how soon they were before Oswald's shooting. None of them make mention of Carroll, Pappas or O'Leary or that Oswald was asked any questions by any members of the media at that time or that he referenced the ACLU.

The confusion between and within Ike Pappas, Maurice Carroll and Jerry O'Leary's statements and absence of proof in Pappas' recording begs the ultimate question – were they up on the Third Floor to see Oswald be taken into the elevator at all?

If they weren't then it could be that Ike Pappas actually was telling the truth in his very first statement to the FBI, on December 2nd, when he made no mention of the Third Floor or his being up there. It also would have meant that after that, he lied when he told the DPD and then the FBI that he was up on the Third Floor just prior to Oswald being brought down to the basement. And because both Carroll and O'Leary mentioned Pappas by name in their statements to the FBI, they must have lied too. Why? And if so, why did the DPD not come out and refute their Third Floor accounts?

Let's look at the most active of the three in terms of interviews over the years – Ike Pappas. On YouTube, there are two interviews that he gave in 1993. One was to the National Press Club and another appears to have been as part of a panel discussion. To the National Press Club, he does not mention being up on the Third Floor at all in the minutes prior to Oswald's transfer commencing. Yet in both, he goes into detail about an interaction that he had with Jack Ruby just after the Friday midnight 'press conference' of Oswald. In the panel interview, Pappas did refer to being up on the Third Floor with Jerry O'Leary as both had the idea of scooping all of the other reporters by asking questions of Oswald when he was brought out up there to start the transfer. According to Pappas, the extent of his and O'Leary's thinking around this included 'practicing running down the stairs' to ensure they gave themselves as much time to ask Oswald questions before he was put in the elevator and then race him / the elevator down to the basement to not miss the happenings down there. Practicing running down the stairs? It was not mentioned by Pappas or O'Leary back then and it appears to be a 'laughable' attempt well after the fact to explain away the unfeasibility of the stairs vs. elevator story. Unfortunately, in both interviews, Pappas provides details regarding his movements prior to Oswald's shooting and after which are provably incorrect when compared to photographs and footage. Jerry O'Leary's statements regarding the shooting are somewhat unclear also. His statement infers that at the time Oswald was shot, he was standing near to where Ruby emerged from. Yet he cannot be seen walking out into the basement like Pappas and Carroll were in pre-shooting footage. So, if he was with the other two reporters when coming down from the Third Floor but was not with them when walking out to the basement, how did O'Leary get to be where he said he was during the shooting?

We have already referred to Maurice Carroll's 2015 book to refer to for his most recent recounting of events that morning but unfortunately nothing can be found from Jerry O'Leary in terms of any further accounts over the years. He had a long and storied career in Washington D.C. by all reports but evidently didn't wish to go on record with his recollections. Perhaps his being affiliated with the CIA[12] had something to do with his silence on the matter. Other than self-prestige, what was the motivation for these reporters fabricating the stairs vs. elevator story? And was there a link to it and what would take place down in the basement?

The area where the bottom of the ramps intersected with the walkway Oswald was led out along and with another ramp down into the basement car park was very cramped. See the below photographs courtesy of University of North Texas Libraries, The Portal to Texas History, to gain a sense of the area's dimensions:

Facing the basement car park and taken from the point where Oswald was shot.

Facing towards the jail office and where Oswald was shot.

Taken from halfway down the Main Street ramp, facing the junction where Oswald was shot.

Taken at the top of the ramp down into the basement car park and facing the Commerce Street ramp.

We have followed the accounts of media personnel arriving at City Hall and the initial concentration of activity up on the Third Floor. Let us move onto what was a momentarily confusing event that did get straightened out relatively quickly. In the minutes prior to Pappas and Carroll entering the basement, the aforementioned WBAP-TV cameramen John Tankersley and David Timmons pushed a large camera on wheels out from the jail office toward the basement car park. They had been on the Third Floor filming an interview with Chief Curry but were prompted to get to the basement because the armoured truck had arrived and was backing in. Riding down in the elevator with them and the camera were Detectives D.G. Brantley, D.L. Burgess and Homer McGee. In their statements for the DPD investigation, McGee[13] and Brantley[14] would confirm that they rode down with two WBAP-TV employees and their camera. Burgess provided a statement to the DPD but it was only to ask him if he knew Jack Ruby. It is not evident if he was asked anything further about the trip down to the basement.[15] Because the camera was mounted on top of a wheeled tripod and Tankersley and Timmons were pushing / pulling it at the bottom, it began to show signs of toppling as it got closer to the ramp. Seeing this, WBAP-TV director, Jimmie Turner ran over to help them safely wheel it the rest of the way down into the basement car park. Unfortunately, it was to no avail as they had left it too late to set it up and have ready before Oswald was brought out so they left it out of the way and helped other cameramen out. Separately, watching this whole episode play out were Detectives W.E. Chambers,[16] Wilbur Jay Cutchshaw[17] and Roy Lee Lowery.[18] All would note three men as pushing the camera into place but seeing only two men handling the camera after the shooting. In his only statement, Chambers told the DPD that he referred his observation onto Capt. Glen King. However, King makes no mention of the entire instance in any of his statements.[19] Lowery and Cutchshaw both testified that they went up to the two cameramen, Tankersley and Timmons, to ask who the third person was that was pushing the camera out with them before the shooting. Tankersley and Timmons allegedly said they didn't know who the third person was. This alerted Lowery and Cutchshaw to the possibility that it could have been Jack Ruby that used the opportunity to help wheel the camera in place as cover for getting into position to shoot

Oswald. This theory could not have held much water as the camera was only brought into the basement four minutes prior to Oswald emerging, which was also when Jack Ruby was confirmed as being at the Western Union transferring money. Detectives Brantley and McGee only ever testified to two cameramen in the elevator with the camera – and neither person was Jack Ruby. Further to that, neither Tankersley nor Timmons testified to being asked by any officers about who the third person was that helped them get their camera into place. And if they were, they would have told whoever asked them that it was Jimmie Turner because he was their director for that morning. The incident would be revisited during the Warren Commission hearings but per it and the DPD investigation findings, the contention that Jack Ruby snuck in posing as a cameraman basement petered out. The HSCA analysed it as among some of the possible ways that Ruby could have entered the basement but deemed that it was not feasible for the reasons above. Making it conclusive, in the KRLD-TV pre-shooting footage of the basement, the WBAP-TV camera can be seen being pushed out from the jail office by only two men, three minutes prior to Oswald being brought out.[20] And Lowery and Chambers can be seen watching on. At that point, it was not showing any signs of toppling over so it is almost certain that Turner only rushed over to help wheel it down the steeper driveway into the car park, making him the third person pushing it at that time. But somehow, in the chaos of the shooting, an untruth that Ruby might have been one of the men with the camera was born but easily discounted thanks to the footage and lack of corroboration from the WBAP-TV personnel and Glen King.

We will now revisit the DPD schematic that indicates where people, marked as numbered circles, were standing when Oswald was shot.

In the below section, the only numbered circles included are members of the media that were acknowledged by the DPD.

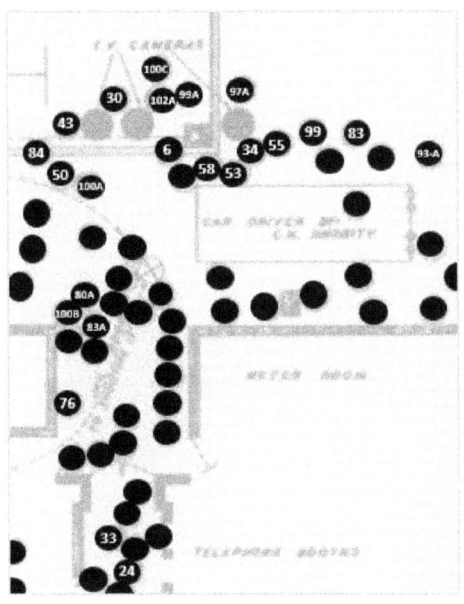

Jack Beers - 6
Maurice Carroll – 100B
James R. Davidson - 24
J.B. English - 30
Warren Ferguson - 33
Bob Fenley - 34
Robert L. Hankal - 43
Robert Huffaker - 50
'Japanese Reporter' – 100A
Robert Jackson - 53
Frank B. Johnston - 55

Seth Kantor - 58
Ike Pappas – 80A
Francois Pelou - 83
Tom Pettit – 83A
George Phenix - 84
David F. Smith – 93A
John Tankersley – 97A
Robert Thornton - 99
David Timmons – 99A
Jimmie Turner – 100C
Homer Venso – 102A

However, there were.. *twenty four* additional members of the media that either testified for the FBI or Warren Commission as to where they were, or somebody else confirmed their presence, but did not appear on the DPD's schematic of the scene. Why? How? According to the statement Detective Dhority gave for the DPD,[21] when Oswald was taken back to the jail office after being shot, Captain Fritz gave him the order to have the supervising officer make a list of those present. Evidently that was Captain Talbert as that's who Dhority relayed the order to. Some form of a list was done as the majority of people are accounted for on the schematic so how could so many people be looked over? It would be entirely understandable if a small handful were but not twenty three. What possible explanation could there be?

The Forgotten Ones

Using statements and footage of the shooting, we are able to pinpoint where at least sixteen of these members of media were standing but not shown in the original schematic map produced by the DPD. They have been added in their alleged positions into the same map section on the next page:

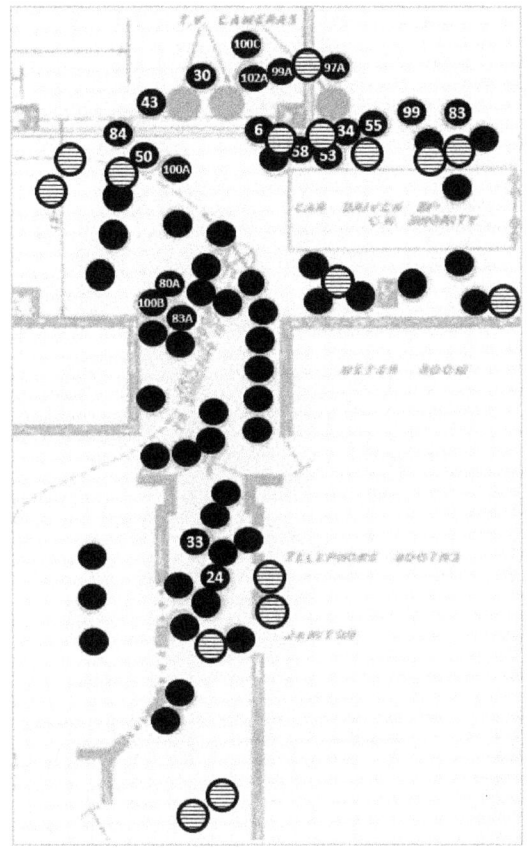

This leaves eight 'misfit' members of the media who were confirmed as being present but never had their location at the time of Oswald's shooting pinpointed. Where could they have possibly been standing amongst the crowd of media and DPD personnel as Oswald was shot? More frustrating was what might they have witnessed before, during and after it. We will focus on these people later in this chapter.

Let us section off this map to better examine who the members of the media were that were not accounted for in the schematic and why we can approximate where they were positioned.

The first 'area' we'll focus on is behind where Ruby stepped out from to shoot Oswald. In other words, the bottom of the ramp from Main Street. The media personnel we can speculate on being here were reporters Terence McGarry, Jerry O'Leary and Peggy Simpson.

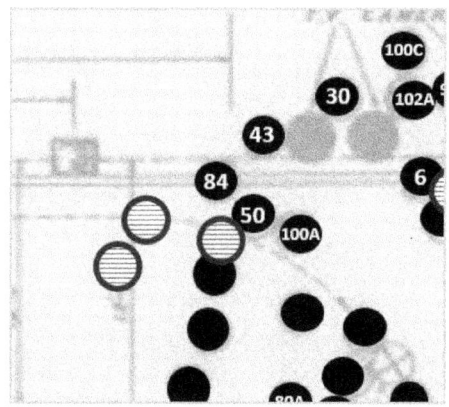

Terence McGarry, one of a number of UPI reporters alleged to be present at the scene, was not acknowledged at all by the DPD but he did testify to the FBI where he was at the time of the shooting.[22] McGarry said that he 'moved to a spot in the middle of the car ramp just north of the hallway where they would bring Oswald out.' The ramp through the basement ran north to south, and if McGarry was where he said he was, this puts him in the vicinity of where Jack Ruby was standing just prior to shooting Oswald. Yet, he did not tell of seeing anyone come down the ramp behind him.

Jerry O'Leary stated to the FBI that, after coming down to the basement from the Third Floor, he stood at the bottom of the ramp. His account of the shooting encompassed him being aware of a car reversing toward him as

Oswald was brought out and wondering if it would stop. He then 'became vaguely aware of a short fat man moving in a gliding from his (O'Leary) right starting possibly 8 – 10 feet from him (O'Leary) and moving across an area possibly a distance of ten fee directly to Oswald'. The issue of O'Leary being able to race the elevator down to the basement from the Third Floor on foot down the stairs aside, as previously stated in this chapter, he was not filmed coming out into the basement like fellow 'Third Floor to Basement reporters' Ike Pappas and Maurice Carroll were. Where he said he was standing in proximity to Detective Dhority reversing the car towards him and being back far enough so Ruby would have been on his right lines up but it is troubling that he cannot be seen getting into that position according to his timeline of movements that morning. Was O'Leary really there or had he seen footage of the shooting to know of the car reversing to make a qualifying reference to it instead.

Peggy Simpson of the Associated Press is one of the reporters who was confirmed as being present by the DPD but was not called on to testify by them, the FBI or the Warren Commission. As such, we can only rely on accounts that she has given in more recent times to speculate where she would have been situated when Oswald was shot. In an interview she gave to the Sixth Floor Museum's 'Oral History' project in 2005, Simpson said that 'Ruby was to her right and just 'came out and shot (Oswald).[23] She rushed to the payphones across from the jail office and called back to her bureau and recounted what she had just seen and was still seeing. Acknowledging the time that had passed between the actual events and when she was recounting them, Simpson clearly places herself very close to Jack

Ruby before he shot Oswald. Trying to identify her is helped by the fact that she was the only female reported as being at the scene and we know she was not in front of Ruby or even beside him because she cannot be seen in any photographs or footage. This means she could have only been behind where Ruby was standing. However, in the footage from various angles of Ruby being wrestled to the ground, she cannot be seen rushing to where the bank of pay phones were. Granted, it is difficult to make sense of who is who in all the footage because of the chaos that broke out. It must be noted that Peggy Simpson can be seen in footage during the aftermath of the shooting among other reporters as one of the DPD officers was being interviewed.

In a report dated July 20 1964, for a separate line of enquiry, the FBI noted that there were two public payphones in the basement across from the jail office – RI 1-0379 and 1-0439.[24] This detail makes the next two reporter's accounts compelling when compared to Simpson's.

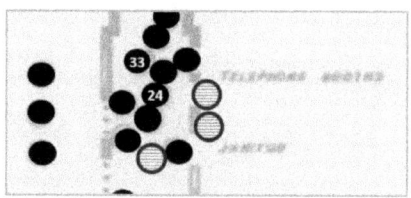

Karl King, another UPI reporter was acknowledged by his colleague, Terence McGarry as being present and 'keeping a line open to UPI'. King was not acknowledged by the DPD, FBI, Warren Commission or even the HSCA. In 2003, King also gave an interview for the Sixth Floor Museum 'Oral History' project during which he described how tense and quiet the atmosphere was down in the basement out of anticipation for Oswald to be transferred.[25] He covered off on the shooting by remarking how quiet it still was because nobody was asking questions of Oswald when he came out. King said that the New York bureau, that he was on the phone with, could hear the shot as he was describing the scene. He then recalled seeing Ruby's 'pork-pie hat' and Oswald crumpling over.

Bill Lord was a television reporter for ABC. He wasn't acknowledged or interviewed by the DPD but he did provide a statement to the FBI.[26] In it, he stated that on the morning of the shooting he was not asked to show his identification by the DPD and in terms of whether he saw any 'unauthorised people' he said he couldn't provide any names of anyone but that it would not have been difficult for such a person to enter. In his statement, he did not say where he was at the time of the shooting but there is an audio recording of him commentating from down in the basement on one of the payphones across from the jail office about a minute after the shooting. How does his time on a phone approximate with Peggy Simpson and Karl King's?

The New York Times' **Gladwin Hill** arrived at City Hall November 25th at 9:45am. According to his statement to the FBI, he went up to the Third Floor and talked to Chief Curry who told him that if he (Curry) had not told the press the night before that Oswald would be transferred at 10am, he would have transferred him earlier.[27] At 11am, Hill came down the elevator from the Third Floor with DPD detectives. As he walked out to the basement, he was challenged by a police officer and asked for his credentials. This was the first time that whole weekend he was required to do so. Oswald was soon brought out and Hill said he saw officers were filing in behind. In regard to the shooting, Hill stated that he was unable to observe anything. The fact that he noted to the FBI that he saw Ted Mann, Gene Bonds (most certainly and phonetically Gene Barnes) of the ABC and reporters Ed Haddad and Gene Blake present and that he was unable to witness the shooting indicates that he was behind it and closer to the jail office when it took place. Hill said he left the basement immediately 'through another exit'. If this was the case, it would have most likely been up to Commerce Street with Gene Barnes and Ted Mann as they were using the same off-duty DPD officer as a driver that weekend.

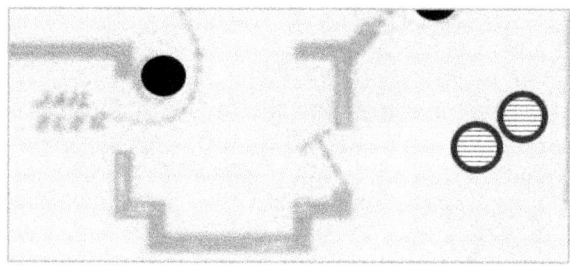

Directly opposite the jail office elevator were cameraman **Gene Barnes** and sound technician **Ted Mann.** Both were sent out to Dallas from Los Angeles by their employer, NBC Hollywood in the wake of Kennedy's assassination. Barnes employed off-duty DPD officer George Riley Spears to be their driver for the weekend. As such, he drove them to City Hall that morning and parked his car outside on Commerce Street. Barnes and Mann were only interviewed by the FBI and gave the same account when it came to their movements before and during the shooting. According to Barnes'

FBI statement,[28] his plan was for them to film Oswald coming out of the elevator and then leave to follow the convoy by car (being driven by Spears) to film Oswald arriving at the County Jail. For this, he and Barnes set up further down the hallway from where the other television cameras had set up. While most were told to move out to the car park to ease congestion, Barnes and Mann must have been allowed to stay because they were so far out of the way. Mann also provided a statement to the FBI and he[29] along with Barnes both suggest that as soon as Barnes had filmed Oswald being brought out of the elevator, they left to get back up to Commerce Street.

In the case of **Peter Worthington**, a reporter for the Toronto Telegram, we do not need corroboration from anybody else to prove he was present at the scene of the shooting because he can be seen in footage standing next to Captain Fritz when Ruby shot Oswald. All that we have from Worthington over the years before his passing in 2013 are retrospective accounts of his time in Dallas that weekend. An article that he wrote in 2011 for the HuffPost Canada,[30] 'I Saw Lee Harvey Oswald Gunned Down' provides the most extensive account. In it, interestingly, he said he was working on the knowledge that Oswald would be transferred to the County Jail at 5pm on Sunday November 24. But he went to City Hall to find out the 'lay of the land' ahead of the transfer. Then he could return to his hotel to catch up on sleep he had not had since arriving in Dallas. When he got there, he said that he was able to enter the basement without having to show credentials. He also saw TV cameras and journalists down there. He started chatting with a plainclothes cop, all the while hoping it would help him blend in as he was aware he hadn't shown his credentials in the first place. He then described 'sheriffs, escorting Oswald who was wearing a sweater, had a bruise mark on his face, and was furtively darting glances side to side.' He then described a 'hunched figure wearing a fedora' lunging at Oswald before hearing a 'sharp pop of a handgun.' This is about as much as we can refer to from Peter Worthington and even then, the passage of time makes this, and anyone else's, that little bit less reliable. The only other thing of note that Worthington wrote in this article was hearing cheers from the crowd up on Commerce Street when word had got out that Oswald had been shot.

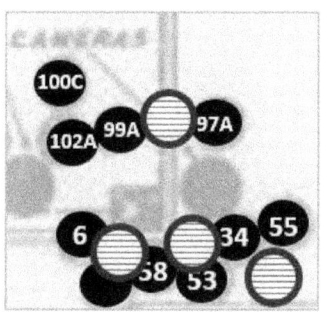

Positioned directly across the ramp from where Oswald would be shot is where the highest concentration of media personnel was. In amongst this group were prolific photographers Jack Beers and Bob Jackson. This is also where most of the television cameras (black circles in the above map section) filmed the shooting. Starting at the figure between, '99A' (Timmons) and '97A' (Tankersley), I contend that this was UPI reporter **Henry Rabun**. In his statement to the FBI, it was acknowledged that was 'of a short stature' so when he came down to the basement twenty minutes prior to Oswald's shooting, he stood on 'a railing around the parking area just in front of the swinging door leading to the hallways of the jail office.'[31] Looking at the layout of the jail office and its hallway leading out to the basement car park and Rabun's description sounds as if he was standing on the railing where the cameras were. This was obviously not the case otherwise he would have been in the way of the cameras there and would have jostled Beers & Jackson out of their positions. To keep his orientation in line with the swinging door near the jail office, I suspect he would have been still standing on the railing but on the one that ran down into the car park. Regarding his memory of the shooting, he only recalled seeing a blur to his right before hearing the shot.

On the corner of the railing that Henry Rabun was standing on was **Izzy Bleckman**, a cameraman who was first introduced in Chapter Four. In his statement to the FBI, he said he had actually positioned himself at the jail office and was able to take a photograph of Oswald as he came out from the elevator.[32] Once he got his picture, he ran out to the basement to film Oswald emerging. His statement is corroborated by pre-shooting footage from another camera as it does show him quickly moving from the jail office to the other side of the ramp at the same time as Ike Pappas and Maurice

Carroll walked to their positions. The upward angle of the film he took also indicates that he was crouching or kneeling in front of the other cameras.

KLIF-Radio reporter **Gary DeLaune** was not acknowledged by or interviewed by the DPD, FBI or Warren Commission. No other witnesses recalled seeing him either, but he did record audio of the moments before and during the shooting. After the shooting, according to the Sixth Floor Museum interview he gave in 1998, he immediately left the basement and ran back to KLIF-Radio to report on the shooting and have his recordings from the basement broadcasted.[33] Audio recording the moments in the basement before and during the shooting as well as a panting DeLaune can be found on YouTube. Curiously, despite saying during his initial report on the air that City Hall was cordoned so no one could leave, he was somehow still able to. In the same 1998 interview, DeLaune said he was standing next to Jack Beers and Bob Jackson at the time of the shooting, as marked in the above map section. Yet, during the 'Oswald Has Been Shot!' panel seminar for the Sixth Floor Museum in 2013 that he was on with James Leavelle, Fred Rheinstein, Robert Huffaker and Bob Jackson, DeLaune was seated next to Jackson and did not mention standing next to him at the time of the shooting.[34]

Steven Alexander gave a statement to the FBI but there is no mention in there about his observations during the shooting.[35] It only focused on his observations prior to the shooting. There are no accounts or records of interviews from Alexander in the years since either. We do have his footage which was clearly taken over the roof of Dhority's car so we can confidently place him before Robert Thornton ('99') in this schematic section.

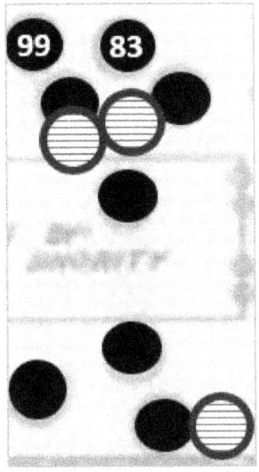

Reporters **Thayer Waldo** and **Lowell 'Jay' Duncan** are placed together in front of figure '99' (Thornton) in the map based on Waldo's testimony. Waldo, who has already been mentioned in this book, testified to the FBI of being down in the basement and talking with an ABC reporter named 'Duncan' while waiting for the transfer to start. However, the only reference to a 'Duncan' in all investigation records is 'William 'Glen' Duncan' of KLIF-Radio who Jack Ruby contacted to offer to help broker interviews at City Hall. A 'Lowell 'Jay' Duncan' was a reporter for the ABC and, there is minimal to be found as to whether he was allegedly in the City Hall basement at the time of Oswald's shooting.[36] But there aren't any interviews to be found with him at any point in time and he is not named as being present by anybody except Waldo. Thayer Waldo's account of what he witnessed during the shooting is also tenuous. In his statement to the FBI, after mentioning he was standing with 'Duncan' he said they were standing behind the '3rd Car' (presumably Dhority's) before it reversed to meet Fritz, Oswald and company.[37] Waldo then said that 'Duncan', who was holding a microphone and tape recorder, asked Oswald as he went past if he 'had anything to say?' Waldo then described seeing a man lunge forward to his right to Oswald. He then saw a white flash and an explosion. He said he knew immediately what had happened because he 'was standing so close.' This account to the FBI can be discredited for a few reasons. Oswald never got as far as the '3rd Car' to then walk past anyone near there. It was Ike Pappas who asked Oswald that question at the last second so did Waldo just get him badly confused with Jay Duncan? And if that was the case, was Waldo standing near to Ike Pappas to hear this being asked therefore close enough to know immediately that a shot had been fired? It is as if Thayer Waldo's account is somehow blurred beyond any recognition. Unfortunately, the Warren Commission didn't ask him if he wished to clarify or correct his statements, like they did with so many others. Instead, they focused on his impressions of City Hall in the preceding days as well as his interaction with Lt. George Butler just prior to the shooting – which we will touch on later in this book.

Detroit Times reporter **Tony Ripley** is another example of someone who's statement to the FBI is incredibly ambiguous and not particularly helpful in pinpointing where he was at the time of the shooting.[38] Like most reporters that morning, he first went up to the Third Floor to find out what the status of Oswald's transfer was. Hearing that it was yet to happen, Ripley left the way he came into the building from the Commerce Street entrance and, with a couple of other reporters, one of which I suspect was Thayer Waldo, was able to enter the basement down the ramp. He recalled that there hadn't been a designated area for reporters to stand within so, without any instructions from the police, he stood against the wall and was about twenty feet from Oswald at the time of the shooting. He did not see the shooter and only recalled seeing a blur at the time. Based on Ripley's statement, I think he was standing along the wall at the bottom of the Commerce Street side of the ramp as indicated.

We now come to the 'misfit' members of the media who we know were present when Lee Oswald was shot but they either never provided any statements, their positions were unaccounted for by the DPD on the schematic map yet actually were acknowledged by either Dallas police or other witnesses as being present at the scene. As such, they have not been included in the above schematic sections.

Gene Blake, a reporter for the Los Angeles Times, was acknowledged by Gladwin Hill as being present in the basement yet there is very little to be found on Blake as he did not give any statements to the authorities. The only thing to be found is an article that he wrote on November 25.[39] In it, he wrote that he was ten feet from Oswald when he was shot and that he peeked into the ambulance window to see Oswald after he had been put in there. He noted that he was unconscious. Once the ambulance had been taken away, Blake said he asked Captain Fritz who the man was that shot Oswald. Fritz apparently said it was Jack Ruby, a local dance club owner.

Ten feet from Oswald means Blake could have been in any number of positions to Oswald's front or sides.

Also mentioned by Gladwin Hill is **Ed Haddad.** He arrived in Dallas on the afternoon of the assassination. The statement that he gave to the FBI only focuses on his perspective of Dallas City Hall on the Friday and Saturday of that weekend.[40] Haddad noted that he was not asked for identification by police that weekend. He also recalled how the press would surge in on Oswald as he was being led through the corridors and that because of how lax security was, he could have been slain on the Friday and Saturday as well. Ed Haddad's statement concludes with the one reference to Sunday: 'Haddad knows nothing concerning the security measures taken by the police on Sunday, November 24 1963'. Because of this and a lack of any other testimony or record regarding Haddad, it is hard to be definitive as to whether he was actually present for Oswald's shooting and that Hill's reference to him in his statement may have meant that he merely saw Haddad at City Hall that weekend.

Paul Sisco with UPI was acknowledged by the DPD in their investigation but not interviewed. He is perhaps most well known as the reporter who hired a taxicab and kept it waiting up on Main Street while he was down in the basement to cover Oswald's transfer. The ironic thing was that Sisco was only interviewed once by the FBI in the week following the shooting,[41] yet the cabdriver, Harry T. Tasker, would testify for the Warren Commission[42] and be referred to in 1978 by the HSCA. This is because Tasker was parked on Main Street and adjacent to the ramp the minutes before, during and after Oswald's shooting. He was close enough to hear the shot, in fact. Tasker did not see Jack Ruby or anyone resembling him approach the ramp and enter down it. Sisco's statement to the FBI offers no clues as to where he was at the time of the shooting. The most interesting thing he noted was that in the minutes prior to Oswald being brought out into the basement, Sisco noted that 'about six police officers armed with rifles came out of the interior area of the building to take guard up on Main Street.' This is not evident in any of the raw footage still available from the television cameras that were down in the basement before the shooting. Sisco would not be the only person to make reference to police carrying arms before and after the shooting either.

Daily Oklahoman reporter, **James N. Standard** was also acknowledged by the DPD as being present at the shooting, but also not interviewed by them for their investigation. The one statement that Standard gave to the FBI offers little insight other than the inference that he was able to enter the basement using the entrance through the door from the police identification section.[43] From what we have already covered in terms of the layout of the basement, this was more than likely the entrance down from Commerce Street to the basement where the assembly room / press conference room was. Before he was allowed out into the basement, he was stopped by two police officers and asked for identification. He only had his credit card and a group insurance card proving who he was employed by. One of the officers did not want to let him in but the other said he could after he searched him. There is no indication as to where Standard was located at the time of the shooting.

Reporters **Milt Sosin** (The Miami News), **Hank Machariella** (Daily Tribune) and **Burt Rhinehart** (UPI) were acknowledged by the DPD as being present for Oswald's shooting,[44] but they were not interviewed by them, the FBI or the Warren Commission. And the only reference to KRLD-TV cameraman, Gene Pasczalek being present was from KRLD news director, Robert Hankal. However, such was the ambiguity to Hankal's DPD statement,[45] it does not even say either way if Pasczalek was in the basement or not. But given a KRLD cameraman filmed the arrival of the armoured trucks, we can conclude that it was Pasczalek situated at the top of the ramp. Ben Molina was a floor man who Nelson Benton testified to as being down in the basement but Molinas himself, during an interview many years later, said he was not present.[46] And Robert Hankal also mentioned Molina being with Pasczalek. **Geoff Edwards**, a radio station reporter from Los Angeles told NBC's Tom Pettit on-camera in the minutes after the shooting that he was standing over to the left when it happened but merely looked and slightly nodded in the direction he was referring to - at the top of the driveway into the carpark from the ramp. Edwards did not give any statements to the DPD, FBI or Warren Commission and his presence at the scene of the shooting was not mentioned by any other witnesses. In a 2013 interview with Ken Levine,[47] Edwards said that he entered 'Dallas Police Headquarters' on the morning of Oswald's transfer and, having been asked to show credentials at the top of the ramp, he walked down to the back of the 'van' Oswald was to be transported in. He was then yanked back away by an officer. He only acknowledged that the majority of the press were 'outside a guard rail' and that Jack Ruby 'somehow made his way through the group, and well, the rest is history.' Geoff Edwards is yet another example of a reporter present at the shooting of Lee Harvey Oswald who does not wish to provide any detail of what transpired even after so much time having passed. Memory may be a factor but witnessing such a historic event would also not be the easiest thing to forget either.

In their own unique category are three newsmen accounted for on the DPD schematic but other than their known position there is literally no trace of any statements.

Associated Press photographer **David F. Smith** took photographs from his front-on position, but he was not interviewed for any investigations and no word from him, or AP, to this day can be found other than crediting him with the photos that he took that day.

NBC broadcaster **Tom Pettit** who was positioned next to Ike Pappas on Oswald's immediate left during his final steps. Pettit can be seen in literally every film and photograph taken during the shooting sequence from the frontal perspective. The effective silence on and from both Tom Pettit is as frustrating as it is perplexing. Carry out a search on the internet and the sum of what can be found on Pettit are articles announcing his death in 1995. Despite his long and illustrious career, no interviews can be found that could have provided any insight into what he saw in regard to the events of November 24.

There is another figure that is just as enigmatic as Tom Pettit and that's the person referred to (in less than politically correct parlance compared to nowadays) in the DPD investigation as the 'Jap reporter'. Evident in footage taken outside of the Commerce Street ramp is a **Japanese man with a camera** around his neck. He is then seen entering the top of the ramp by walking past the armoured truck. During footage in the basement prior to the shooting, he can be seen standing in the vicinity of where Jack Ruby would emerge from. He can also be seen standing there when Ruby sprang forward between, he and officer Blackie Harrison to shoot Oswald. It is interesting to watch this man closely when Oswald was shot as he looks to react to it a split second before anybody else as does he darted very quickly backwards, and he is never seen again in any post-shooting footage. Was he able to leave before the DPD close down the basement and took down the names of those present? Additionally, he can be seen in footage, along with other reporters, and Jack Ruby, during Oswald's midnight press conference. So, who was he? A search of the internet will not provide any clues as to who this Japanese man was. On a message board for the 'Steve Warran Research' page,[48] a user suggested that it was Sassa Atsuyuki but comparing a photograph of him with the man at Dallas City Hall and it is obvious they are not the same person. Depending on how the question is worded, ChatGPT posits that it was either 'Yukichi Haguchi' who was in Dallas that weekend on behalf of the Nippon Corporation's media arm or 'Tochiyuki Tanaka' for Mainichi Shimbun, a Japanese newspaper. When asked for sources, ChatGPT concedes that it has no credible sources for any of these men, so we continue to be left to ponder who this man was, what he saw and why there is no trace of he or his reporting from that weekend.

Silence and Disparity

While we have not examined the statements and whereabouts of all members of the media present in relation to Lee Oswald's shooting, in this chapter, by focusing on lesser-known and acknowledged figures present that morning, we have been able to see just how equally unreliable and under-utilised the media were in terms of testimonies that they gave about Lee Oswald's slaying. We will revisit the media in different contexts throughout the remainder of this book but by questioning some of the more commonly known aspects from that morning i.e. the three reporters who raced the elevator down the stairs, we can begin to appreciate how brittle the peripheries of the orthodoxy of the Oswald shooting really is. And by all means, there is no doubt that being on the scene of an event such as a shooting would be traumatic to varying degrees for anyone, but we can use Tom Pettit as an example of many others that were present at the Oswald shooting who, by virtue of their profession and reason for being there, were obligated to report and recount the historic event they witnessed that day yet would ultimately stay mute about it. It is evident that the bulletins from those reporters on the scene flowed during the immediate aftermath of the shooting. But what might have been a respectful silence after the initial fallout of the shooting and during the investigations took hold and stayed in place ever since. Retrospective accounts, regardless of substance, were scarce except for the odd exception such as Maurice Carroll's shallow account in his 2015 book. And even within the immediate investigations themselves, there are too many instances of inconsistencies, misrepresentation and ignorance when it comes to who from which media outlet was there to see what.

'JFK – The Book of the Film'[49] perhaps offers some perspective on this front. It contains the screenplay of the Oliver Stone film plus resources and numerous articles debating for and against the film. The critical articles demonstrate that the establishment media of the early 90's set about attacking the film since its early stages of production and they were not afraid to wheel in relics of the case such as Warren Commission and legacy media figures to do so. Does this correlate with the literal radio silence from the media in the 1960's in regard to asking any key critical questions regarding the killings of President Kennedy and Police Officer J.D. Tippit? No doubt and the cone of silence extended over what took place in the Dallas City Hall basement on November 24 as well. Yes, it is true that a great deal of testimonies and statements from those in the media did not flatter the Dallas Police Department when it came to inconsistent or non-existent security measures and associations with Jack Ruby but that appears to be where the harshest of criticism lays. Was it not more important to attribute how Ruby was able to access the basement using the multitude of witnesses and hold the DPD independently accountable for facilitating the transfer so publicly in the first place?

What is also clear is that the testimonies that members of the media gave to the FBI manifested as statements only. Because we do not have access to the actual transcripts of what was said we can only speculate how faithfully the statements summarised all testimonies.

The blanket narrative reported about the Kennedy assassination, including the killing of his alleged killer, continues to this day and it is not too dissimilar to the all-points alignment of mainstream and corporate media across the world during the COVID-19 pandemic. Any critical voices that questioned the wisdom and science of lockdown measures and vaccine mandates were marginalised and discredited by the mainstream media. And the 'Twitter Files' expose' proved how far the arm of the government extended when it was revealed how much pressure was being exerted on

Twitter by the FBI and the White House to censor dissenting voices and outlets.

With the benefit of time, we know that such a force existed during the time of President Kennedy's assassination with the CIA's Operation Mockingbird which was focused entirely on manipulating and managing the media of the day. Mark Lane and Jim Garrison are but two examples of lightning rods for criticism and censorship when it came to their questioning the mainstream narrative regarding the Kennedy assassination.

If nothing else, this book will prove that from the forty six members* of the media who were at the scene, emerged an incoherent and deficient account of what happened.

We will never know if or how much pressure was applied to the media to not veer far from the established narrative but given the fact that there is little that makes sense about how the shooting took place, their silence ever since is a dereliction of their duty as observers and reporters, and of their employers, and it should be seen as a blight on their legacies.

---

*Dallas Morning Times reporter Hugh Aynesworth claimed that he was present to witness President Kennedy's assassination, Lee Oswald's arrest and murder. If this were remotely true, it would have made him the only witness of all three events. But in the instance of Oswald's shooting, no one within the media or the authorities named Aynesworth as being present. And, while not wishing to speak ill of the dead, with his less than honest conduct in subsequent years regarding Marina Oswald and the Garrison investigation considered, the late Aynesworth is beyond questionable and, frankly, not worth acknowledging beyond this footnote.

CHAPTER NINE

POLICE

So far, our orbit over the shooting of Lee Oswald has circled over the layout of the City Hall basement, high level preparations for security down there and certain narratives from those in the media and in utility roles. In all instances, there have been numerous references to regular and reserve Dallas Police personnel within specific contexts, but the time has well and truly arrived for them to be introduced as a whole as it's on their shoulders that most of the controversy and questions regarding Oswald's shooting sits upon.

Let us start with the reserve personnel and how it sits within the Dallas Police structure. Most Police departments across the United States had, and still have, a group of reserve officers that could be called on at times of large-scale events, emergency, or catastrophe to lend manpower to regular police personnel. There were reserve personnel that assisted on the day of President Kennedy's motorcade through Dallas. Much like an auxiliary function for the Dallas Police Department, in the early 1960s, the reserves were three hundred strong comprising of members of the community who were strictly volunteers.[1] Like the army, the 'Reserve Battalion' was made up of companies. Within each company were three platoons and within each platoon, were three squads. In late 1963, the Reserve Commander was George Tropolis. Under him were Reserve Captains Charles O. Arnett, R.L.

Crump, J.E. Marks, and O.S. Muller. Captain James M. Solomon of the Dallas Police was the Reserve Coordinator who oversaw DPD liaison, training, and selection with Captain of Personnel, William R. Westbrook. The process that a person had to complete to become a functional Reserve Officer appears to have been a stringent one. It started with completing an application that gathered an applicant's details regarding their background, schooling, employment and where they had lived. This information would be used to have a criminal or credit check carried out. Having passed that stage, reserve captains would interview applicants and as a result, the applicant would either make it to a training program or be rejected. The role of a reserve officer attracted people of all backgrounds and vocations. In 1963, reserve officers had an array of blue- and white-collar jobs. The calibre of anyone who applied to become a reserve officer was tested not only by the multi-stage application process but also the longevity of the training program (one night per week over eight months) that each person had to complete before they 'earned their badge' as it were. So much so that the Dallas Police were proud of the sixty percent completion rate because it meant that only the most dedicated, skilled, and honorable people ought to have got through. But as we'll discover, it turned out that some reserves would be right in the thick of the action when Lee Oswald was shot.

On the night of Saturday November 23, ranking reserve officers such as Lieutenants Barney Merrell and Ben McCoy were tasked with calling on other reserves to present to City Hall the next morning by 9am. The calls would continue the next morning. When the reserve officers reported for duty Sunday morning, they did so in the assembly room in the basement at

City Hall (which we know had doubled as a press conference room that weekend) and assigned out as needed.

Turning to the DPD hierarchy now and up on the Third Floor, after Chief Curry's first phone call that day with Sheriff Bill Decker, as detailed earlier in this chapter, he, his Deputy - Charles Batchelor, and Deputy Chief M.W. Stevenson discussed how Oswald would be transferred to the County Jail. Apparently having discussed the threat received to Oswald's life by a group attack, yet without a definitive time and route to move Oswald on, all agreed that using an armoured car would still be the best option. Batchelor was tasked with arranging this so he called the 'Armored Motor Car Services' and spoke with the company's General Operations Manager, Harold J. Fleming. According to his testimony to the Warren Commission, Fleming said that he had met with Batchelor within a month prior to inquire about a permit issue. And when he called Fleming, Batchelor said that he referred to the same conversation.[2] As a result, Fleming arranged for two of the company's drivers, Don Goin and Edward C. Dietrich to meet he and operations manager, Marvin 'Bert' Hall at the company's terminal. Once there, Fleming contacted Batchelor back to say they would be arriving shortly. Fleming also stated that he told Batchelor not to give him dimensions for the ramp as he already knew the truck that the police wanted would be too large to fit down it. Fleming and Hall decided on taking two trucks – a larger one 'No. 46', that Batchelor indicated as required, and a smaller one as a backup because '46 had just had a new battery installed and they actually had to jump start it in the company's garage earlier that same morning.

Basement Search

As Curry, Batchelor and Stevenson were deciding on how to transport Oswald to the County Jail, Captain Cecil Talbert took the initiative by instructing one of his lieutenants, Rio Pierce to call in the officers of three patrol squads and report to the basement for assignment.[3] Talbert then caught up with Stevenson and Captain George L. Lumpkin over coffee in the lunchroom of the Second Floor and discussed the transfer with them – particularly which way through Dallas that Oswald would be taken along to the County Jail. Having speculated on the most likely route, Talbert conveyed this information to Sergeants Putnam and Dean as they were who he delegated responsibility of security arrangements in the basement to.

Between 9am and 9.15am, enough police personnel consisting mainly of reserves, had gathered in the basement and were ready for their next instructions. But before the basement could be searched, it had to be sealed. In order to do this, all non-police personnel in the basement were supposedly asked to leave. As covered in Chapter Seven, it was City Hall workers Harold Fuqua, Alfreadia Riggs and others who were ordered to leave due to security precautions. However, contrary to widely held opinion, those in the media were not told or asked to leave. According to his statement to the FBI, Steven Alexander, a videographer who was at Dallas City Hall for NBC, was in the basement at the time of the search and was never asked to leave while it was being searched.[4] He said that he observed 'several officers searching the basement including looking in the trunks of parked cars and the air conditioning grills in the hallways'. He said that he even asked one of the officers why they were doing it. He said he was told that it was because the police had received threats on Oswald's life. Adding further weight to his claims is the fact that he referenced several City Hall workers (Fuqua, Riggs, Kelly & co.) being moved out of the basement by police officers and the two elevators up to the Annex Building being sealed – presumably by reserve officer Brock. Throughout this whole time, Alexander said that no part of the basement was closed off and there is nowhere in his statement that he was ever asked to leave either.

Because Steven Alexander's account of the search of the basement by the DPD flies in the face of the narrative established, it must be qualified and cross-referenced against any testimonies given by other members of the media.

United Press International reporter, Henry Rabun arrived at City Hall at 7am and, like Alexander, he was not asked to show any identification or credentials. Rabun testified to the FBI that he sat in the jail office for most of the morning in wait.[5] He said he would go up to and return from the Third Floor every now and then to gather any updates or developments regarding Oswald's transfer. Nowhere in his statement was it mentioned his not being allowed back in the jail office or that there was a sealed search of the basement taking place.

While Rabun was in the jail office and might not have been able to confirm if the search out in the basement was taking place or not, we have one more account to consider. KRLD-TV reporter, Robert Huffaker testified to seeing 'officers searching the cars in the parking area in the basement prior to the time Oswald was brought out of the jail'.[6] However, Huffaker's statement is not definitive in terms of timing. His 2013 book, 'When the News Went Live: Dallas 1963' does not offer any clarity either.[7]

Other than Alexander, Rabun and Huffaker, no other member of the media made any reference to the search of the basement taking place. But it is also important to remember that there was a portion of the media personnel that witnessed Oswald's shooting that were never interviewed for any investigations.

However, it turns out that there were very few references in any DPD personnel's statements regarding the basement search and it being sealed beforehand. In terms of clearing people out prior to the search, according to his statement to the DPD, Lt. Pierce instructed Sergeant Patrick T. Dean to remove all unauthorised people from the basement until it had been searched.[8] In his statement to the FBI, Pierce made a similar inference when he said all 'civilian' employees were removed from the basement.[9] And it was Pierce's superior, Captain Talbert's understanding that all personnel other than regular and reserve officers would be cleared out according to his statement for the DPD investigation.[10] If Alexander, Rabun and Huffaker's claims are to be believed, only the City Hall workers were cleared out but not any members of the media. Why? Did the ever media-conscious DPD want their efforts of searching the basement to be seen and reported? Likely so. It does not matter either way. Conveniently for the DPD, the ambiguity of who was a civilian and who was not seems to have enabled the story to germinate that the basement was secured prior to a full search being carried out when it was not. So, in the immediate wake of Lee Oswald's shooting, at least it would be known that the DPD did carry out their due diligence. While it may seem like a small detail in the scheme of things, this is just another example of a 'crinkle' in the narrative that we have been able to iron out having closely examined it.

Regardless, before the search began, Sgt. Dean and Putnam did assign some regular and reserve personnel to guard the basement as marked on the map below:

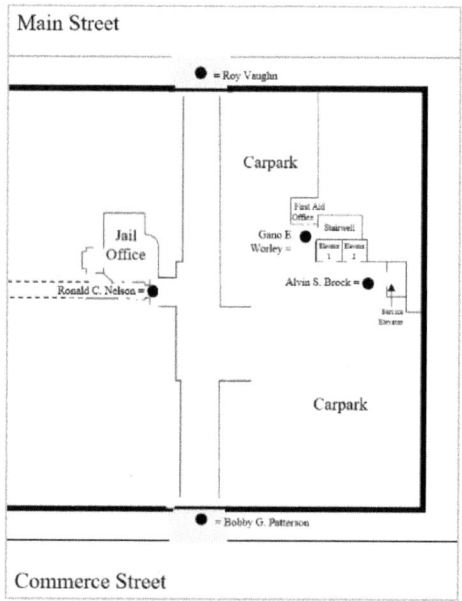

Copyright Paul Abbott

Given the most likely points that people could enter the basement were down the Commerce Street and Main Street ramps, as well as down the corridor from the lesser-referred-to Harwood Street entrance, Officers Bobby G. Patterson, Vaughn, and Ronald C. Nelson were instructed to not let anyone pass them that were not police or press. And even then, members of the press would need to produce credentials. Reserve Officers Worley and Brock were assigned to the outside of the stairwell and elevators respectively on the eastern side of the basement car park - in addition to the Annex

Building above apparently being closed off to the public. However, as already covered in Chapter Six, the basement was still far from sealed when we consider the many other ways it could have been, and was, accessed by 'unauthorised' persons that morning.

For the remainder of the basement search, Dean oversaw a group of, mostly, reserve officers (as many as 30 as stated in some testimonies) searching the basement from top to bottom. Below is a list of reserve officers that I have deduced were most likely involved in the search:

Charles O. Arnett (assisting Dean)	Alvis R. Brock
Robert T. Davis	J.R. Hopkins
J.C. Hunt	Jerome Kasten
J.C. McCain	Ben McCoy
, Montgomery	D.J. McDonald
William J. Newman	Donald Suits
Gano E. Worley	

According to those involved in the search, all parked cars were examined including under their hoods and in their trucks. Crevices across the ceiling, including air ducts were searched as well as around any air conditioning systems on the ground – which lines up with Steven Alexander's observations. The only thing that the search turned up were a couple of rifles in some of the parked cars that belonged to police personnel. These were removed by officers and taken away for safe keeping. To account for the remaining reserve officers that would be present for the events as they unfolded that morning, they were:

James D. Brockway	arrived at 11:00am
Arthur W. Capps	arrived at 9:45am
Roland A. Cox	arrived at 10:00am assigning reserve officers in the assembly room
Kenneth Croy	
Oliver W. Harrison	arrived at 10:00am
Harold J. Holly	arrived after Oswald had been shot
Harry M. Kriss	arrived at 9:45am
Logan W. Mayo	arrived at 9:45am
Barney Merrell	assigning reserve officers in the assembly room

As time came closer to 10am, when Chief Curry said Oswald would be transferred, members of the public began to gather outside the Commerce Street ramp exit, waiting to catch a glimpse of Oswald, however and whenever he would emerge. This necessitated Patrol Officers D.L. Pate, Leonard E. Jez, R.A. Watkins, L.C. Taylor, and most of the reserve officers listed above who did not participate in the searching of the basement, being assigned to help with keeping the crowds across the street from the ramp. In contrast, leading all the way up to the time of the shooting, only Officer Roy Vaughn would be at the Main Street ramp entry to guard it. And to be fair in this regard, there were minimal bystanders there presumably as it was common knowledge that all vehicles leaving the City Hall basement only did so up the Commerce Street ramp.

With the search of the basement car park completed, thoroughly, by all accounts, Dean called together all patrol officers that had since arrived for a briefing of assignments at some time just after 10:45am. See the table below for which officers were assigned where along the presumed transfer route:

Officer	Location
D.K. Erwin	Commerce and Pearl
T.R. Burton	Commerce and Central Expressway - now Cesar Chavez Blvd
Thomas R. Gregory	Central Expressway & Main
Gerald L. Tolbert	Elm and Pearl
L.L. Fox	Elm and Harwood
Marvin L. Wise	Elm and St. Paul
Jerry Raz	Elm and Stone
Alvis S. Brock	Commerce and Central Expressway
Warren E. Hibbs	Elm and Akard
Kenneth K. Anderson	Elm and Field
M.E. Ferris	Elm and Lamar
Don Francis Steele	Elm and Houston

Because the County Jail was situated on Houston Street, and its close proximity to Dealey Plaza, where many members of the public were gathering at the site of President Kennedy's assassination, this meant Officer Steele would be joined by additional personnel including Reserve Officer J.C. Hunt and Captains H.L. Hatley & R.H. Lunday to keep crowds at bay for Oswald's arrival.

This accounts for where most of the patrol officers were just before and during Oswald's shooting. Their instructions were to stop the traffic at their given intersection as the convoy transporting Oswald approached. After the convoy passed through their intersection, they would fall in behind it on their motorcycles to escort it the rest of the way to the County Jail. However, when reports of Oswald's shooting emerged, officers along the route were alerted to it either over the police dispatch or by members of the public. They were then all summoned to Parkland Hospital to assist with security there.

So far, we have broadly accounted for the DPD reserve officers, patrolmen and the search of the basement. As plans matured, some of their postings and instructions changed so we will cover this in a later chapter.

This brings us to the Dallas Police detectives. In some respects, they are perhaps the easiest category of personnel to surmise as most had minimal to no involvement in the security measures and plans to transfer Oswald. As had been so since 2pm on Friday November 22nd, the detectives from Capt. Fritz's Homicide and Robbery Bureau, had been working on the Oswald case. Apart from questioning witnesses and gathering evidence for the Kennedy and Tippit killings, the detectives would participate in interrogations and move Oswald around City Hall as needed. On the Sunday morning, it was Detectives Leavelle, Graves and Montgomery who would escort Oswald with Fritz to start the transfer. Excluding Leavelle, Graves and Montgomery, and Detectives Charles W. Brown and Charles N. Dhority (who were both behind the wheel of cars intended for the convoy), there were 26 detectives who had been called upon to assemble down in the basement from approximately 11am by their superiors. Before then, most had been going about their normal work duties. These detectives would arrive down in the basement in drips and drabs just before and after 11am, but most would testify to Captain O.A. Jones giving them the order to form a cordon on either side of the corridor for Oswald to be led through. In the photographs and footage taken of Oswald as he was led out of the jail office, the majority of people that can be seen are detectives, with the exception of reporters Tom Pettit and Ike Pappas and Lt. Wiggins in the white police hat directly behind Oswald. There was also Acting Detective William J. 'Blackie' Harrison who is most visible reaching out to Ruby in the Bob Jackson photograph (see Chapter Four).

As we did with the assembled media personnel in the last chapter, let's account for where DPD personnel (regular and reserve) were around Oswald (X) on the schematic at the time of the shooting. On the next page after that is a listing grouping each DPD officer by division or bureau.

Compared with the accounting of media within the same vicinity (**forty six**) per the last chapter, it is alarming to consider the **forty six** police personnel listed as present at the scene on the next page. If this was the case, and we have gone to great lengths to conclude as much, we have uncovered the fact that for every member of the media, there was one member of the DPD present! This means that the basement was far from secure in terms of the balance of DPD manpower. Perhaps this is why there has been such a cloud of silence over and regarding members of the media present that morning.

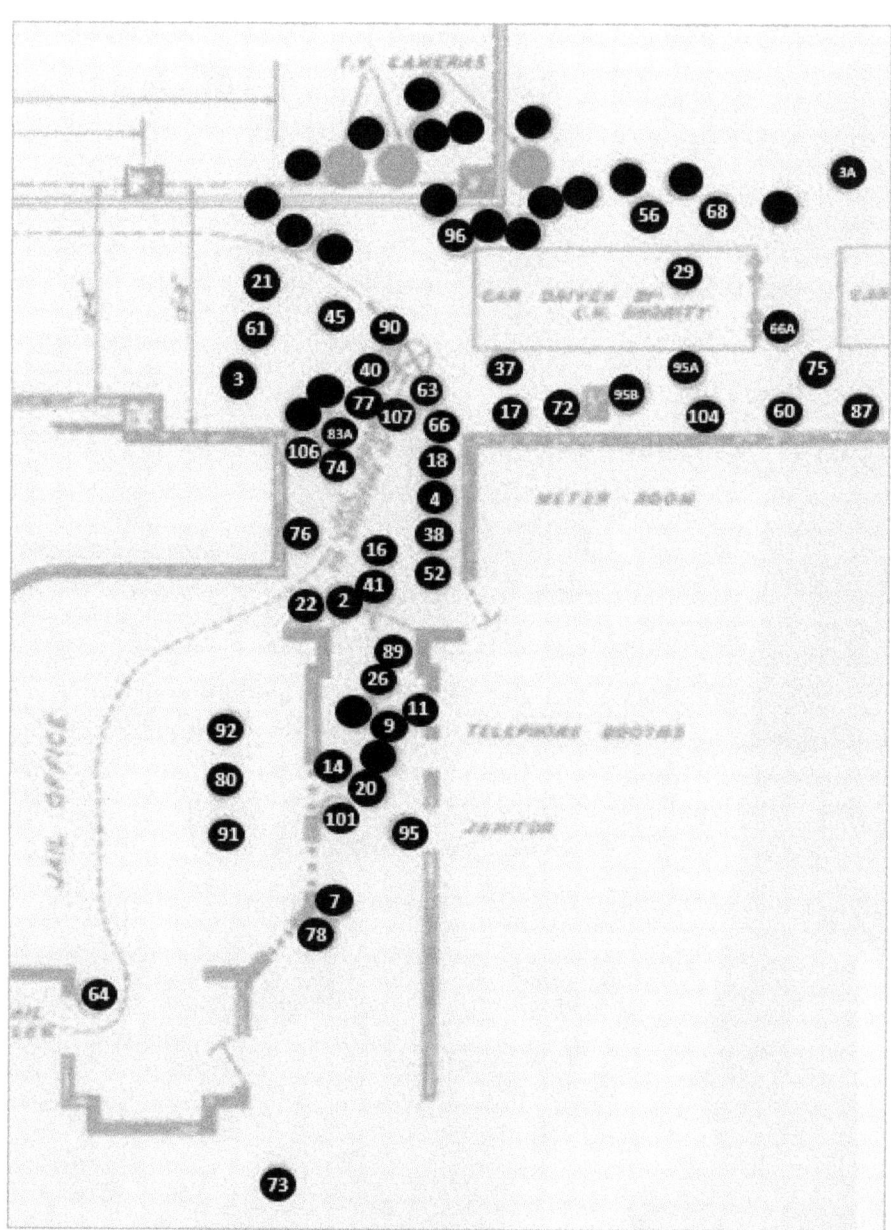

Auto Theft Bureau
Detective Don Ray Archer - 2
Detective Barnard S. Clardy – 17
Detective Harold Dawson - 26
Detective Thomas D. McMillon – 74
Detective James C. Watson – 106

Burglary and Theft Bureau
Detective Daniel G. Brantley – 7
Detective Vernon C. Campbell – 14
Detective Homer Lee McGee – 73
Detective Ivan R. Stephens – 95
Lieutenant Richard E. Swain – 96
Detective I.F. Van Cleave – 101

Forgery Bureau
Capt. Orville A. Jones – 56
Detective W.E. Chambers - 16

Headquarters Division
Officer Carroll G. Lewis - 64
Officer Willie Slack - 91
Lieutenant Woodrow Wiggins – 107

Homicide Robbery Bureau
Capt. J.W. Fritz – 37
Detective Charles N. Dhority – 29
Detective L.C. Graves – 40
Detective James D. Leavelle – 63
Detective Lesley D. Montgomery – 77

Juvenile Bureau
Detective Wilbur Jay Cutchshaw - 22
Detective C. Goolsby - 38

Acting Detective William J. Harrison – 45
Detective Roy Lee Lowery – 66
Detective Louis D. Miller - 76

Patrol Division
Detective D.L. Burgess – 11
Officer Ronald C. Nelson - 78
Detective James K. Ramsey – 87
Detective Homer B. Reynolds – 89
Detective R.C. Wagner – 104

Special Service
Detective Buford Beaty – 4
Detective Billy S. Combest – 18
Detective J.D. Hutchinson – 52

Supervisory
Capt. Charles Batchelor – 3A
Capt. Glen D. King – 60
Capt. George L Lumpkin – 66A
Deputy Chief M.W. Stevenson – 95A

Traffic Division
Officer C.A. Greeson – 41

Reserve Division
Reserve Charles Arnett – 3
Reserve J.D. Brockway – 9
Reserve A.B. Craig – 20
Reserve Kenneth S. Croy – 21
Reserve Harry Kriss – 61
Reserve Barney Merrell - 75
Reserve Donald Suits – 95B

While the DPD schematic in its original form is a useful resource, as previously stated in the context of media personnel, it is far from ironclad in terms of accurately attributing where every person at the scene of the shooting was. However, in terms of the regular DPD personnel, it is fairly accurate when cross-referenced with testimonies and statements. For most of the detectives listed as present, it also helps that we have film and photographic records to visually account exact positioning.

Coffee and Cigars

Among the worst that we have uncovered in the conduct of the DPD is a gross lack of communication, lax security measures and a disproportionate amount of DPD personnel to media personnel. Yet we are still early in our examination of who and what was evidentially negligent or suspicious. There is one member of police who was an outlier in terms of acting overtly suspiciously in the hours leading up to Oswald's transfer – Active Detective William J. 'Blackie' Harrison. He was on secondment from the Patrol Division to the Juvenile Bureau in November of 1963. A member of the DPD for sixteen years, it was how well that Harrison related with young people that he was given the new posting. But it is unclear how soon prior to the weekend of November 22nd his transfer took place. In any event, it meant he would be requested to join the other detectives in his bureau down in the basement for when Oswald's transfer would begin. After the shooting however, Harrison would be one of three DPD officers who would undertake a lie detector test in the months following.

Harrison would give statements to the DPD and FBI that focused on his movements during and after the shooting, which we'll get to later. However, he also testified for the Warren Commission and it was in that, that the questionable movements of his from earlier in the morning of Sunday November 24 emerged. According to his WC statement, he arrived at Dallas City Hall at 8am on the Sunday.[11] He went up to the Third Floor where he was based having noted no cameras set up in the basement. With assignments not yet made, he and Detective Louis D. Miller, who had also just been transferred into the Juvenile Bureau a month prior, let Detective C. Goolsby know that they were going to get a coffee – which was a fairly common practice at the time. Staying with Harrison's statement, he and Miller walked to the Delux Diner just a block west down Commerce Street. While there, Harrison inferred that they only stayed long enough for a cup of coffee before he received a call on the phone at the diner. He said it was Goolsby back at City Hall telling him and Miller to come back. Louis Miller would corroborate going to the diner with Harrison and that they stayed for 30 minutes and didn't talk about anything in particular. Miller confirmed that Harrison took a call there as well.

Like Harrison, Miller gave a statement to the DPD in the weeks after Oswalds' murder and made no mention of going for a coffee on the morning of the shooting either. In fact, it was well into his testimony for the Warren Commission, and only after Counsel Burt Griffin spoke with him off the record, that Miller spoke of the Delux Diner and Blackie Harrison.[12] What is also interesting is that Miller testified that he did not know who called Harrison at the Delux Diner – nor did he ask as he presumed it was someone from back in the 'office'. The person that Harrison alleges called him,

Detective Goolsby only gave the one statement for the DPD investigation and it contained no reference to calling Officer Harrison and Detective Miller back from the diner either. But Detective Cutchshaw told the Warren Commission testimony that Goolsby did make the call.[13] And he did it with Assistant Chief Stevenson having told him and others in the Juvenile Bureau to stay put as they'd want security set up down in the basement soon.

Continuing with Harrison's Warren Commission testimony, when they walked back to City Hall, he mentioned a man by the name of Johnny Miller recognising him and stopping him for a chat just outside. Apparently (Johnny) Miller and Harrison were acquaintances who Harrison would stop by the house of every now and then for a coffee while he was out on patrol. Who Johnny Miller was is anybody's guess but reading the transcript of Harrison's testimony about this interaction, while walking back to City Hall with another man who also happened to be named Miller, makes for some confusing reading. Particularly when WC counsel Griffin asked Harrison 'Does Miller know Ruby, to your knowledge?' The other 'Miller' (Louis) with Harrison didn't testify to this interaction to the Warren Commission either. Was Harrison walking with a man named Miller only to bump into another man named Miller just a coincidence? And that it was sloppy practice by Counsel Burt Griffin not to clearly differentiate one Miller from the other in that part of the questioning? Perhaps it had just slipped from Louis Miller's mind by the time he came to testify to the WC as well.

According to Blackie Harrison, when he returned, he went about normal office duties in the Third Floor office of the Juvenile Bureau by answering calls and looking over what had been assigned to him. He noted reporters coming in and out of the office to use any phone available as well.

Harrison's statement reads as if he then went from the Third Floor office to get a cigar from the vending machine down in the sub-basement locker room. He said that no one else was down there at the time and that, interestingly, he hadn't used his assigned locker for the last 2 ½ or 3 years.

Looking at the timeline of Harrison's movements that morning and in the three hours since he clocked on at 8am, he first walked to a nearby diner for a coffee with another detective. Then, having been called there and told to return, he said he ran into an acquaintance to stop and have a brief chat with on the way back. When he returned to his desk, he got back to some work before going down to buy a cigar from a vending machine. From there he came back up to the Third Floor office and was there when the order came for all detectives to go down to the basement at approximately 11:10am.

But Detectives Cutchshaw and Lowery both gave different accounts to the Warren Commission. According to Lowery, Harrison met them down in the basement as they had just come down from the Third Floor.[14] He also mentioned that Harrison had walked from the corridor leading to the sub-basement. And according to Cutchshaw, when he saw Harrison down in the basement after all personnel arrived for Oswald's transfer, he even asked Harrison 'where he had been?' Harrison replied that he went to the 'café' and got some cigars after he came back. And in his statement to the FBI three months prior to his WC testimony, Cutchshaw actually named who he walked down to the basement with at 11am – Capt. Frank M. Martin, Detectives Miller, Lowery and Goolsby.[15] Harrison was not mentioned therefore it is safe to assume he must not have been with them. This bolsters the theory that Harrison went straight down to the locker room after the diner and could have been down there for any period of time.

Could he have been the man that porters Alfreadia Riggs and Harold Fuqua encountered and who encouraged them to leave by inferring the transfer wouldn't be able to be watched on the TV? If so, why? We have uncovered how easy the basement was to access from stairs down from Commerce and Harwood Streets so we know Harrison could have easily walked straight down to the locker room and not return to his desk that morning. Recall that there was a bank of payphones there so what business could he have had being down there? And is there any link to his time on the payphone in the diner?

What is clear is that there was no mention by anybody during the initial DPD and FBI investigations of Blackie Harrison going down to the locker room to get a cigar. It was only ever referred to in testimonies to the Warren Commission a few months later. Let's trace the timings of the testimonies and what was said by who to lay out how the cigar story emerged:

- Detective Miller was the first to testify to the WC at 9am on March 25, after a false start during the afternoon prior. He was prompted to discuss the diner, but he made no mention of Blackie Harrison meeting another man named Miller on the way back or he (Harrison) going to get a cigar after coming back.
- Detective Lowery gave his testimony at 11am on March 25. Yet he only recalled Harrison joining him and the other detectives when he walked to them from the corridor that led to the sub-basement.
- Harrison also gave his testimony on March 25 at 3:45pm. His testimony contained the first reference to his going to the locker room to buy cigars from a vending machine.

- Detective Cutchshaw gave his testimony at 10:30am on March 26 and he was the only other person, as well as the last, to mention Harrison getting cigars.

Blackie Harrison would be seen in photographs and footage of the shooting both holding and placing a cigar to his mouth. Was his buying them beforehand some kind of ploy to substantiate his being down in the locker room? for however long it may have been. If so, why? There is much more to explore when it comes to Blackie Harrison, and Louis D. Miller, but we will do so in their relevant contexts throughout the remainder of this book.

Having introduced the cohorts of people and personnel that were present at the scene of the shooting and laid out the conditions in the basement and on the Third Floor at Dallas City Hall, we now come to the crux of this book - the moments just before, during and after Lee Oswald's shooting to form the most comprehensive picture of what happened.

PART THREE

SHOOTING

CHAPTER TEN

COUNTDOWN

Given there were some ninety people (media and police) in the direct vicinity of where Oswald would be shot, we will use as many statements and visual records as possible to examine the incident.

It is worth focusing on the forty minutes in and outside of the basement prior to Oswald emerging first. After the search of the basement by Sgt. Dean and the reserve officers, police vehicles began to enter the basement. Sgt. Putnam[1] said that an unmarked car with two detectives entered and was searched. A patrol wagon, driven by Officer Carroll G. Lewis had also returned from the dog pound. Both vehicles were thoroughly searched in full view of the waiting media.

At this time, we should bring our attention back to reserves Gano Worley and Alvis Brock. As established in Chapter Nine, they were posted at the eastern side of the basement car park – Worley at the bottom of the stairs up to the Annex Building and Brock in front of the elevators when the basement search got underway at approximately 9:15am. At 10:45am, once the basement search had finished, Brock was reassigned from the elevators to the intersection of Elm and Ervay. Brock's testimony to the Warren Commission[2] confirm he received his reassignment at the time that the patrolmen, per the table in Chapter Nine, were receiving theirs.

It appears that Worley was left alone at his post in the front of the basement stairs. But he would tell the Warren Commission that he saw another reserve officer in his immediate area after 'the other officer' guarding the area with him (referring to Brock, whom he did not know the name of either) left.[3] That said, he did note Reserve Capt. Arnett and Reserve Officer Ben McCoy nearby to him as well.

Who was the man standing near to Worley after Brock left? And did he stay there? It may seem strange that Worley couldn't name Brock or the other reserve. Yet it comes up in a few instances across other reserve officer statements – that they could not identify other reservists.* This may be understandable when we consider that reserve officers were only required to volunteer for eight hours per month to remain on the roster. So, when we consider there were some three hundred people to choose from, it would be very unlikely that reserves would be posted with the same fellow reserve officer/s during their monthly roster too often, if at all, therefore, making it difficult to remember other's names.

---

*Reserve Harold Holly was another example of this. He claimed to the DPD that another reserve officer told him after Oswald's shooting that Jack Ruby was able to enter the basement because he was wearing a press pass – despite no press pass being mentioned as found on him after shooting Oswald. However, Holly could not identify the reserve who told him this. He was shown personnel photographs and allegedly chose Reserve William J. Newman – who was standing in the basement under the Commerce Street ramp for most of that morning. Newman strongly denied Holly's claims.

In all statements he would give, Worley said that he was reassigned away from his basement post approximately 10 to 15 minutes before Oswald emerged and was shot.

He stated that it was Ben McCoy who instructed him to go to the intersection of Commerce and Central Expressway. Again, as per the table in Chapter Nine, we established that Patrolman T.R. Burton was also posted there so why the need to send Worley there as well when most other intersections were allocated only one patrolman? In his statements to the DPD[4] and FBI,[5] Burton doesn't shed any light on Worley, or a need for him, at all. The closest he comes to acknowledging anyone else being with him was when he said how Capt. Talbert came by and told him and his 'partner' about the shooting. Burton was then ordered to Parkland Hospital.

What did McCoy testify to regarding ordering Worley away from his posting down in the basement? He told the DPD that it was Sgt. Dean who asked for someone to be sent to 'Commerce and *Pearl* to work the signals as the light was stuck' so McCoy said he sent Worley.[6] However, it was Commerce and Central Expressway where Worley said he was sent to. Adding to the confusion is the fact that Reserve Captain Arnett mentioned the faulty signal at Commerce and Pearl to the FBI and the need to 'furnish one man to help direct traffic'.[7] The thing was, there is no other specific reference from anyone else about faulty traffic lights at the intersection of Commerce and Pearl – including Sgt. Dean. Reference and meaning to it appears to have started with Arnett and stopped with McCoy.

The obvious questions regarding both Alvis Brock and Gano Worley start with why were they transferred away from guarding points of entry into the basement that were adjacent to where the Oswald transfer was about to embark from? And who was the unknown reserve officer that was still near Worley before he was moved? How long were they there for and in what capacity? Were they standing guard to cover after Brock and Worley?

Charles Arnett offers no explanation about who this person might be. And neither does Ben McCoy, despite giving the DPD the most amount of detail about so much else to do with that morning. I think that this person was reserve officer William J. Newman, who was stationed nearby at the engine room door at the Commerce Street side of the basement car park. He did not testify to covering any areas away from his own post either.

Moving forward to the arrival of the armoured trucks on Commerce Street. KRLD-TV footage filmed by Gene Pasczalek shows the larger truck, being driven by Bert Hall, reversing into position at the top of the ramp. The backup truck, driven by Don Goin, was parked further down Commerce Street. Accompanying this footage is commentary by Robert Huffaker from down in the basement. It is evident in the footage that the truck parked at the top of the ramp had left the smallest of gaps between it and the sides of the ramp. Members of the media can be seen walking past it on the east side to go down to the basement. Three and a half minutes later, the footage cuts to George Phenix's camera down in the basement which is focused on the rear compartment of the armoured truck and some personnel searching it. Lieutenant Vernon Smart told the DPD[8] and FBI investigations[9] that he searched it with Charles Batchelor, who confirmed as much in his WC testimony.[10] Patrol Division Lieutenant George Butler said that he searched the truck with Batchelor and Dean.[11] But Dean's testimonies and statements do not corroborate this.

While searching the truck, Batchelor said that they planned the seating configuration. The KRLD-TV footage filming all of this really is raw because off-the-air dialogue involving Huffaker and CBS news director, Nelson Benton can be heard. It is also useful because it provides a timeline from the moment the armoured truck arrived until the moment Oswald is shot. For the record, it arrived exactly thirteen minutes before the shooting, which happened at 11:21am – putting its arrival at 11:08am.

Staying with this footage and it pans rightwards to focus on the corridor leading out from the jail office. Over an hour after the announced time of Oswald's transfer and the activity and anticipation of those gathered is clear. Next, it shows the wheeling out of the WBAP-TV camera by John Tankersley and David Timmons only – three minutes prior to Oswald emerging. Seeing all of the DPD and media personnel milling about, including the unknown Japanese reporter, it's interesting to note that female reporter, Peggy Simpson is nowhere to be seen at all prior to the shooting.

The next event the footage captures is an important one. A second or two under the one-minute mark before Oswald is brought out, an unmarked car is seen being guided onto the ramp toward Main Street. DPD and media personnel such as the unknown Japanese reporter, Robert Huffaker and Tom Pettit step aside to let it come through. Blackie Harrison is also front and centre (with a lit cigar in hand) helping the car negotiate the congestion. Lieutenant Pierce told the Warren Commission[12] that Chief Curry and Assistant Chief Stevenson instructed him at 11:15am to source a car and some uniformed officers to drive it as the lead car of the convoy to the County Jail. Curry wasn't in the basement at the time and neither he nor Stevenson corroborated Pierce's claims. Sgt. Dean must have known of the order Pierce was apparently acting on because he would ask Sgt. Putnam, who was assisting with security in the basement, to go with Pierce. In any event, Pierce found a car and pulled it out. Before the car reached the ramp, according to Lieutenant Billy Joe Maxey, Pierce waved him over and asked him to ride along so he obliged by getting in the backseat. In the KRLD-TV footage, Putnam can be seen clearing the way at the base of the ramp. When it was clear, he jumped into the front passenger seat.

Main Street Ramp Entrance

With Lt. Pierce now driving up the ramp to Main Street, it is important to set the scene there as it was the lynchpin to the established narrative of how Jack Ruby accessed the basement to shoot Oswald.

As already stated, as the basement search began, Officer Roy Vaughn was posted at the mouth of the ramp on Main Street to prevent anyone without police or press credentials entering. According to his statement to the FBI, this was at 9:30am.[13] Also in this statement, Vaughn said that he let in:

- Patrolman Watkins who had four juveniles in his custody,
- the 'City doctor' (presumably medical intern Fred Bieberdorf),
- Officer Lewis driving the paddy wagon back from the dog pound,
- Officer G.K. Springer who was driving a squad car,
- the 'City Mechanic', (Tom Chabot or Colbert, it's not clear in witness statements) who he saw speaking with Sgt. Dean in the basement for a few minutes before coming back up,
- and members of the media (who most likely were Curtis Gans, Oliver Oakes (who would both leave prior to the shooting) and Paul

Sisco of UPI, Robert Thornton from WFAA and 'someone from the Associated Press')

Vaughn also stated to the FBI that, at 11am, a crowd began forming around the top of the ramp. No one asked to be let in, they just seemed to be curious about what was going on down in the basement. Joining Vaughn at his post was former African American Dallas police officer, Napoleon J. Daniels. He would give statements to the DPD,[14] FBI[15] and Warren Commission[16] and as is evident in them, was a questionable character from the outset.

Daniels left the DPD in November of 1962 due to conflicts of interest with tenants in one of his apartments. His next job saw him become a real estate broker. He claimed that he was on his way to Dealey Plaza on the morning of November 24 when he saw a crowd forming around City Hall. He said that he recalled the fact that Lee Oswald was to be transferred from there that morning so he parked his car in the vacant lot between the Annex Building and another building. Walking along Main Street, he saw that there was only one officer standing at the top of the ramp so he walked over to him. In his first account of events, he told the DPD (on Nov. 29) that the time was 11am when he reached Roy Vaughn and started speaking with him. Vaughn corroborated Daniels' arrival and his talking with him but he stated the time as being 10:15am.

Daniels recalled to the FBI that there were no other spectators standing around. However, he did mention a man named 'Alonzo' or 'Alphonse' that he recognised as being a former shoeshine boy in the police locker room. He was wearing a grey suit and had a camera hanging from his neck. Could

Daniels have been referring to Alfreadia Riggs? Recall that he and Harold Fuqua walked past the Main Street ramp on their way around to access the locker room. The uniform for City Hall workers was grey so that lines up with Daniels' description and he wasn't far from recalling Riggs' first name either. If this was him, the reference to Riggs having a camera is interesting as no one else, including Riggs, mentioned this. However, Daniels said the man he saw tried to take a photograph down the ramp but that Vaughn stopped him from doing this. Neither Vaughn, Riggs nor Fuqua testified to this.

At this point, we must refer back to two other people that were positioned on the other side of Main Street – cabdriver Harry Tasker and Patrol Sergeant Don Flusche to round out the picture.

Tasker was seated in his cab across Main Street per the instructions of UPI's Paul Sisco. Despite the best efforts by Warren Commission Counsel Leon Hubert to seemingly confuse the issue,[17] Tasker stated that he was parked with his car back at a 45-degree angle to the curb so he was facing the ramp. He positioned himself as such because he was keeping an eye out for Sisco coming back up from the ramp. He said he left his cab once to look for 'his reporter' but he went straight back to resume his wait. When asked about the police officer he saw standing at the ramp, Tasker confirmed that he only ever saw him standing in 'about the middle of the opening of the door'. Hubert asked for clarification so Tasker told him that the police officer was standing just beyond the opening of the ramp.

Don Flusche with the traffic division was on duty on the morning of November 24. He was not called to City Hall to assist with Oswald's transfer. But, knowing the transfer was taking place, he told the HSCA in

1978 that he parked his car across Main Street from the 'police and courts building' – the Annex Building, as it's been referred to in this book.[18] He stood out of his car and with the radio on to monitor proceedings. He said that he knew Jack Ruby personally and never saw him walking along Main Street or enter down the ramp of City Hall. Don Flusche was not interviewed by the DPD, FBI or Warren Commission. He reported his movements on Main Street at the time of the shooting and his observations and lack thereof of Ruby to his superior, Lt. Earl Knox but he never heard back about the matter.

See the diagram below for Tasker, Flusche, Vaughn and Daniels' positioning at the time when Pierce would drive up from the basement:

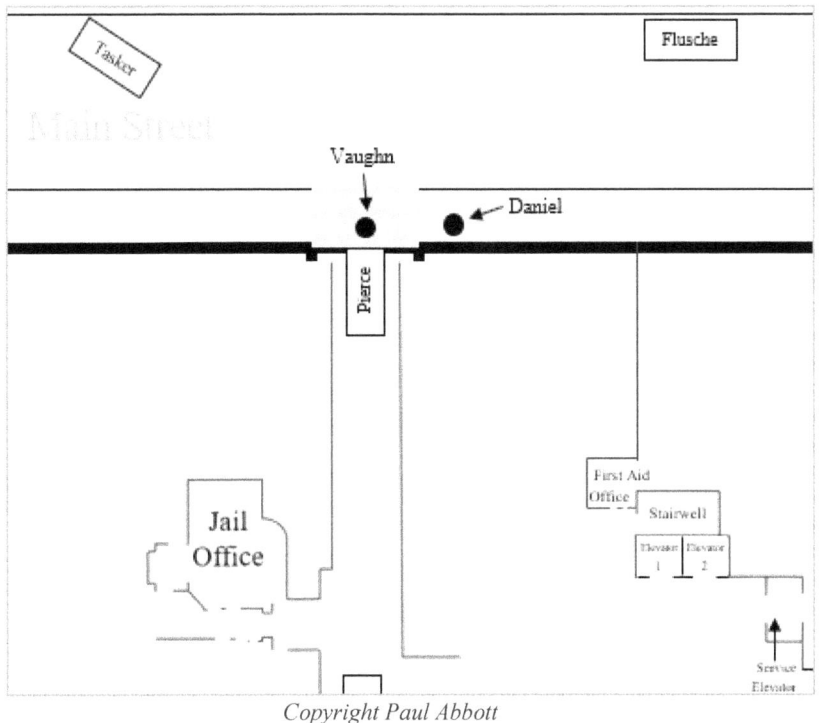

Copyright Paul Abbott

With Lt. Pierce approaching the top of the ramp, Roy Vaughn stated to both the DPD[19] and Warren Commission that he stepped to his right to let him emerge and help guide him out onto the street. Tasker stated to the Warren Commission that he saw Vaughn step out onto the street to let a car out but in either statement, he couldn't recall if this was before or after the shooting. Napoleon Daniels flip-flopped about between his statement on this front. He told the DPD that Vaughn stepped out into the middle of Main Street to stop traffic so the car that had come up the ramp could get out, and additionally to the FBI, even though there were no cars to stop. What did the occupants of the squad car say? Pierce told the Warren Commission that Vaughn did step out into the street and to the right to let him out. Putnam saw Vaughn stationed directly in front of the ramp where the sidewalk joins the street. Sgt. Maxey, seated in the back told the DPD that he saw Vaughn standing at the right side of the top of the ramp.

How far does stepping out onto Main Street mean? With people standing on either side of the ramp, including Napoleon Daniels, and given how vigilant he had been so far that morning, it is hard to fathom that Vaughn would have walked too far from his post.

Tasker, Vaughn and the three DPD personnel in the car noted people standing on either side of the ramp at the time but the only person to say they saw someone enter down it after the police car drove away was Daniels. And reading all of his statements, it is hard to make sense of what he said he saw. To the DPD, he said that he stepped out into the street to have a better look down the ramp. When he did so, he said he saw a white male, approximately 50 years of age and wearing a dark suit walking from the east, which was coming from the Western Union office, on Main Street. The man was not wearing a hat so he was able to describe his light coloured, thinning hair. He watched the man walk straight down into the ramp. He told the DPD that he was adamant that Vaughn could not have missed seeing him either because he (Vaughn) was standing in the middle of the ramp mouth at the time. He said he assumed that Vaughn must have known who the man was and that's why he didn't do anything to stop him. Daniels never identified who he saw as being Jack Ruby. He said that two minutes later, he heard a shot down in the basement. Vaughn must have found out what had been stated about him to the DPD because Daniels said Vaughn called him at his home on Monday November 25. He said that Vaughn asked him if he saw anyone enter the basement while Pierce was driving the squad car out. Daniels said he told him he hadn't. He also didn't mention the man he did see because he was still sure that Vaughn did see him and allowed him to pass. In his Warren Commission testimony, Daniels admitted that he wasn't sure if he saw the man enter the basement before or after the shooting after all.

Daniels would testify to the HSCA some fifteen years later adamant that the man he saw go down the ramp was Jack Ruby,[20] which does little to resolve how questionable he was at the time. Below is the polygraph test that he was given by the DPD. With the benefit of hindsight, we know that such tests are far from an exact science but in the context of the time, they were used to detect if a person was lying when answering questions. Daniels clearly did not pass his, according to the DPD investigation:

1. Have you told the complete truth in the statement you gave? Answer: Yes. Indication: False
2. Have you deliberately made up any of this story? Answer: No. Indication: False

3. Do you think the person you stated you saw enter the basement at that time was Jack Ruby? Answer: No. Indication: True.
4. Did you actually see the person you described come from the direction of the Western Union? Answer: Yes. Indication: False.
5. Do you think this person entered the basement of the city hall after the squad drove out? Did not answer this question.
6. Have you seen the person you described in your statement around city hall before? Answer: Did not answer this question.
7. Have you given a true description of the person you stated you saw enter the basement of the city hall? Answer: Yes. Indication: False.
8. Did you actually see the person you describe enter the basement of city hall? Answer: Yes. Indication: False.
9. Did you get a good look at this person? Answer: Yes. Indication: False.

What all of this means is that nobody in the vicinity of the Main Street ramp entrance conclusively saw Jack Ruby enter the basement that way. The closest that anyone comes is Jimmie Turner seeing Ruby emerge at the bottom of the ramp. But before we can close this tangent off fully, we must acknowledge the questionable account of reserve officer William J. Newman – who was situated at the Commerce Street side of the basement car park. To the DPD, he gave *four* statements which was more than most.

- The first statement, dated November 26, had him saying when he reported for duty that day (9:30am) and who to (Merrell), any other personnel that he saw in the vicinity (reserves Suits and Croy) and that he did not know Jack Ruby or see him at the scene of the shooting.[21]

- In his next two statements, one of which was not dated, he said that he recalled seeing a man going over the railing where the media were but he was not sure if it was before or after the shooting. He described the man as wearing a suit but couldn't remember if he was wearing a hat or not.[22]
- Newman's fourth statement for the DPD, on December 1, had him adding that he saw a white male run from down the ramp from Main Street one minute before the shooting only to then blend in with the crowd.[23]

Newman would soon give a statement to the FBI on December 5.[24] In it, he conceded that he could not see all the way up the ramp to Main Street because of how low the basement ceilings were. He still spoke of seeing a man come down the ramp but wasn't sure if the man had been checked for identification at the top.

Finally, to the Warren Commission, Newman, under oath this time, went into more detail about how he was posted to guard the entrance to the engine room in the sub-basement (under the Commerce Street ramp) after having helped search cars parked in the basement, presumably as part of the Sgt. Dean-led search. Of the man he saw coming down the ramp, he told the WC that he saw him climb back through the railing but didn't think to tell anyone. He then alleges seeing a camera crew run up to the man in a panic before a brief scuffle broke out. Newman alleges that the man said he wasn't trying to escape, he was only trying to get away from the immediate scene.[25] This infers that Newman's sighting of a man coming down the ramp was *after* the shooting because, firstly, nobody reported a scuffle breaking out within the media gathered prior to the shooting. And after the shooting, who knows what went on during the chaos.

Either way we cut this statement, it still does not make sense because why would someone who entered the basement, and then the car park through the railing, only to get into a scuffle, say that he wasn't trying to escape? We'll come back to Reserve Officer William Newman later but it is still safe to say that nobody in the basement saw Ruby walk all the way down the ramp from Main Street that morning.

With the Pierce car en-route along Main and Harwood Street to the Commerce Street ramp, let us turn our focus to the remaining seconds back down in the basement.

The raw KRLD-TV footage remains crucial for us to understand the timings of movements in the brief window of time after Pierce's car left and Oswald emerged and shot. According to the footage, it was 56 seconds from when Pierce's car drove up the ramp until Oswald was brought out. This dashes any notion that minutes lapsed from when Ruby entered the basement to when he shot Oswald. We know that the element of coincidence was leveraged by the authorities with explaining Ruby's miraculous timing but we can now take a new lens to it when we consider that prior to being in the basement, he was at the Western Union signing a money transfer. The time on the receipt for the transaction was 11:17am so if Oswald was shot at 11:21am, Ruby actually had up to four and a half minutes to leave the Western Union, walk the short distance to City Hall and access the basement.

Under a Minute

Keeping with the film being taken of the jail office corridor and there is a lot to see in the 56 seconds after Pierce's car left and when Oswald came out. Blackie Harrison took the position he would be in when Ruby lunged out. That's not to say he stood perfectly still. He ambled on the spot and, crucially, looked back to the direction of the Main Street ramp a few times. This is crucial because he testified to knowing Jack Ruby for 12 to 13 years. If Ruby was walking down the ramp after Pierce's car left, Harrison would surely have noticed and recognised him as he came to stand right near him – hat or no hat. But watching Harrison and he is as cool as a cucumber just taking the whole scene in. The next flutter of activity comes with Detective E.R. Beck emerging from the jail office direction. He had been instructed by Fritz to go down the basement along with Detectives Brown and Dhority to get the cars in the convoy ready.[26] Ducking around him was Izzy Bleckman getting into place to take his footage of Oswald emerging. Behind him was Ike Pappas in his light trench coat and tape recorder & microphone in hand. Pappas looks to be speaking into his microphone as he gets in place. Listening to the recording of this and comparing the timings of when he emerged and when Oswald did and it all lines up. Directly behind Pappas when he emerged out into the basement was Maurice Carroll who moves off to the left and where he would be visible in the Beers photograph.

It is not clear exactly how soon or late it was decided that Oswald would be driven in a squad car to the County Jail and not in the armoured truck. By trying to make sense of their statements, it is clear that the decision was made between Chief Curry and Capt. Fritz as the latter thought it best to still use the armoured truck in the convoy but only as a decoy. Detective Graves testified that he recalled hearing Fritz discussing the concept with the Secret Service's Forrest Sorrels in the minutes prior to Oswald being brought down.[27] The decision must have been made earlier enough for word to get down to the basement because several personnel who were down there testified to knowing about it before Oswald's transfer began. Lt. Pierce was told about it when he was given his orders by Curry and Stevenson to drive the lead car out in front of the armoured truck. Sorrels provided the additional detail that the car that Oswald was in would simply turn out of the convoy and drive directly to the County Jail. The plan sounded logical but it clearly did not factor in the live television cameras and reporters in the basement who would have seen Oswald get in a different vehicle to the armoured truck, therefore broadcast this over the radio – negating the entire point. In fact, this very point was made to Batchelor by WC counsel Burt Griffin but he just bristled that he didn't make the decision.[28] Regardless, the scene had been set for Oswald's transfer to begin.

CHAPTER ELEVEN

SHOOTING

Oswald stepped off the jail elevator with Detectives Leavelle and Graves on either side of him. Before them was Lt. Swain, Detective Montgomery, then Capt. Fritz. The footage that James Davidson took through the jail office window shows that Fritz then conferred with Swain for a couple of seconds. Swain testified that this was because Fritz was telling him to ride in Brown's car as there wouldn't be room for him in Dhority's.[1] Swain then walked out of the jail office. Graves and Leavelle began to walk with Oswald but Davidson's footage cuts and resumes once Oswald is out of the jail office. Lt. Wiggins stated to the DPD that Fritz asked him, while still in the jail office, if everything was ready.[2] Wiggins said that he stepped outside the jail office to look out to the basement. Fritz then came out of the jail office anyway as did the detectives with Oswald right behind him. Wiggins would fall in behind, as is apparent in the Davidson footage.

What is clear from the footage taken directly ahead is that Lt. Swain is the first of the personnel with Oswald to emerge. He walks through the cordon that has been formed by detectives and looks to the right to where the vehicles are situated on the ramp. He can then be seen giving a gesturing motion as if directing Brown and Dhority back. While he is doing this, Fritz can be seen coming out at the top of the cordon. He is walking slowly in front of Detectives Archer and Cutchshaw while looking back to the jail office. Only Detective McMillon, who was several feet in front of Fritz, so not the closest to him by any means, testified that he answered 'yes' when Fritz asked nobody in particular if everything was ready.[3] Unfortunately, none of the front-on footage shows Fritz during this time either but this is because the three TV cameras that filmed the longest, were obscured by the line of media personnel and detectives.

The moment that Fritz starts to follow Swain, a car horn can be heard. Could this have been either Brown or Dhority, who were the only two people known to be behind the wheel of a car in the vicinity? Brown makes no mention of sounding his horn or that there might have been the need to. But Dhority does. In his statement to the DPD,[4] he said that he was having 'trouble with reporters in his way' so could it have simply been him who sounded his horn to get them to move? He didn't say but that could have been the case when we consider Lt. Swain only got to his position and started gesturing the moment the horn sounded. There is literally no mention from anybody present at the scene that either of the cars' horns sounded either. So why else would a car horn be honked at this time? Might it have been a signal to indicate that Fritz had emerged therefore Oswald must not be far behind him? Because of how low the ceilings were in the basement it is incredibly difficult to approximate where else the horn could have come from down there.

When organising the cordon of detectives that Oswald would be led through, Sgt. Putnam and Capt. Jones instructed all personnel to fall in behind Oswald as he moved through. This, presumably, was to contain and protect him, particularly from the rear, as he got closer to the car. The order was also given that none of the press ask Oswald any questions. The only person who would contravene this was Ike Pappas, when he stepped forward and thrust his microphone toward Oswald in front of Graves and asked if he had anything to say. However, it is understandable as we know that he only got into position seconds before Oswald would come out meaning he wasn't around to hear this order given.

It is clear in footage and photographs of the scene that almost every detective was looking at Oswald as he walked past. This runs counter to standard protection and crowd control techniques, and common sense - that eyes should be peeled across the immediate scene for any threats. This would then enable a quick response to any form of attack. Numerous references were made by DPD personnel that the camera lights made it hard for them to see forward which adds to the incompetence of the preparation and regard for security by the DPD. The bright lights are incredibly evident in film and footage of the shooting so they no doubt were a hinderance for observation of the scene. But they had been on from at least the time that the armoured truck arrived so nobody could say they didn't have time to adjust their sight to them. And only one detective, Thomas D. McMillon (in the black fedora as evident in the Beers photograph) showed any sign of following instructions by changing his position after Oswald passed. He correlated this in his testimony to the Warren Commission.[5] The only other person was Detective Billy H. Combest who tried to move in behind Oswald (also evident in the Beers photograph as the second person back from Leavelle's right shoulder) by taking a step to follow the moment he was shot. It is also clear in Beers' photograph that none of the detectives positioned themselves to prevent reporters Tom Pettit and Ike Pappas, both in light coats and holding microphones, from getting close to Oswald.

Interestingly, speaking of the media, Detectives Beaty and Combest and Reserve Sergeant, Kenneth Croy would tell the FBI in their statements that when Oswald emerged, the media surged. This is hard to detect in any of the footage. Furthermore, reporter Maurice Carroll (also visible in the top far right of Beers' photograph) would tell the FBI that 'newsmen and television reporters on both sides surged toward him (Oswald).' The obvious problem with this is the fact that there were no members of the media on the opposite side to Carroll. The only reporter remotely across from Pettit, Pappas and was Peter Worthington and he was downwards along the ramp wall – effectively around a corner when Oswald was brought out. What scene was Carroll recalling here? He further discredited himself in this statement when he said that where he was standing was 'two or three deep with newsmen' when this was clearly not the case.

News director, Robert Hankal would also give a questionable statement about this moment. He told the FBI that he heard someone say 'He's coming' as if to indicate Oswald was on his way out. Then some shuffling began and he noted a number of police officers locking arms in front of 'the camera'. He must have been referring to his KRLD-TV camera as 'the camera' because Hankal said that an officer stepped aside at his request. At no time, in any footage or according to any statements, were there any police officers standing in front of the area where the media and cameras were. What scene was Hankal recalling here?

Also evident in all footage and photographs is the lack of protection in front of Oswald. Instead of maintaining a closed and guarded distance, Capt. Fritz was no less than five feet in front of Oswald during the short walk through the cordon. This literally left Oswald wide open for attack from the front, as is most apparent in the Beers photograph. On this aspect alone, he should have been held to the highest of accountability. But he was not and it does not even get mentioned in any part of the findings of the investigations.

Some have purported that in the last second before being shot, Oswald actually looked at Jack Ruby. And others have taken this to mean that the two knew each other. It is clear in Frank Johnston's photograph and the Bleckman and Phenix footage that Oswald did turn his head to his left in the last second before being shot. Unfortunately, there's a cut at this moment in Homer Venso's footage so we cannot use his central position as a reference. However, given he was filming from just behind Ruby's position, George Phenix's footage gives us the best perspective. It could well be that Lee Oswald and Jack Ruby knew each other so Oswald recognised him in that split second. However, using the Phenix footage, I offer the more likely possibility that perhaps Oswald was turning toward where he heard Ike Pappas ask, 'Do you have anything to say?' Pappas would have asked the question with Oswald's escort, Graves, in the way so when Oswald could better see past him, he looked toward Pappas holding his microphone. Then Ruby lunged forward at him.

(Jack) (You) (Rat) Son of a Bitch etc.

Let's pick the scene back up from the moment captured in Jack Beers' photograph. According to some, Jack Ruby yelled out when he lunged forward to shoot Oswald. However, oddly so, it was only Detectives Archer (2) and McMillon (18) – as indicated in the below map portion - who would contend this. And even then, they had Ruby yelling two different phrases:

- Archer told the DPD investigation and testified at Jack Ruby's trial that he heard Ruby yell 'Son of a bitch'[6] and to the FBI he said he heard 'You son of a bitch'.[7]
- McMillon told the FBI that he heard Ruby yell 'You rat son of a bitch. You shot the president' as he shot Oswald.[8]

How can two people hear two completely different things at the same time? Particularly, as both were behind Oswald and the detectives, per the below schematic section:

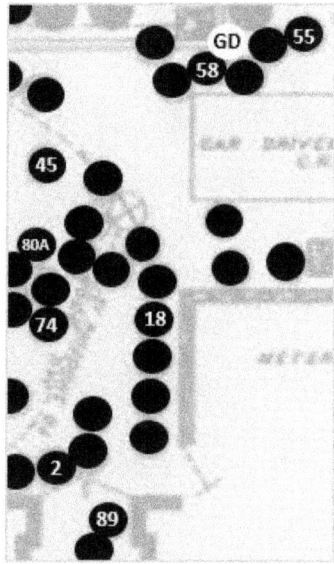

- Detective Combest (18), also shown in the same schematic section, stated to the FBI that when he saw Jack Ruby emerging, he himself yelled 'Jack Ruby, you son of a bitch, don't'.[9] Per the Beers photograph, Combest's vision of Ruby would have almost entirely been impaired by Leavelle and Oswald so how could he have seen

enough of Ruby to know what he was going to do and then warn him not to do so.
- Interestingly, reporter Seth Kantor (58), and photographer, Frank Johnston (55) are the only people who come close to corroborating what Combest said. Both were standing in front of where Oswald was shot. Kantor stated in an affidavit for the DPD investigation that he heard an officer shout 'Jack, you S.O.B.'.[10] And Johnston testified at Jack Ruby's trial the following March (and only then) that he heard someone say 'You s.o.b.' as the gun went off.[11]
- Blackie Harrison (45), in his statement to the DPD, said that he yelled 'Jack!' when he saw Ruby lunging past him. Yet, Harrison did not make the same claim in his statements for the FBI and Warren Commission.
- and perhaps most strangely, Detective Reynolds (89) told the FBI that as soon as he heard the shot, he recalled hearing Detective Leavelle, who was standing right next to Oswald, yell 'You S.O.B'[12] However, Leavelle did not testify to saying this.

Putting a question mark firmly on all of these contentions is the fact that no audio accompanying the TV cameras picked up anything being said either. Furthermore, reporters Ike Pappas (80A) and Gary DeLaune (GD) had their tape recorders recording the scene. No utterances to the effect of what Archer, McMillon, Combest, Kantor, Johnston and Harrison alleged as being yelled or said can be heard in their recordings. And Pappas himself would testify that his microphone had a range of four metres which, given he was standing just to the right of Ruby and back slightly at the time, would have picked up anything Ruby, Combest, Harrison, Kantor… or anyone in the immediate vicinity said or heard. So, again, we must ask, what scene were these people observing? Getting minor details wrong can be forgiven but testifying that something was said when it clearly and evidently was not, is a whole other story.

In terms of chronicling the exact moment that Oswald was shot, we have the Bob Jackson photograph as well as the footage from the news cameras. But before we refer to those, I have used the schematic and witness statements to compile a list of the people who had the clearest line of vision for when Oswald was shot. They are indicated by number in the schematic section below, followed by a summary of their accounts:

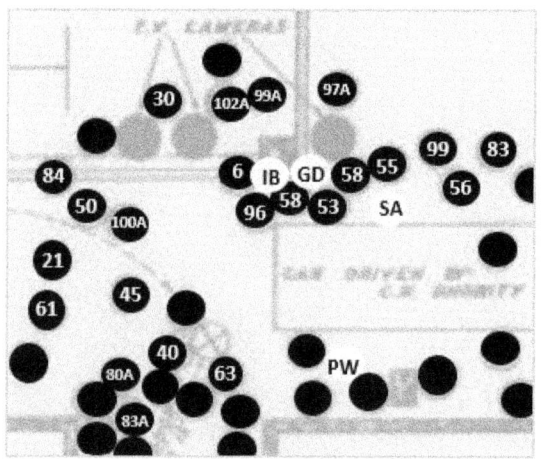

Steven Alexander – SA:
Filmed the shooting but never gave a description of what he observed.

Jack Beers - 6:
Was focused on Oswald through the viewfinder of his camera so he only ever saw the back of Jack Ruby. His initial reaction was that he thought Ruby was a detective who went berserk and shot Oswald.

Izzy Bleckman - IB:
Was also focused on Oswald through his camera. He recalled an individual, he would later find out was Jack Ruby, 'cut through the photographers, TV cameramen, etc. a short distance to his (Bleckman's) right and proceeded to shoot Oswald.'

Reserve Kenneth Croy - 21:
Was standing behind where Ruby emerged from. He was paying attention to the reporters immediately in front of him when he remembered a blurred figure. He said that he tried to reach out for the man, who was moving as if crouched with a football, but was off balance so all he could reach was the bottom of the man's coat.[13] He then heard a shot. The Beers photograph disproves Croy's account of reaching the bottom of Ruby's coat as his nor anyone else's can be seen near it.

Gary DeLaune - GD:
Would state many years later that he only recalled seeing a blur when Ruby stepped out and shot Oswald.

J.B. English - 30:
Filmed the shooting but never gave a description of what he observed.

Bob Fenley (misspelt as 'Finley' by DPD) - 34:

Gave a statement but did not provide a description of the shooting.[13]

Detective LC. Graves - 40:

Testified to the DPD that he and Leavelle paused with Oswald at the time to wait for Dhority to back the car up – however, this is not evident in any footage. Ruby then stepped out and, according to his statement to the FBI, fired at Oswald from a distance of fifteen inches away.

Acting Detective William J. 'Blackie' Harrison - 45:

As he saw Ruby move past then in front of him, Harrison said he reached out to try and stop Ruby. According to his FBI statement, he even got as close as being able to put his hand on Ruby's right arm the moment he shot Oswald. Just looking at the Beers photograph we know this was not the case.

Robert S. Huffaker - 50:

His attention was on Dhority's car reversing toward him. He only saw Oswald fall and he couldn't tell who shot him at first.

Bob Jackson - 53:

Was focused on Oswald's face. When Ruby emerged, his initial thought was that someone had moved into his line of vision and interfered with the photograph. He didn't see Ruby or the gun either.[14]

Frank B. Johnston - 55:
Took a photograph of Oswald being led out but was distracted by Dhority's reversing car so he didn't actually see the shooting.[15]

Seth Kantor - 58:
He said he saw someone come into his view with a gun in his hand. That's when he heard someone shout 'Jack, you S.O.B'.

Reserve Harry Kriss - 61:
Was watching Oswald's face when a shot rang out. He also recalled seeing a blur but it was not clear because of how bright the lights were.[16]

Detective James Leavelle - 63:
Like Graves, he said that they paused to wait for Dhority's car to pull up and that Ruby then lunged out and shot Oswald. He pulled back on Oswald out of instinct then reached out to Ruby.

Ike Pappas – 80A:
Told the FBI that he was conscious of someone moving by him on his left two or three feet away. He then heard a shot and saw Oswald fall to the ground.

Francois Pelou – 83:
Never gave a description of the shooting. He only recalled Oswald looking at the man who was about to shoot him.[17]

Tom Pettit – 83A:
Never gave a description of the shooting.

George Phenix - 84:
Recalled almost being knocked down by someone bursting through the crowd. Then he heard a shot.[18]

Lieutenant R.E. Swain - 96:
He was guiding Dhority's car back so he only heard a gunshot.

Robert Thornton - 99:
Never gave a description of the shooting.

Unidentified Japanese Reporter – 100A:
Visible taking a photograph of Oswald at the moment Ruby lunged past but never gave a description of the shooting.

Homer Venso – 102A:
Filmed the shooting but never gave a description of what he observed.[19]

Peter Worthington - PW:
Never gave a description of the shooting.

Because of the overall lack of clarity in witness statements and precise positioning, as well as how quickly the shooting happened, this list cannot, by any means, be taken as complete. However, the point remains that the lack of information and details across all of the statements (from those that were actually asked for their account) is incredibly vague and non-descript. Of course, it is easy to be critical when having not been at the scene so there are several factors that should be noted before we get too deep with our judgement of these observations, and lack thereof.

For a start, it really was a split-second event. Ruby lunged out at Oswald and shot him straight away at point blank range. Most of the people that had a direct line of vision were members of the media. That is because the shooting took place closer to most of where the media were gathered and after Oswald had been led through the cordon of detectives.

And if we consider the media a little more, it would be worth arguing that what each photographer and cameraman saw was captured in their photographs and footage so what more could they add? One detail that is interesting to note among multiple witnesses was Dhority's car. A number of people stated that they were watching the car reversing at the crucial moment that Oswald was shot. Can we just assume this is another unfortunate coincidence that may have prevented the record from having more witness accounts to draw on? We must also note that there was another car horn blast just prior to when Ruby emerged to shoot Oswald. Again, coincidence or something sinister?

Let's pull back and refer to the footage and the Bob Jackson photograph. In all, it is very clear that when Ruby emerged, he was in a low 'hunched' position as some described when he lunged out between Pappas, Harrison and the unknown Japanese reporter. Moving in one smooth motion (recall Jerry O'Leary)… 'gliding', Ruby is holding a revolver in his right hand and it was clearly inches away from Oswald when it was fired into his abdomen.

The gun used to shoot Oswald was a .38 Special Colt Cobra which was a lightweight, 6 round, double-action trigger revolver. It was modified with a hammer shroud, and, for a snub-nosed revolver, it packed a good punch. In the confines of the basement, the shot sounded like a roar in all audio recordings of the shooting. Despite being shot at point blank range, the bullet did not exit Oswald's abdomen. According to the autopsy, the bullet entered just under Oswald's left seventh rib and would be recovered near his rear eleventh rib.[20] See the diagram *(right)* of a rib cage transposed on Oswald in Johnston's photograph just prior to being shot to show the bullet's path.

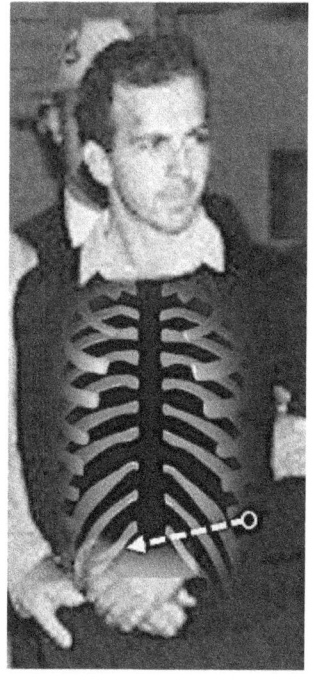

Ruby clearly shot at a slight downward angle as the bullet travelled front to back, through Oswald's spleen, the top of the stomach, the aorta, the diaphragm, through the top of the kidney and the liver. If the intent was to damage as many internal organs as possible to cause the most amount of harm, Ruby's shot could not have been more precise. Because of the position of all cameras in front of Oswald and the lack of definitive witness statements, we cannot be precise in how close the revolver was when fired. The autopsy did not report any signs of 'tattooing' or small burns on Oswald's skin around the entry wound to indicate the gun was in contact with him when fired. Only fibrous debris from the clothing he was wearing was found in the wound so we can presume the shot was fired from a matter of inches. Recall Detective Graves saying that he thought it was from fifteen inches away.

All at once, Oswald's abdomen curled up in recoil and his mouth gaped opened per the Bob Jackson photograph. His head then lifted up as he let out a guttural groan. Detective Don Archer told the DPD investigation that he heard Oswald say, 'Oh no!' at this point, but like his other contention that Ruby shouted as he shot Oswald, there is no evidence to support this claim either. Oswald fell backward before groaning once more. Detective Leavelle reacted by pulling back on his arm that was handcuffed to Oswald's. He and Detective Graves together reached out to hold back Ruby, who appeared to try and lunge again at the stricken Oswald. Then all hell broke loose.

Chaos Theory

The eruption of hysteria was instant. Handcuffed to the now prone Oswald, James Leavelle crouched over him as Billy Combest, who was standing just behind Leavelle's right shoulder at the time the shot was fired, stepped to him. In footage, Oswald can be seen laying still on the ground below them. His body appears to be orientated parallel with the ramp.

Immediately after Ruby fired the shot, a crowd of officers literally swarmed all over him. See the amended schematic section *(next page)* to illustrate the concentration of DPD personnel around Oswald and Ruby according to their statements. Per the footage, Dhority's car has also changed as it reversed back enough to have made contact with Ruby's left leg just after he shot Oswald. Despite the mass of bodies, some people are easier to identify in the footage than others.

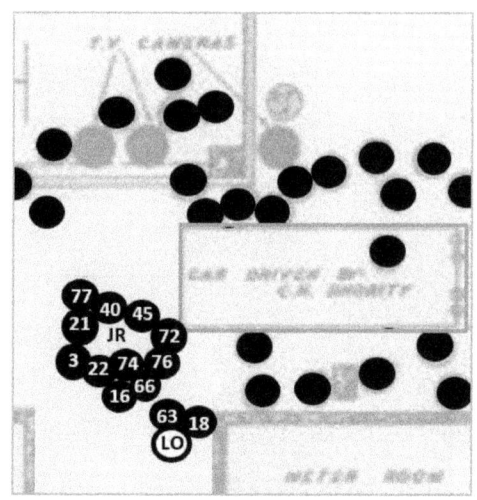

Reserve Charles W. Arnett - 3:

Stated to the FBI that he grabbed Jack Ruby's left arm.

Detective W.E. Chambers – 16:

Stated that he tried to grab Ruby's arm.

Detective Billy H. Combest – 18:

Stood with Det. Leavelle and helped take Oswald away. *He is clearly visible in footage.*

Reserve Sergeant Kenneth Croy – 21:

Tried to grab Ruby's gun but was not successful. He testified to the DPD that he saw himself in TV footage of the event.

Detective Wilbur Jay Cutchshaw – 22:

Stated to the FBI that he grabbed Ruby's left wrist.

Detective L.C. Graves – 40:
Twisted Ruby's right wrist with his left hand while he pried the at the gun with his right hand. *He is clearly visible in footage.*

Acting Detective William J. 'Blackie' Harrison – 45:
Helped force Ruby to the ground. *He is clearly visible in footage.*

Detective James R. Leavelle – 63:
Took Oswald to the office with Det. Combest. *He is clearly visible in footage.*

Detective Roy Lee Lowery – 66:
Assisted with taking Ruby away, as far as to the jail office door.

Detective Thomas D. McMillon – 74:
Stated to the FBI that he grabbed Ruby's right arm. *He is clearly visible in footage.*

Detective Louis D. Miller – 76:
Stated that Ruby was hit from behind so he was pushed toward him (Miller). *He is clearly visible in footage.*

Detective Lesley D. Montgomery – 77:
Shuffled around the pack of people as they swarmed on Ruby. *He too is visible in footage.*

Detective Graves is pictured in the above photograph by Jack Beers, attempting to pry the revolver out of Ruby's right hand. Ruby's socks can be seen at the bottom of the photograph and Blackie Harrison has his back to the camera.

Compared to the melee on Ruby, there were only two DPD personnel that attended to Oswald so at least they can't be accused of not being consistent in terms of their lack of regard for him! But why was there such a massive pile-on of police personnel on Jack Ruby? The suddenness of his actions and an instinctive response to a shot fired in a crowded and confined area perhaps justifies it. But as is clear in the footage, DPD personnel huddled all over each other with Ruby somewhere in the middle. It is also clear that Graves had the biggest struggle to remove the revolver from Ruby's right hand. It is as if he's pulling Ruby toward the Main Street side of the basement to release the revolver. Thomas McMillon told the FBI that he heard Ruby saying, 'I hope I killed the rat son of a bitch' while being subdued. Others would testify to hearing Ruby saying something similar in the jail office.

According to footage, Lee Oswald and Jack Ruby were evacuated out of the area within sixteen seconds. Left in their wake was a confused crowd of police and media personnel. Efforts to control the scene are evident in the footage as well as in statements. The tops of the ramps were sealed with explicit orders not to let anyone in or out.

So, was the mass-grapple with Ruby just about disarming and subduing him? Within a second of his shooting Oswald, Ruby is barely seen again amongst the bodies of DPD personnel. But when footage of the scene is slowed down, a very interesting sight can be clearly seen.

Early in the DPD wrestle with Ruby, Louis Miller is seen approaching Oswald from his position. He is the hatless man with a receding hairline. When Miller has reached the point where Ruby's head is, he very quickly places some kind of dark sheet or covering over Ruby's head. In fact, just a frame or two prior to this, Ruby's hatless head can be seen before it is covered.[21] And we do not see Jack Ruby's face or head after this moment because once he was disarmed, he was swept away to the jail office. It happens in a split second but it is visible to see when slowed down - that Miller covers Jack Ruby's head with something. Why? What was to hide from the dozens of people surrounding them as well as the media and their cameras? Miller's explanation for his contribution to the melee on Ruby was that he said that Ruby was 'propelled' toward him.[22] But there was no explanation about why he covered Oswald's shooter and how he was prepared to do so.[23]

The questions cannot stop here because it has never been adequately scrutinised or addressed why the stricken Oswald was not put straight into Dhority's car and rushed to the nearest hospital. It would have been as simple as either reversing the car up the Main Street ramp to leave the basement as the quickest option or at least having the armoured truck and

Brown's car in front of Dhority's drive out onto Commerce Street to open the way. Instead, the wounded Oswald was taken back to the jail office where he too would be out of view of the media and cameras.

Jack Ruby was restrained in the jail office by being pinned down on the floor and, depending on whose account we refer to, was handcuffed there and then. According to most accounts, Blackie Harrison, Thomas McMillon, Don Ray Archer, Bernard Clardy and Glen King took Ruby up to the Fifth Floor jail but as in almost all aspects of this case, it is hard to be definitive on even this front due to differences in statements.

Using witness statements, and the Davidson footage, we can at least be definitive about where Ruby and Oswald were situated behind counters in the jail office once, they'd both been taken in there. See the layout of the jail office in the below for indications of positioning:

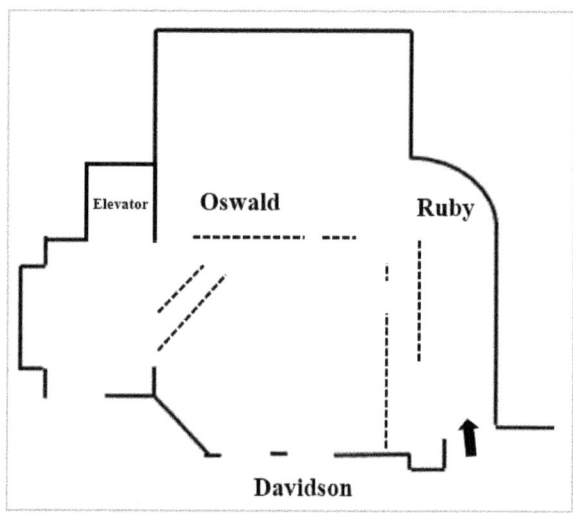

Copyright Paul Abbott

First Aid?

Twenty-five-year-old medical intern and City Hall First Aid officer, Fred Bieberdorf attended the wounded Oswald and unfortunately for clarity sake, his accounts are both unclear and inconsistent. For starters, inexplicably, he was not interviewed for the DPD investigation. In his statement to the FBI on December 6, he said that he arrived at the City Hall basement on the morning of November 24 at 9:30am and reported to the First Aid office in the eastern side of the basement.[24] This is in the same area that Reserves Worley and Brock were standing guard at.

At 9:45am, he said he was requested by an officer to vacate the office and leave the basement area. This at least correlates with when City Hall employees, Harold Fuqua, Alfreadia Riggs, Edward Kelly and others were told to leave as well. His statement then has him saying that he moved to the intersection of the hallway underneath City Hall. According to the layout of the basement, this would have been the area just west from the jail office along the hallway leading to Harwood Street. Bieberdorf's statement to the FBI skips forward to his movements after the shooting. In it, it has him saying that he had an unobstructed view out toward the basement parking area and that he was able to watch Oswald being brought out.

He then said that he heard a gunshot and that it took him... several minutes... to reach the vicinity of the shooting. This does not sound at all plausible as where Bieberdorf was standing was barely twenty feet from where Oswald was shot. And while there was chaos and confusion to contend with, it could not have taken him several minutes to cut through to get to Oswald. Footage of the aftermath does not show an impenetrable wall of people to prevent Bieberdorf's access either. The statement then says that when Bieberdorf got to the point of the shooting, he found that Oswald and Ruby had been moved from the scene so he 'searched the area for several minutes more before proceeding to the jail lobby.' But he then needed to identify himself to a detective to be let in. Wilbur Cutchshaw testified that it was he who let the doctor in.

In the jail office, Bieberdorf saw Ruby lying face 'up' in one part of the jail office and Oswald in the same position halfway between Ruby and the elevator. When Bieberdorf got to Oswald, he couldn't detect a pulse, breathing or any heartbeat. He also noted that his pupils were dilated so he assumed that he had died. Oswald's shirt had been lifted up to reveal a 'small puncture wound' under his ribs on the left side. No external bleeding was evident. Bieberdorf then said he was able to feel the bullet just below the skin's surface on Oswald's right side. Because of how noisy it was in the office, Bieberdorf thought that might have been why he couldn't hear a heartbeat so he commenced 'massaging the sternum' (CPR in modern terms) – which surely must be beyond the last resort as a course of treatment to give someone who has just been shot in the abdomen or torso. While he was doing this, some ambulance attendants soon arrived and entered with a stretcher and Oswald was loaded into an ambulance. Confusingly, Bieberdorf's statement to the FBI said that it took place five minutes after he had heard the shot. This contradicts what he apparently said earlier about it taking him 'several minutes' to get to the location of the shooting and more minutes for him to find Oswald.

More incredibly, Bieberdorf said he rode in the back of the ambulance with Oswald and kept administering CPR. He had also put an oxygen mask over his mouth. However, 'five blocks' from the hospital, Oswald started thrashing around and attempted to take the mask off of his face. No one else who rode in the ambulance corroborated this. And five blocks from the hospital? Which route was being taken? Or was this some obscure way of measuring the distance. The quickest way to Parkland Hospital at the time (and still so these days, according to Google Maps) is along any road out of the CBD and onto Stemmons Freeway. If Bieberdorf marked the location as being a certain number of blocks away from the hospital when Oswald started 'thrashing around', was the ambulance driving through suburbs and not the freeway to get Oswald to Parkland? The statement to the FBI concludes with Bieberdorf staying with Oswald while he was being rushed into emergency.

The time that passed between December '63 when Fred Bieberdorf gave his statement to the FBI and March '64 when he both testified at Jack Ruby's trial[25] and soon after, to the Warren Commission[26] either did wonders for his memory, scrambled his account even more or a combination of both. I'll let you be the judge.

First and foremost, his testimony to the Warren Commission was largely used to clarify details in the FBI statement. For example, correcting the spelling of his surname and the fact that Jack Ruby was actually lying face down, not up, in the jail office. Thankfully, perhaps, WC counsel Leon Hubert had Bieberdorf confirm where he was at the time of the shooting. See the chart below from the Warren Commission with an 'x' circled at the bottom to signify where he confirmed his location:

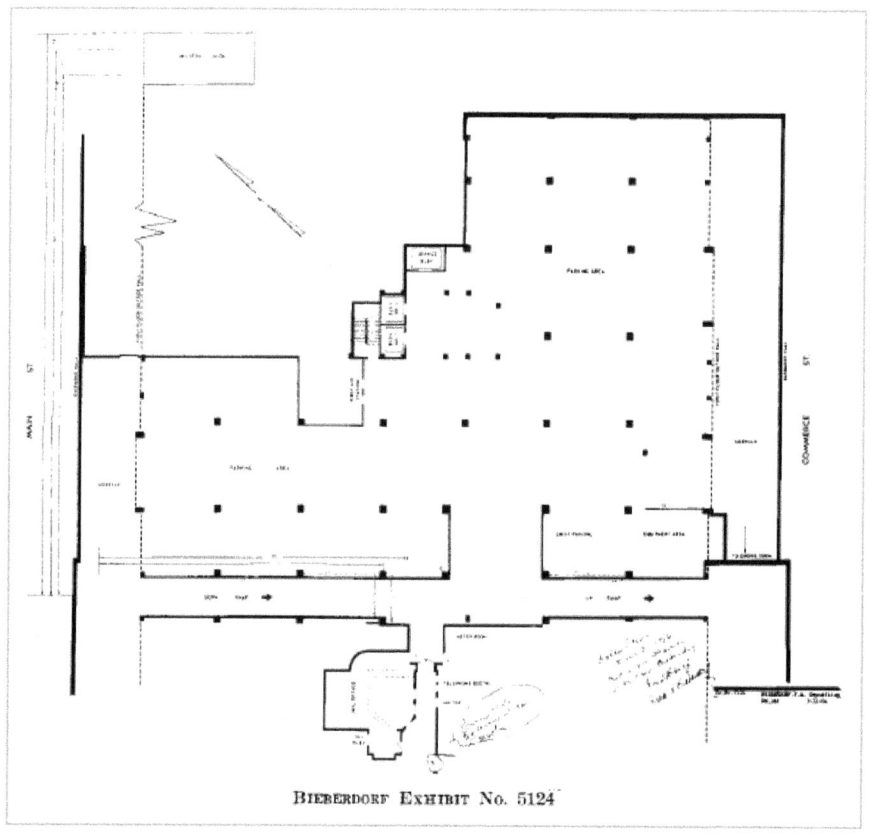

BIEBERDORF EXHIBIT No. 5124

The clarifications continued with Bieberdorf saying that it actually took '1-2 minutes' for him to reach the scene of the shooting and 'a few seconds' to work out where to go to treat Oswald. This sounds a little more likely but it still doesn't read as though Bieberdorf was stating these times with any conviction. He then explained at length about the seating configuration in the ambulance but it's a shame he was not more informative on most other aspects. Of more significance, he stated that Oswald was still alive upon arrival at Parkland and that until halfway into the journey to the hospital, he thought Oswald had died.

In terms of earlier that morning, Bieberdorf confirmed that he was asked to leave his office at 9:45am and that the officer checked in there before having him lock it. Bieberdorf stated that he spent the majority of the time in the sub-basement locker room and it appears as though he walked through the car park and the jail office corridor to get there. Let's examine this aspect a little further, as frankly and frustratingly, there is little more of worth in the rest of his statement after this point.

At least Bieberdorf going to the locker room when he had been ordered away from his base of work makes sense. It would be much easier and comfortable to kill time down there instead of standing around in a hallway for an hour and a half. So, on the presumption that he did go to the locker room, could Bieberdorf have been the person that porters, Fuqua and Riggs encountered when they went down there to watch TV? I don't think so because they surely would have recognised Bieberdorf as he was asked to leave the basement at the same time they were. And being in the positions they were in, for as long as they had been, they would have known who he was, what his job was and where his office was to therefore recognise him in the locker room. But they did not name him or his position in any of their statements so we cannot account for this person as Bieberdorf. Counsel Hubert didn't press him about anything to do with the locker room and perhaps most interesting was the fact that Leon Hubert took Bieberdorf's testimony on the March 31st and those of Harold Fuqua and Alfreadia Riggs... the very next day on April 1st. Having heard Bieberdorf's account the previous day and then hearing how it mirrored aspects of Harold Fuqua and Alfreadia Riggs in a couple of crucial ways – having to leave the basement and ending up in the sub-basement locker room – would it have been too much for him to press them a little further as to the identity of the man they encountered down there?

Adding to his statements in the first four months after the Oswald shooting, Fred Bieberdorf also sat down to give an interview for the Sixth Floor Museum's 'Oral History' series in 2007.[27] So again, considering the passage of time, it is interesting to still review. Of note, he said that when he heard the shot, he recalled waiting for a few seconds to be sure before making his way to the 'jail lobby'. He said he saw that there was a group of people over Jack Ruby but virtually nobody by Lee Oswald – who was 'supine'. This infers that he got to the scene much sooner and not out to where he thought the shooting happened only to find nobody there to treat – like he testified some forty years earlier. Moving forward in the interview and Bieberdorf was asked about the ride to the hospital in the ambulance with Oswald. He said that they went along Stemmons Freeway and the journey took about ten minutes. He said that he thought it would be a good idea to give Oswald oxygen but the wrench to open the valve could not be found so none could be given to him. He said this laughing – clearly not regarding the gravity of the situation this comical episode was taking place during. Callousness aside, this story counters what he told the Warren Commission that he *did* administer oxygen to Oswald in the ambulance.

Now for the real kickers. When Oswald's shooting was brought back up in the interview, Bieberdorf said that Oswald was 'shot in the jail office' and when pressed a little further he said that it was 'just inside the door to the parking garage.' He then said that Oswald must have been 'dragged just a few feet' to the position he would treat him at before the ambulance arrived. In all footage, photographs and witness statements, Oswald was shot away from the jail office and much closer to the 'parking garage' (to use Bieberdorf's term for the car park). What did he mean by Oswald being shot in the jail office? Could this mean something more than the mother of all Freudian slips, mix ups or confusion after so many years?

But any confusion Bieberdorf had in 1963 and '64 is clearly shared by some of the DPD and media personnel in some of their statements at the time. Network floor director, Robert Hankal was standing near to where Ruby emerged from at the time of the shooting and he told the Warren Commission on April 17 that he heard people asking Oswald after he'd been shot if he killed the president and his saying that he hadn't.[28] No one else present uttered a single word to this effect in their statements. Detective Graves, who was holding Oswald's left arm when he was shot by Ruby actually gave a completely alternative version of events regarding Oswald and the ambulance. See the snippet from his (undated) DPD statement:

> REPORT ON OFFICERS DUTY AT TIME PRIOR TO OSWALD'S MURDER
>
> L. C. GRAVES - 2522
>
> Sunday, November 24, 1963, was the day set for the transfer of Lee Harvey Oswald to the County Jail. The time set for the transfer was 10:00 AM. Shortly before 9:30 AM, J. R. Leavelle, C. N. Dhority, and I brought Oswald down from the fifth floor jail for final questioning by Capt. Fritz. Agents Sorrel and Kelly from the Secret Service, others present during the questioning were Mr. Holmes from the U. S. Post Office Department, Detectives L. D. Montgomery, C. N. Dhority, J. R. Leavelle, and I. Chief Curry was present only a few minutes at the beginning of the questioning and at the end just prior to Oswald's removal to the basement. Before leaving our office with Oswald, Capt. Fritz instructed J. R. Leavelle to handcuff his left arm to the right arm of Oswald. I was to walk by Oswald's left side.
>
> Oswald was immediately placed in an O'Neal ambulance and rushed to Parkland Hospital, where he underwent surgery within 10 minutes after his

[circled text:]
> Oswald was immediately placed in an O'Neal ambulance and rushed to Parkland Hospital, where he underwent surgery within 10 minutes after his

40

According to all visual records and witness statements, Oswald was not immediately placed into an ambulance and rushed to hospital. But if he was to stand any chance of surviving, he definitely ought to have been. Graves made no such claim to the FBI and Warren Commission. Still, all other witness accounts about the handling of Oswald immediately after he had been shot had him being taken into the jail office – except for one other.

Enter Detective James K. Ramsey, who was the only person to say (to the DPD[29]) that Ruby was handcuffed during the scuffle out in the hallway before being taken to the jail office. He also said that he saw a powder burn around Oswald's wound when he saw him in the jail office. He would be the only person, including the pathologists who conducted the autopsy on Oswald, who made this claim. Yet in his statement to the FBI, it had Ramsey saying that after helping to take Ruby to the jail office, he came back out to the hallway and saw Oswald lying on the pavement.[30] The statement then has him contending that an ambulance arrived along with the city doctor so he (Ramsey) helped Oswald onto a stretcher and load him into the ambulance. It is one thing that Ramsey clearly contradicted himself but no footage, photographs or witness statements corroborate what Ramsey stated to the FBI so how could his account to them be so different to what he told the DPD?

To add, Detective Wilbur Cutchshaw testified to the FBI that Oswald was taken *into* the jail office on a stretcher after being shot, so one must ask…what scenes were he, Graves and Ramsey and Cutchshaw witnessing to testify to seeing things that clearly did not take place?

O'Neal Ambulance service was called immediately after the shooting. Who exactly made this call lays with either despatcher, Frances Cason or Lt. Woodrow Wiggins – and it's entirely possible that both could have done so. According to ambulance driver, Michael Hardin, he arrived at the City Hall basement three minutes after he was notified.[31] For the record, using the KRLD-TV footage, the ambulance arrived four and a half minutes after the shooting. And while Fred Bieberdorf stated to the FBI that he couldn't detect a pulse on Oswald, Detectives Combest and Leavelle, who brought Oswald back into the jail office, as well as Det. Stephens, each stated to the FBI, Ruby Trial and the DPD, respectively, that Oswald appeared to be conscious. This at least tallies with Robert Hankal's assertion that Oswald was being asked to give a statement while he lay mortally wounded.

So, what we have is yet another key aspect of the shooting of Lee Oswald that was never explained clearly. Instead, accounts of his immediate treatment are riddled with contradictions.

Perhaps adding yet another layer of insult to literal injury is the fact that once Oswald was loaded into the ambulance, it had to wait forty-two seconds for the armoured truck to move out of the way at the top of the Commerce Street ramp before it could start its journey to Parkland Hospital. And there are contradictions with who rode in the ambulance as well. With ambulance driver, Michael Hardin and his rider attendant, Harold Wolfe, noted as givens, the below lists who said they rode in the ambulance and whom they testified as such to:

- Fred Bieberdorf   DPD, FBI, RT*, WC
- Det. Charles N. Dhority DPD, WC
- Det. L.C. Graves   DPD, RT
- Det. James Leavelle   DPD, RT

---

*RT refers to Jack Ruby's trial in March of 1964.

See the below diagram of the ambulance and who was seated where on the way to Parkland Hospital according to Fred Bieberdorf's clarified account to the Warren Commission:

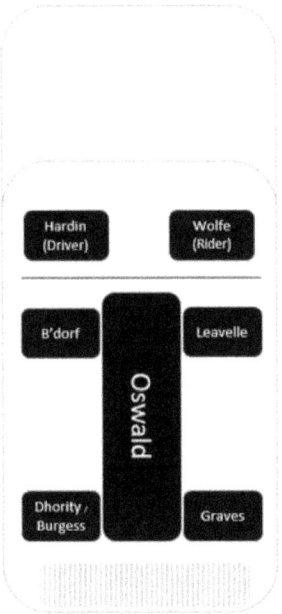

Copyright Paul Abbott

The reference to 'Dhority / Burgess' has been included because Graves stated that it was Detective Burgess who rode in the ambulance but this does not corroborate with what the others in the ambulance said. Nor did Burgess tell the DPD in his one and only statement, that he rode to the hospital either. This is still noteworthy as Graves ought to have known who Dhority was as they both reported to Capt. Fritz and had both been part of the movements with Oswald up on the Third Floor just prior. So, are we to put this down to just another case of Graves getting 'mixed up'?

We have now uncovered new depths of incompetence by the Dallas Police on the immediate treatment of Oswald after he was shot. Disregarding the contradictory accounts of Ramsey and Graves, it is clear that they could not have done anything more to lessen his chances of surviving the shooting. Dr. Charles Crenshaw would admit that if he had been treated properly from the time the ambulance arrived, by being provided with Ringer's Lactate to ensure circulation would not be cut off, Lee Oswald could have lived.[32] But in a sign of the times, ambulances back then were nothing more than wagons with the rear seats removed to make room for a stretcher and, unlike ambulances of today, contained the most arbitrary of rescue equipment. And their drivers were little more than cab drivers with a licence to speed so even if the O'Neal ambulance was parked at the scene when Oswald was shot, the best way it could have been used was to evacuate him immediately. Instead, by all timings considered, Oswald's flight to Parkland was delayed by five minutes and the lack of clarity in the record begs the question, was there a genuine and concerted effort to hinder Oswald getting the proper treatment as quickly as possible so as to ensure he would not survive the shooting? And further to that, what exactly happened in the basement and the jail office in those minutes before Oswald would finally be taken to hospital? Was Fred Bieberdorf's access to Oswald also hindered?

More broadly, the lack of detail in witness statements has meant that what was a very quick and swift action in Lee Oswald's shooting is something that is very hard to follow and make sense of. Lack of detail and clear contradictions have robbed the record of having a clear narrative to outline the incident with.

When we consider how dramatically Jack Ruby was set upon after the shooting and that he was clearly concealed and swept away from the scene, we must be suspicious and continue asking questions.

CHAPTER TWELVE

SHOOTER

With Lee Oswald's removal from City Hall to Parkland Hospital, we are now able to devote focus to the man apprehended for his shooting, Jack Ruby. We already know that he was concealed and rushed from where he shot Oswald to the jail office. There, Ruby was pinned on the floor face down and the most common consensus was that he was handcuffed before being briefly searched then led to the elevator. For the briefest of moments in the Davidson footage for WFAA-TV, we see Blackie Harrison begin to lead Ruby toward the elevator and they are joined by more personnel by the time they reached it.

In their statements, Detectives Clardy, Archer, Harrison, McMillon and Capt. Glen King would all say they accompanied Ruby to the Fifth Floor – and most would corroborate each other's presence. What is clear is that James Davidson continued to film through the jail office window and he was able to capture Jack Ruby being led through the jail office to the elevator.

There are some cuts in the footage but, interestingly, Ruby is no longer wearing a jacket or tie (presuming he was actually wearing a tie when he shot Oswald). Yet none of the DPD personnel would state that articles of Ruby's clothing were removed while he was in the jail office being pinned to the floor and before he was handcuffed.

On the Fifth Floor, McMillon searched Ruby and placed anything he found on him in his (Ruby's) hat. In his statement to the Warren Commission, McMillon said that all he found were dollar bills and postcard pieces of paper that said, 'Impeach Earl Warren'. Ruby was then stripped down to undershorts. Archer testified that around the same time he said to Ruby 'Jack, I think you killed him'.[1] He said that Ruby replied by saying that he hoped he killed 'the son of a bitch' and that he intended to shoot Oswald three times but couldn't because the police moved too fast.

Ruby's own words in February 1964, in an article he co-wrote with William Read Woodfield,[2] may provide some more insight. In it, he recalled saying to the DPD as they piled on top of him, "You don't have to beat me – my brains out. I'm Jack Ruby. What am I doing here? What are you guys jumping on me for? Why am I here?" According to this same article, it was when he was taken to the Fifth Floor jail and was told that he'd shot Oswald that he had first realised what he had done.

Jack, why?

The Secret Service's Forrest V. Sorrels was a veteran agent who had headed up the Dallas bureau, in various structures, since 1938. In that capacity, he had been part of the advance plans for President Kennedy's visit to Dallas on November 22nd including surveying venues for him to speak at a luncheon for that day and ultimately deciding on the motorcade route to Dallas' Trade Mart just off Stemmons Freeway.

While Oswald was being held at Dallas City Hall that weekend, Sorrels observed and participated in his interrogations. On the Sunday morning, he was up on the Third Floor and standing in Deputy Chief Batchelor's office at the time that Oswald's transfer got underway. With Sorrels* was Secret Service Inspector, Thomas J. Kelley and together they were watching the crowd down on Commerce Street. Curiously, Kelley would testify to the Warren Commission on three separate occasions but not once was he asked about November 24 and Oswald's shooting. Inexplicably, Chief Jesse Curry was in his office nearby, taking a phone call from Mayor Earle Cabell at the same time. Sorrels told the Warren Commission on May 6 the following year that it was a police officer who told them that Oswald had been shot in the stomach.[3] It is not known what Kelley did but Sorrels stated that he (Sorrels) rushed down to the basement. When he arrived there, Lee Oswald was being treated and Jack Ruby had been taken away. Sorrels then picked up a nearby phone and dialed his headquarters in Washington D.C. to convey the news to Deputy Chief, Paul Paterni that Oswald had been shot by a man named 'Jack Rubin'.

After that, he returned to the Third Floor and went to Capt. Fritz's office. Sorrels testified that it was Sgt. Dean who came for him and took him up to the Fifth Floor so he could speak with Ruby.

---

*Referring to President Kennedy's motorcade route on the previous page, Sorrels testified to the Warren Commission that the reason it did not stay on Main Street to access Stemmons Freeway beyond the railway overpass was because Stemmons could only be accessed by Elm Street. This was demonstrably false as there were no road configurations or median strips to prevent crossing over from Main Street at the time. At the very most, the route would have had the presidential motorcade violate a local traffic law by making the crossing only – which did not apply to presidential motorcades. Ergo, the fact that President Kennedy was assassinated in a section of Dealey Plaza (closest to the Texas School Book Depository) that he need not have travelled through has been one of the largest sources of suspicion about the incident ever since.

When he encountered him up there, Sorrels noted that Ruby was only wearing shorts and he was standing in an empty area.

Actually, it was the corridor between the empty jail cells. In there with him were two uniformed officers (one of whom was K.H. Haake, who is perhaps also known to JFK assassination researchers familiar with the Nov. 22nd Red Bird Airport incident). Sorrels would also make mention of two plainclothes officers in the room as well. In all likelihood, these would have been Detectives Clardy and McMillon. Detective Archer remained on the Fifth Floor but it's not clear how long for.

Continuing with Sorrels' testimony to the Warren Commission, he said that Dean introduced him and he (Sorrels) started by telling Ruby that he wanted to ask him some questions. Ruby may have expected to have been given access to reporters after his act of shooting of Oswald because he asked if he was asking 'for newspapers or magazines?' Sorrels just said for himself. He told Ruby that he had been up on the Third Floor looking out of the window when he saw an old Edsel car that was parked down on the street and 'all painted up with 'Honest Joe' on there'. According to his testimony, Sorrels then told Ruby he knew a number of Jewish merchants. Why was this important enough for Sorrels to mention to Ruby but also recall it much later after the fact? Who or what was Honest Joe's?

'Honest Joe's' was a pawnbroker dealership in Dallas that was established by a Jewish man from Chicago by the name of Rubin Goldstein in 1931. According to Greg Doyle's article in the Third Decade, 'Who Was Honest Joe?'[4] 'Honest Joe's' was tied up with all kinds of 'seedy businesses and characters around town and that Goldstein himself, had linkages within organised crime and law enforcement. In fact, one of the pallbearers at his funeral in 1972 was Detective Charles N. Dhority. As if the world was not small enough already, Rubin Goldstein also happened to be the appraiser for Jack Ruby's estate. Furthermore, regarding the weekend of the assassination, several witnesses in Dealey Plaza testified to seeing an 'Honest Joe's' truck parked in front of the Texas School Book Depository just before and during President Kennedy's assassination. It particularly stood out because no other cars were permitted to access that location and the truck reportedly had a (presumably) ornamental .50 calibre machine gun on the cab roof. If this is true, can it just be coincidence that 'Honest Joe's' had a presence at both the shootings of President Kennedy and Lee Oswald?

With Sorrels having dropped a less than subtle reference to 'Honest Joe's', like it was some kind of password, Ruby allegedly said 'that's good enough for me. What is it you want to know?' Sorrels said he then said two words, 'Jack, why?' regarding Oswald's shooting.

Ruby said that he was in a newspaper office placing ads for his business when President Kennedy was shot so he canceled the ad and closed his business for three days out of respect. He also said he heard a eulogy for Kennedy at a Jewish synagogue, a letter of sympathy written for President Kennedy's daughter, Caroline, being read out and that his sister had been hysterical having been operated on as the reasons for his actions. Ruby also told Sorrels that when he heard Mrs. Kennedy was going to have to appear for a trial, he thought to himself, 'why should she have to go through this ordeal for this no-good-so-and-so.' Sorrels also asked Ruby why he had a gun on him that day. Ruby said it was because he carried large sums of money for his business. Warren Commission Counsel, Leon Hubert asked

Sorrels if Ruby mentioned how he got into the basement area where he shot Oswald. Sorrels was taking notes of his conversation with Ruby and testified that they did not show that Ruby had said any such thing. This is evident in these notes within the Warren Report.[4] The time that Sorrels said he spent with Ruby was between five to seven minutes after which time, he left leaving at least Dean, McMillon, Clardy and possibly Archer alone with Ruby.

This exchange between Ruby and Sorrels is important because it raises the very likely possibility that Sorrels knew or knew of Ruby well enough to a) make a reference to a Jewish businessman and presume that it would mean something to Ruby and b) refer to him by first name. It also brings to a point that researchers have been debating ever since – when or if Ruby detailed how he got into the basement up on the Fifth Floor in the minutes after shooting Oswald. To attempt to settle the score, we will now scrutinise the testimonies that Dean, Archer and McMillon gave about this aspect.

Starting with Sgt. Dean, he said in various statements, including at Ruby's trial,[5] that he spoke with reporters down in the basement just after the ambulance left with Oswald. This footage is available to view on YouTube.[6] In it, he infers that he recognised who the shooter was but would not provide a name. He then left the basement, despite still being in charge of its security, and went to Captain Fritz's office on the Third Floor. There he expected to find Oswald's shooter, who he said he had already recognised as Jack Ruby immediately after the shooting, being detained there. When he got to the Third Floor, Chief Curry ordered him to take Secret Service Agent

Sorrels to the Fifth Floor to speak with Ruby instead – on the pretext of finding out from Ruby how he was able to breach the security of the basement.

Regarding the conversation with Ruby up there, Dean corroborated Ruby asking Sorrels if he was asking questions for newspapers or magazines. Dean also said, presumably after Sorrels left, that Ruby said that it was when he was watching Oswald at the Friday midnight press conference that he 'thought' of shooting Oswald if he got the chance. And that he wanted the world to know that Jews had guts. With Sorrels not being able to recall Ruby stating how he entered the basement to shoot Oswald, this infers that Ruby only did so after he left. We must look to the others that were present and left with Ruby – Sgt. Dean, Detectives Clardy, McMillon and Archer* – and what they reported *initially*.

Sergeant Dean:

In his first report on Oswald's shooting, on **November 26**, Dean stated that after Sorrels had finished asking Ruby his questions, he (Dean) asked Ruby how he was able to enter the basement.[7] He said that Ruby stated that he did so down the Main Street ramp and that he did so three minutes prior to Oswald being brought out.

Detective Archer:

Yet, in his first report, on **November 24**, Archer only mentions helping with bringing Ruby up to the Fifth Floor and removing his clothes.[8]

---

*Why were the two uniformed officers, Haake and his unknown colleague, present with Ruby on the Fifth Floor that afternoon, not asked what they heard him say?

He named Dean, McMillon and Clardy as being present as well as the coming and going of Forest Sorrels and later, FBI Agent Hall as well as staying with Ruby until 3:30pm that afternoon, when Homicide began interrogating him.

Detective Clardy:

Similarly to Archer, in his first statement on **November 27**,[9] Clardy details being a part of the group of DPD personnel to take Ruby to the Fifth Floor jail, remove his clothes and search them. Clardy named McMillon and Archer as being present as well as Sorrels and Hall's questioning of Ruby but Dean is not mentioned in this statement.

Detective McMillon:

In his first report, on **November 27**, McMillon virtually echoes what Clardy stated including not mentioning Dean as being on the Fifth Floor with them with Ruby.[10]

It is evident that Dean was the only person among those present with Ruby on the Fifth Floor to state that Ruby told of how he entered the basement. Archer, Clardy and McMillon did not refer to it at all in their original DPD reports, despite it being an incredibly important detail in the scheme of things.

However, each would mention Ruby's stating how he got into the basement in their follow up reports for the DPD investigation (Archer – November 30,[11] Clardy – December 1[12] and McMillon – November 30[13]). And all three would add the new detail of Ruby also remarking how he could not have timed his entry into the basement any better to shoot Oswald.

We know that the FBI began questioning witnesses almost straightaway for what it assumed was its own investigation (before dovetailing into the Warren Commission) so, did the detectives tell them anything more or different about Ruby's alleged admissions on the Fifth Floor? Not particularly. Archer[14] Clardy[15] and McMillon[16] largely kept to the same version of events for the FBI that they initially gave the DPD. But in his statement to the FBI on December 5, McMillon did mention that Ruby admitted entering the basement down the Main Street ramp.[17] And what about Dean? He kept the same line, only by this time, he added that Ruby mentioned recognising one of the officers of the police car that was coming out at the top of the ramp when he passed – Lt. Pierce. The inference being that Ruby could have only known such a detail if he really had entered the basement that way.

With all the above considered, what we have is a clear case of Dean manufacturing the fact that Ruby told him up on the Fifth Floor so soon after the shooting how he entered the basement. The fact that the three detectives who were also present did not corroborate this in their initial reports all but confirms it. They clearly came to Dean's defense after the fact by corroborating what he said in their follow up reports and subsequent testimonies to the FBI, Ruby's trial (McMillon and Archer only) and the Warren Commission.

Why is the fact that Dean falsely contended that Ruby admitted how he entered the basement down the Main Street ramp and Detectives Archer,

Clardy and McMillon followed suit after the fact so important? Aside from it being evidence of corruption and collusion, it was their testimonies at Ruby's trial (all with the exception of Clardy) which focused on Ruby's supposed admissions that would be pivotal to his being found guilty of premeditated murder and sentenced to death. If Ruby thought he had friends in the DPD that he could rely on, he was sorely mistaken.

Dean left Ruby with the detectives on the Fifth Floor and returned to the basement. According to journalist, David Hughes' testimony to the DPD[18] on December 11, he was at home when the shooting took place so he came straight to City Hall and, somehow, got close enough to interview both Officer Roy Vaughn and Patrick Dean. Of Dean, Hughes said he gave a 'precise' account of where he was during the shooting, what he witnessed including seeing Jack Ruby come down the Main Street ramp*, according to his statement to the FBI.[19] The statement seems to have had Dean paraphrasing Ruby saying this. Dean also added that when he was arrested 'immediately after the shooting, he (Ruby) related that he had been to Western Union where he sent a money order to Ft. Worth.' Dean also told Hughes that Ruby told police that the main reason he did it was out of sympathy for Jackie Kennedy and Officer Tippit.

---

*If Dean was where he said he was just before and during the shooting, standing at the back of the Armored Truck and facing down to where Oswald would emerge, he could not have possibly seen Ruby early enough to know that he entered from the Main Street ramp. This was because the low ceilings would have made it impossible.

The article would come out on December 8 quoting Dean and he went to great lengths to deny most of what he said. But by then, the foundations for Ruby's supposed premeditation had well and truly been laid.

Back up on the Fifth Floor and the next official to interview Jack Ruby, was FBI Special Agent C. Ray Hall, a veteran of 21 years. Hall would have Ruby in his presence for almost all of the time between 12:40pm to 3:15pm that afternoon. Still present were Detectives McMillon and Clardy. This is confirmed by the fact that Hall spelled their names out for the Warren Commission during his testimony on May 28.[20] According to Hall, all that Ruby said about how he entered the basement was that he did so on the Main Street side and that the ramp was the only way to get into it. Why would Ruby be so cryptic instead of simply telling Hall that he walked down the Main Street ramp, particularly if he had just told Dean and co?

I think it was because he really did not want to get anyone in the DPD in trouble – whether they were part of a plot with him or because of how close he felt to them. Little did Ruby know what Dean would quote him as saying followed by McMillon, Clardy and Archer. That neither McMillon nor Clardy stepped in to tell Hall that Ruby had just admitted entering the basement down the Main Street ramp infers that Ruby said no such thing prior to that point.

Hall stated to the Warren Commission that just prior to 2pm, an officer called up to the jail and announced that there was an attorney downstairs that wanted to talk to Ruby. Hall said that he indicated that Ruby was available immediately so he accompanied him as he was taken down to the Fourth Floor to meet the attorney, Tom Howard. Recall from an earlier chapter in this book that Howard was standing just outside the jail office up until the moments that Oswald was shot. Ruby and Howard spoke through a screen for ten minutes, during which time it's likely that Howard fed him the strategy of attributing shooting Oswald as an act of grief because it would be a theme that Ruby consistently leaned into in interrogations thereafter.

After his time with Howard, First Aid Attendant, Fred Bieberdorf, who by that time had returned from Parkland Hospital, checked over Ruby for any injuries. Ruby had some abrasions on his head, arm and wrist. After this, Hall resumed his questioning of Ruby back up on the Fifth Floor.

At 3pm, and dressed in prison whites, Ruby was taken to the Homicide Bureau on the Third Floor to be interrogated by Capt. Fritz. Accompanying him were Detectives Archer and McMillon and Agent Hall. Archer and McMillon left at this point but Hall stayed with Ruby until 3:15pm, according to his Warren Commission testimony. Let's review the relevant portion of Fritz's testimony to the Warren Commission's Joseph Ball on April 22nd:

> **Ball:** What did Ruby say to you, do you have the exact time?
>
> **Fritz:** Well, he told me, I told him, I, of course, wanted to know something about premeditation because I was thinking about the trial too and I told him I wanted to ask him some questions and he said, well, he first said, "I don't want to talk to you. I want to talk to my lawyers," and he said, I believe he told me too that he had been advised by a lawyer, and I asked him

some other question and he said, "Now if you will level with me and you won't make me look like a fool in front of my lawyers, I will talk to you." I didn't ask him one way or the other, but I did ask him some questions and he told me that he shot him, told me that he was all torn up about the Presidential killing, that he felt terribly sorry for Mrs. Kennedy. He didn't want to see her to have to come back to Dallas for a trial, and a lot of other things like that.

Ball: Did you ask him how he got down to the jail?
Fritz: Yes; I did.
Ball: What did he say?
Fritz: He told me he came down that ramp from the outside. So, I told him, I said, "No, you couldn't have come down that ramp because there would be an officer at the top and an officer at the bottom and you couldn't come down that ramp." He said, "I am not going to talk to you anymore, I am not going to get into trouble," and he never talked to me any more about it.
Ball: Did you ever talk to him again?
Fritz: I don't think I ever talked to him after that. I talked to him a little while then and I don't believe I ever talked to him after that. I asked him when he first decided to kill Oswald, and he didn't tell me that. He told me something else, talked about something else.
Ball: What was that time, you said you could give us the time?
Fritz: Yes, sir; I can give you the time. 3:05.

Ball: What time?

Fritz: 3:05.

Ball: 3:05 in the afternoon?

Fritz: Yes, sir.

Ball: Did you know that Archer or Dean or Newman had talked to Ruby?

Fritz: I didn't know that they had talked to him. I knew that some officers had talked to him, but I didn't know who they were.

Ball: Were there any reports given you by any one of these three men, Dean----

Fritz: They weren't given to me. Those reports were given to the investigative team that the chief setup headed by Captain Jones and some of the inspectors and they gave me a copy. I have copies of it.

The 'Newman' that Fritz refers to is most likely to have been McMillon as he's confirmed by other's testimonies as having escorted Ruby down from the Fifth Floor Jail.

Forrest Sorrels comes back into the picture as it turned out that he was present for Ruby's interview by Fritz – and he continued to make notes (per the time noted – 3:15pm in the copy of them on the next page) of the conversation including one very interesting reference:

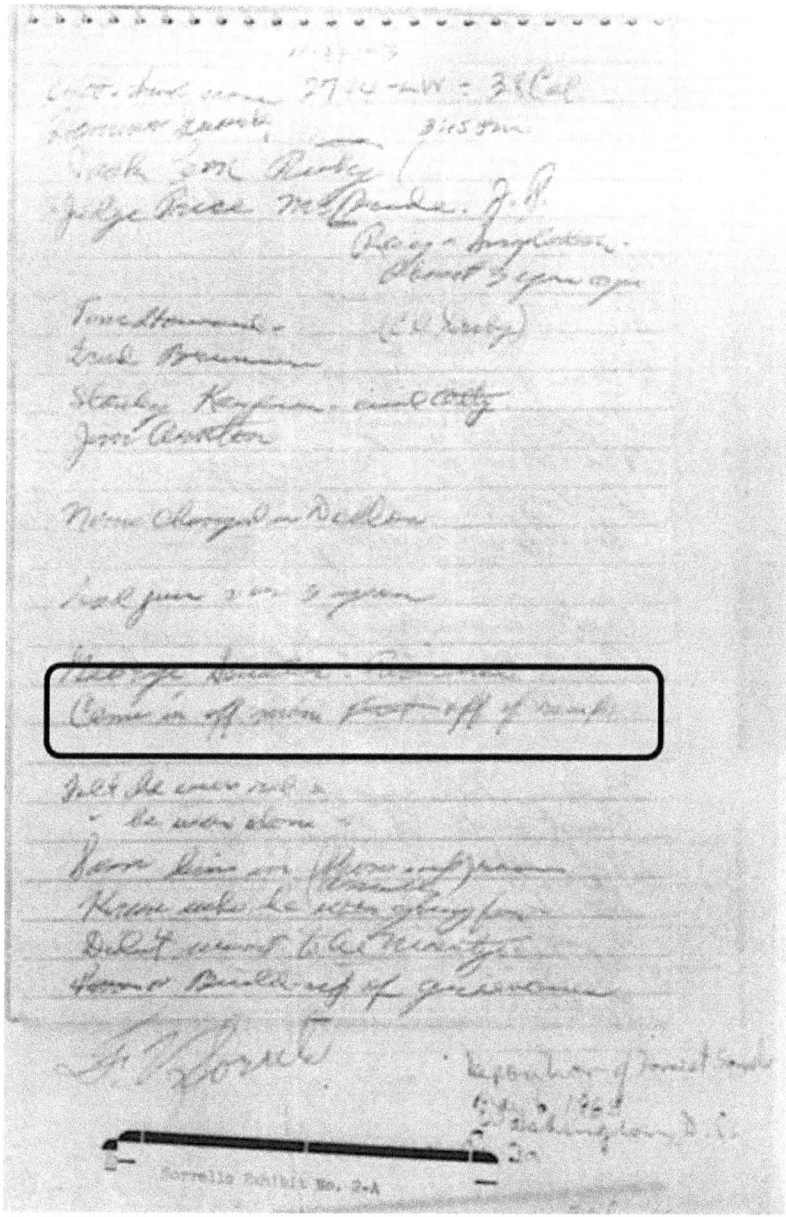

The portion circled on the document says, 'Came in off main street off of ramp'. This all but confirms that Sorrels heard Ruby tell Fritz how he entered the basement. The question now is why did Ruby only mention it at this point but not on the Fifth Floor to Sorrels, Dean and company or FBI Agent Hall?

Between the Fifth Floor conversations and the interview / interrogation on the Third Floor with Fritz, recall that Ruby met attorney, Tom Howard. During their conversation, which interrupted Ruby's interview with Agent Hall, could Howard have given word to Ruby about how to answer the question of how he entered the basement?

Despite the various statements that were attributed to Jack Ruby during and immediately after the shooting, there is little to no evidence that he was anything but evenly tempered when in DPD custody. Considering the footage of the aftermath, there is a lot of yelling and struggling with Ruby but it is impossible to differentiate how much or if he was yelling and struggling. Detective Graves perhaps had the most amount of struggle with Ruby to pry the pistol from his hand but other than that, by all accounts Ruby was easy to handle at all other times. Blackie Harrison, who helped bring Ruby up to the Fifth Floor, would tell the FBI that he remembered noting how calm Ruby was. If that was the case, it is consistent with the account of Fred Bieberdorf when he told the Warren Commission that at around 2pm, Ruby 'assured' him that the bruises and abrasions weren't bothering him and that the police officers hadn't injured him any more than what was necessary because 'they were just doing their job'.

Don Ray Archer is an outlier on this front because he told the FBI, on November 30, that he was concerned that afternoon that Ruby would harm himself but the statement doesn't indicate any further information about what Ruby said or did to prompt Archer thinking this. And anyone else in the DPD that may have shared his concern about Ruby didn't act on it until 6pm that evening as the good doctor-in-training, Fred Bieberdorf was called back to give Ruby a rectal examination. This was due to a concern, all those hours later after the shooting, that he may have something 'smuggled'. According to Bieberdorf's WC testimony, Ruby quipped to him at the time that it was the worst massage he ever had.[21]

A bank of photographs within the Warren Commission of Jack Ruby during his trial in March 1964. (Photograph courtesy of the Warren Commission)

Jack Ruby, the man, the myth... his movements

What is indisputable is how mythologised Jack Ruby became since his arrest for shooting Lee Oswald and his own death just over four years later. With proven ties to organised crime, pre-Castro Cuba gunrunning operations and the FBI as an informant, he has been frozen in time as a mysterious and enigmatic figure. This, along with his own place within the carnage of the weekend of November 22nd 1963, makes him not too dissimilar from Lee Oswald.

Jack Ruby was born in Chicago in 1911, and just like Oswald, he was also raised within a dysfunctional and turbulent family environment that included stints in orphanages.[20] Ruby moved from Chicago to Dallas in 1947 after his service in the army and his most legitimate source of income ever since were the night clubs he ran across the city.

Already in this chapter, we have uncovered links between Jack Ruby and members of the DPD. However, at this point of our examination, it will be wise to examine Ruby's speculated movements from just prior to President Kennedy's assassination until his entrance into Dallas City Hall to shoot Oswald. In doing so, we will see a few different sides to the Ruby 'character'.

Friday November 22nd:

Dallas woman, Julia Anne Mercer was stuck in traffic on Elm Street in Dealey Plaza at **10:50am** on the morning of President Kennedy's motorcade. Causing the delay was a pick-up truck that had stopped with its two right wheels mounted on the curb. From the back of it, a man, aged in his late 20's or early 30's with dark brown hair, approximately 5'9" or

5'10'' in height and about 165 to 170 pounds, carried what appeared to be a wooden brown rifle case up to the fence atop the grassy knoll. She looked ahead to the overpass and saw three Dallas police officers standing near a motorcycle and observing the scene. Mercer drove past the truck and was able to look right at the driver who was a white male, heavy set, about 40 to 45 years of age and wearing a green jacket.

In light of what would happen there just over an hour later, Mercer went to the FBI the next day and reported what she saw take place there. She was shown photographs of Lee Oswald but did not identify him as the man carrying the rifle case although she did note that the man had the same build as him. She was also shown mugshots to try and identify the driver of the truck. She picked out four photographs and ultimately picked the photograph of Jack Ruby as the man she saw behind the wheel of the pick-up truck. She knew then and there that the man she identified was named 'Jack Ruby' because that was what she saw written on the back of the photograph when one of the FBI agents turned it over. Bear in mind Mercer's identification of Ruby took place the day *before* he would be known the world over for killing Oswald. When questioned about this whole episode in early 1968 by New Orleans DA Jim Garrison for his investigation, Mercer told him that when she read a copy of her statement, she saw that the FBI had her saying that she 'advised the person in the truck had a rather large round face similar to Ruby's, but she could not identify him as the person'.[22] To add, Mercer said that the signature notarised as hers on the statement was a forgery. Julia Ann Mercer would not be called upon by the Warren Commission to testify but her conversation with Garrison along with what she witnessed on November 22nd was dramatised in Oliver Stone's film 'JFK'.

Local Dallas petty criminal and Internal Revenue Service informant, Robert Murray Vanderslice would reveal in 1977 that he was contacted by Jack Ruby on the **morning** of Friday November 22nd and asked if he 'would like to watch the fireworks.' This resulted in Ruby and he standing at the southernmost corner of Dealey Plaza where Houston and Commerce Street intersected near the Postal Annex building. They were facing the Texas School Book Depository at the time of the shooting, Vanderslice would allege. He said, in his statement to the FBI in 1977, which was declassified in 2017, about the incident, that 'Ruby left and headed toward the Dallas Morning News building (only a few blocks away) without saying a word'.[23]

Dallas Morning News advertising salesman, John Newnam told the Warren Commission that Jack Ruby arrived there at **12:40pm** and he knew this because he had watched the president's motorcade down on Main Street and had walked back to the office in time to see Ruby seated at his desk waiting.[24] He had ad copy for his Carousel Club that he wanted printed. He noted that Ruby, like everyone else around, looked stunned and in disbelief at the news of Kennedy's shooting.

Just after **1:00pm,** Jack Ruby phoned his sister, Eva Grant, who also lived in Dallas at the time. According to her statement to the Warren Commission,[25] she gathered that he was calling from the Dallas Morning

News because he told her that the phones there were running mad and that people were calling up from all over to cancel their advertisements in the wake of the news. John Newnam corroborates this as having occurred in his testimony to the Warren Commission. Grant also recalled Ruby saying to her, 'Isn't it awful?' about the assassination.

At **1:30pm** reporter Seth Kantor was at Parkland Hospital and on his way to Acting-Press Secretary, Malcolm Kilduff's press conference to advise of the president's death when Jack Ruby came up to him. In a sworn affidavit he stated that Ruby looked very upset and said, 'This is terrible" and "Should I close my places for three days." Kantor said that he replied that he should and kept walking to make the press conference. Jack Ruby denied to the Warren Commission that he was at Parkland Hospital but they did not challenge his denial with Kantor's claims. In 1978, Seth Kantor wrote the acclaimed book 'The Ruby Cover-up' which details this episode.[26]

At **1:50pm,** George Applin was seated on the ground level of the Texas Theater when Dallas police entered and apprehended Lee Oswald. Seeing that Oswald had a gun out whilst being subdued, Applin said that he saw a man seated nearby in the back row so he said to him 'Buddy, you'd better move. There's a gun,' but the man did not move. He just sat still and watched Oswald's arrest. Applin recounted this to the Warren Commission but he said that he had not seen the man since.[27] However, investigative reporter Earl Golz interviewed George Applin in 1979 about the incident.[28] It was then that Applin revealed that the man in the back row of the theater was Jack Ruby. He told Golz that he recognised Ruby immediately only after his photograph was all over the news after the Oswald shooting. But he kept what he saw to himself because of a magazine article he had read that reported the deaths of people related to the Kennedy assassination. This is also why he did not name Jack Ruby as the man he saw when testifying to the Warren Commission. As stated in Earl Golz's article, Applin's sighting of Ruby at the Texas Theater when Lee Oswald was arrested contradicts the accounts that Ruby and Carousel Club bartender, Andrew Armstrong, gave to the FBI.[29]

However soon Ruby arrived at the Carousel Club, he instructed Andrew Armstrong to notify all employees that the club would be shut for that night. He stayed there and discussed the assassination with Armstrong and labourer employee, Larry Crafard.[30] Ruby would also make a series of calls regarding cancelling newspaper ads for the club and closing for the weekend out of respect to President Kennedy.

Between **3:30pm & 4:00pm,** Ruby was seen standing in line at the Merchant's State Bank. In fact, he was reprimanded by Bill Cox an employee there, for carrying so much cash on him - $7,000.[31] However, there is no record of Ruby making a deposit at all that day.

At around this time, photographer, Ferd Kaufman encountered Ruby on the Third Floor of Dallas City Hall. Kaufman, along with a growing amount of media personnel had descended there over the last two hours since Lee Oswald had been brought in there. Kaufman said that Ruby gave him a business card with 'Carousel Club' written on it. Ruby told him that the card would enable him to be a guest there.⁽³²⁾

Still on the Third Floor of City Hall at around **6:00pm**, reporter Vic Robertson Jr. was near the entrance to the outer office of Capt. Fritz's Homicide & Robbery Division where Lee Oswald was being interrogated. Robertson saw Ruby walk up to the entrance and try to open the door. He was stopped by an officer standing nearby who said, 'You can't go in there, Jack.' Ruby allegedly made a joking remark and walked away back down the hall in the direction of the elevators.⁽³³⁾

Ruby would go to the Ritz Delicatessen to buy food for himself and his sister, Eva, which he then took around to her house. There he was pale and nauseous, according to her WC testimony. How long it was before Ruby went back to his own apartment is debatable but phone records confirmed that he was there at **9:00pm** to call his brother, Hyman, in Chicago and speak with him for seven minutes.⁽³⁴⁾

Ruby was next seen at arriving at a Jewish synagogue between **9:30pm & 9:45pm** as a service was coming to an end.⁽³⁵⁾ He must not have stayed there for too long because at approximately **10:00pm,** he entered Phil's Delicatessen and ordered some rounds of sandwiches. He stayed there and would make various phone calls from there including to City Hall – to tell Detective Richard M. Sims that he would bring sandwiches – and to get the direct number to ring the radio station, KLIF.⁽³⁶⁾

At **11:15pm**, Ruby left Phil's Delicatessen and drove around the Dallas CBD to observe if any other clubs were open. He would arrive at City Hall shortly thereafter and this is when he would testify to the Warren Commission that this was the first time he would go there that day. Dallas District Attorney, Henry Wade conducted a press conference at approximately **11:30pm**. During it, several witnesses would testify to Ruby being present also. When Wade referred to Oswald being associated with the 'Free Cuba.. movement'. Ruby, along with a few others present, allegedly corrected this by saying 'Fair Play for Cuba'. Footage of Wade making the incorrect reference and being corrected is available on YouTube and it is debatable that Ruby's was one of the correcting voices.[37]

Saturday November 23rd:

Just after midnight, Lee Oswald was brought into the makeshift press conference room in the sub-basement of City Hall. Several witnesses would also corroborate Ruby's presence and there are even photographs showing him there at either the Wade or Oswald press conference. When Oswald was led into the room, Jack Ruby was standing only three feet from the doorway according to some statements.

Reporter Ike Pappas stated that he also encountered Ruby at City Hall just after **midnight** and that he was even given a guest pass by him to the Carousel Club. In his 'Oral History' interview, Pappas went into great detail about how he spoke with Ruby and 'humored him by taking his card' so he could get access to a phone. He then said that Ruby turned to Henry Wade, who was talking to other reporters, and asked him if he (Pappas) could use a phone. Wade said he could in one of the offices.

According to William Duncan's testimony the Warren Commission, Ruby contacted him at KLIF-Radio by phone just prior to **1:00am**.[38] Ruby told him that he was at City Hall with sandwiches and cola to hand out. He said that Ruby told him that he had come to KLIF beforehand but the door was locked. Ruby then said that he went to City Hall to try and get a phone number for KLIF from someone there. He then offered to call him back from there to report his findings. Ten minutes later, Ruby did call Duncan back and asked if he wanted to speak with DA Wade. Duncan recalled having difficulty with accessing City Hall so he said he was interested. With that, Ruby put Wade on the line and Glen Duncan conducted an interview with him. This interview can be listened to on YouTube[39]. Forty-five minutes later, Ruby showed up at KLIF-Radio with sandwiches and cola in hand. Duncan put the time as **2:00am** as Ruby was there when a newscast for that time was put out.

According to his testimony for the Warren Commission, off-duty DPD officer, Harry Olsen* and his girlfriend, Kay Coleman, who worked at Ruby's Carousel Club were sitting in a parked car in a parking garage.[40]

Olsen testified that Ruby joined them and spent an hour with them discussing the assassination.

---

*Olsen's own whereabouts at the time of the shooting of President Kennedy and Officer Tippit remains suspicious. He testified to the Warren Commission that he was off duty at the time with his leg in a cast but moonlighting by guarding an estate, a vacant house, that happened to be close to the scene of the Tippit shooting in Oak Cliff. Harry Olsen would give testimony to the HSCA but was not asked about his activities on November 22nd.[42] Harry Olsen quit the DPD soon after in January 1964 and moved to California.

Ruby would corroborate this meeting as taking place in his own WC testimony but in it, he said that he heard a car horn and saw that it was his good friend, Olsen (inexplicably referred to as 'Carlson'), getting his attention.[41]

After this encounter, Ruby went to the Dallas Times to check on how the designs for print advertisements for his Vegas and Carousel clubs was coming along. Whilst there, he kidded around with employees by demonstrating a 'twist board', a fitness contraption, that he had tried launching in Dallas as a business venture.[43]

Next, Ruby went back to his apartment and woke his roommate, George Senator, to discuss the assassination.[44] They left the apartment and drove to the Southland Hotel for a cup of coffee. After that, Ruby called Larry Crafard and told him to get dressed and meet him with a polaroid camera and meet him at the Carousel Club. From there, all three drove out to Stemmons Freeway and took a photograph of an 'Impeach Earl Warren' billboard. After that, Ruby and Senator dropped Crafard back home (who promptly left Dallas later that morning having become fed up of how Ruby treated him) then returned to their apartment where Ruby went to bed and slept until **10:30am – 11:00am**.[45]

At approximately **12:00pm**, NBC News producer / director, Fred Rheinstein and his crew in a mobile TV unit van parked outside City Hall on Commerce Street were about to have lunch. Rheinstein told the Warren Commission that a man, he would later recognise as Jack Ruby, 'put his head through the open window of our remote truck' to look at their monitors.[46] Rheinstein and co. would come to refer to the man as their 'creepy friend' as it would not be the last time some of them would encounter him that weekend

At around the same time, French reporter, Philippe Labro met Ruby on the Third Floor in City Hall during which time Ruby gave him a card for the Carousel Club and invited him to come have a drink some time.[47]

Wes Wise, a sportscaster with KRLD Radio and TV, and future mayor of Dallas, was at the Texas School Book Depository at around **3:20pm**. He testified to the FBI that he was trying to access the building to recreate Oswald's movements after he allegedly shot President Kennedy.[48] When he found he couldn't because the doors were locked, Wise returned to his car. He then had a knock on his window. It was Jack Ruby, who he had known for five or six years. He got the impression that Ruby had approached from the direction of the railway tracks behind Dealey Plaza. The two talked about Kennedy's death in general detail. Wise recalled telling Ruby that he was at the Trade Mart where the president was on his way to. He told Ruby that he had seen two horse saddles there ready to be presented to the president and his wife for their children, Caroline and John Jr., as gifts. Wise said that talk about this and general reactions to the shooting brought tears to Ruby's eyes. Wise said that Ruby then asked him if he knew that Chief Curry and Capt. Fritz were down in Dealey Plaza looking at all of the flowers that people had left there in memory of the president. Wise said he didn't know and he got the impression that Ruby was hinting that he should photograph the scene. Wise and Ruby walked to Dealey Plaza and Wise did take some photographs of Curry and Fritz and thanked Ruby for telling him about it. He said that he also saw Ruby taking photographs of the crowd. Both the defense and prosecution for Ruby's trial asked Wise about his impressions of Ruby's temperament. Overall, Wise answered that he knew Ruby to be emotional and excitable sometimes but he had never experienced that side of him. Wise stated that during the conversation with Ruby, he even kidded him about being able to help KLIF-Radio gain an interview with DA Wade the previous night.

That afternoon back at City Hall, reporter Paul Sisco overheard someone asking somebody else 'what's a night club owner doing here?'[49] Another reporter, Thayer Waldo saw Jack Ruby around the time on Saturday that Chief Curry was telling reporters that Oswald would be transferred to the County Jail the next morning at 10am. At **5:00am,** Fred Rheinstein would see Ruby on one of his monitors in the truck open the door into Henry Wade's office and not come back out.

At **6:00pm,** Ruby went back to the Carousel Club and stayed for about an hour. While there, he had Andrew Armstrong call the club's girls and tell them not to come into work that night either. He then asked Armstrong to stay until 8pm and then he left and went to his sister's house. A little later, at **8:30pm,** one of Ruby's stripper, Karen Carlin aka 'Little Lynn', at the Carousel, called him at his home and said that she needed money to get back to Fort Worth from Dallas that night. Ruby was angry but told her he would meet her at the Carousel. However, Ruby didn't show up so Carlin's husband, Bruce called Ruby back at his home. When he was reached, Ruby had an attendant there at the club at the time, come out and give Karen Carlin $5.00.[50] Reports suggest that Jack Ruby didn't venture far that night, instead he stayed at his apartment and made numerous calls including one to Breck Wall at **11:44pm** who was in Galveston, Texas having left Dallas for there late the previous night.[51]

<u>Sunday November 24th</u>:

WBAP-TV remote operator, Ira N. Walker was in the mobile van outside Dallas City Hall when, at around **8:00am,** a man came up to the truck, peeked in and asked if they've brought Oswald down yet.[52] Just prior to this, his colleague, Johnnie Smith described a man standing near the truck looking up at the City Hall building[53] and camera operator, Warren Richey, who was seated on the roof of the truck saw the same man. [54] All would give similar descriptions of the man and later, identify him as Jack Ruby. However, Jack Ruby's housekeeper, Elnora Pitts called his house, at **8:00am,** as she always would on Sunday mornings to ask him if he needed her to come and clean the apartment. Only this time, when Pitts made the same call that morning, she said the male voice who answered as Ruby did not sound like he knew why she was calling.[55] George Senator said Ruby did not rise from bed until 9:30am that morning.

At **9:30am,** a preacher and radio evangelist from nearby Plano, Ray Rushing, rode up in the elevator at Dallas City Hall as he wanted to provide Lee Oswald spiritual guidance. He would tentatively report to Jack Revill of the DPD that Jack Ruby was in the elevator with him and that they conversed.[56]

At **10:19am,** Karen Carlin called Ruby at his apartment from Fort Worth and asked him to send her $25.00 by money order. Apparently, Ruby had asked her to do so the night before. When they spoke during this call, he said he would wire her the money through Western Union.[57] To do this, having also taken some pills of the weight loss drug (and stimulant), Preludin, he drove into the Dallas CBD with his dog, Sheba in his car, hundreds of dollars of cash in the glove compartment & on his person, his ID and a revolver. Once there, he parked across from the Western Union office on Main Street. Ruby entered there and filled out a money transfer that supervisor, Doyle Lane – who was covering staff who were taking lunch, had given him. Completing the transaction, Lane stamped a receipt '11:17am' and Ruby walked out and turned left in the direction of Dallas City Hall.[58]

What are we to take from Jack Ruby's movements that weekend? At the very least, he was incredibly interested in the assassination of President Kennedy, at times consumed with grief and was doing his best to follow the news like some kind of 'news hound wannabe' or worse, he was involved in the plot to kill the president and was monitoring its aftermath including the incarceration of accused assassin, Lee Oswald. To exactly what degree of guilt or complicity he had regarding President Kennedy's murder, based on the weight of evidence, is deserving of debate because the list of sightings laid out in the last few pages is by no means a complete account. There were many more sightings and accounts of Ruby's movements – most of which overlap with each other so it has been difficult to be certain about what actually took place or are fabrications or embellishments.

What is clear is that none of the DPD who were called on as witnesses to the events on Sunday November 24 leading up to, during and after Oswald's shooting, testified to seeing Ruby around City Hall on Friday or Saturday that weekend. Those that knew Ruby or of him, of which there were between '25 to 50 of the 1,750 men in the Dallas Police Department' according to Chief Curry's more than generous estimate for the Warren Commission.[60] In actual statements provided to the DPD, FBI, Ruby Trial and Warren Commission, approximately eighty DPD personnel admitted to knowing of or being acquainted with Jack Ruby. But maybe Seth Kantor said it best when he said that, come that Sunday afternoon, there wasn't a 'Dallas policeman that said he knew Ruby...'

In the meantime, let us return to the topic at hand by next examining how Jack Ruby *actually* entered the City Hall basement on November 24.

Jack Ruby... Enter Stage *East*

Having left the Western Union office after he transferred money to Karen Carlin, Jack Ruby proceeded west along Main Street. The DPD and WC concluded that he walked all the way to the City Hall basement entrance and *most likely* entered from there but, as already covered in Chapter Ten, this did not happen. Ruby was apprehended and seen being walked through the jail office after the shooting so he obviously got down to the basement somehow. The HSCA put forward the possibility that he entered through the eastern end of the basement car park but would not commit to it definitively. Let's zoom out on the diagram that indicates who was situated near the top of the Main Street ramp to see how feasible this scenario is:

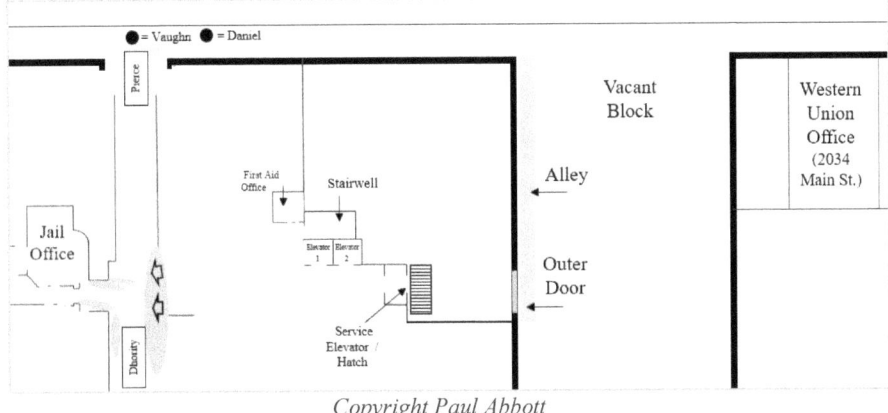

Copyright Paul Abbott

The map now includes where the Western Union office was at the time. This was the last verified sighting of Jack Ruby at 11:17am prior to Oswald's shooting in the basement. The Western Union was on 2034 Main Street and on the same block as the Old City Hall and Annex Building. Dividing the building it was in and the Annex Building at the time was a vacant lot used as a car park.

Also indicated in the above diagram is the outer door that porters Alfreadia Riggs and Harold Fuqua walked out of in their quest for a TV on the morning of November 24. No floorplans or schematics can be found for the Annex Building at the time but an alleyway that led alongside the outside of the building to Main Street was referred to in the testimonies of porters Fuqua and Riggs and in later years during the HSCA investigation.

However, it is not evident when looking at the Annex Building and the outer door (behind the white van), in more recent times, in this Streetview image from Google Maps:

In any event, the outer door that Fuqua and Riggs walked out from was locked on the inside so we can consider it as secure at that point. In terms of securing the basement and the car park, we have already covered the group of reserve officers that Sgt. Dean was leading. To refresh our perspective, let's take things up from this point with testimony that Dean gave to the Warren Commission's Burt Griffin:[61]

> **Griffin:** Who checked the stairway door in the garage that leads up into the municipal *(Annex)* building?
> **Dean:** The stairway door?
> **Griffin:** Yes.
> **Dean:** I don't know of any door that leads up into the... the stairway?
> **Griffin:** There is a stairway...

Dean: That goes down into the subbasement?

Griffin: Well now, over where the elevators are.

Dean: Oh, Oh, yes.

Griffin: You know what I'm talking about?

Dean: Yes.

Griffin: Who checked that door?

Dean: Sergeant Putnam checked it once and I checked it and it was locked.

Griffin: Did you know at the time you checked it that even though the door was locked from the outside, it could be opened from the inside?

Dean: (no response)

Griffin: Let me state this again. Even though the door would be locked from the garage side, that from the stairway side it would be unlocked; were you aware of that?

Dean: I believe we asked the maintenance man about this, and I believe he locked it so as it couldn't be unlocked from either side unless they had a key. I believe Sergeant Putnam called this to the maintenance man's attention, and I recall being there at the time they were discussing it, and I think at that time the maintenance man locked the door so it couldn't be unlocked from either side other than with a key.

Griffin: Do you recall the name of this maintenance man?

Dean: No, sir; I don't know. I didn't know his name to start with. However, I did know he was the maintenance man, by sight.

Griffin: When did you get ahold of this maintenance man?

Dean: Sergeant Putnam, I believe, had gotten--or had thought about this and asked him, or he had gotten in touch with him some way.

Griffin: Was this at the same time you had the 13 men in the garage searching, or at some later time?

Dean: This was during the search.

Griffin: And do you know where this maintenance man was located?

Dean: No, sir.

In actual fact, the stairway door into the basement that Dean said he 'thought' he had locked by a 'maintenance man' could not have been because it was an emergency exit therefore not lockable from the inside. John Servance testified to this to the Warren Commission.[59] The only way it could have been locked was on the basement side to prevent people from coming up to the Annex Building. In all probability, Dean knew this but made up the story of having a maintenance man lock the door on both sides as none of the City Hall workers (Servance, Pierce, Kelly, McKinzie) testified to being asked to do this. Still, the fact that the door could have been opened from within the stairway was not an issue, at least while reserves Brock and Worley were standing nearby on guard. But as we have already discovered, both were reassigned out of the basement on traffic duty on Dean's indirect orders. This means the eastern end of the basement car park was not guarded in the minutes leading up to the shooting.

With the time that lapsed between when Ruby left the Western Union office and Oswald's shooting (four minutes), it is a stretch to consider that Ruby could have accessed the basement through any point off Commerce or Harwood Street. See the below Streetview screenshot from Google Maps that shows where the Western Union office was at the time and where both the eastern door and Main Street ramp were in proximity:

The Streetview perspective really captures how short a distance it was from the Western Union office to either point, indicated by the white arrows, but having eliminated the Main Street ramp scenario, Jack Ruby could have only entered through the eastern outer door of the Annex Building. Once through the outer door, all Ruby needed to do was cross the fire escape stairs, go through the rear hatch of the service elevator and he would have been on the ground floor of the empty Annex Building. All he needed to do was then walk down one flight of stairs, open the door that could not be locked to come out of the stairwell door and he would have been in the basement. From there, with practically all media and police personnel focused toward the jail office as well as the bright lights trained in the same direction, Ruby could have simply walked toward the ramp, shuffled through the railing and (recall Jimmie Turner's testimony) walked down the ramp the rest of the way and be in position for when Oswald emerged. This journey could have easily been done in four minutes. And it could have had him in the basement early enough to have seen Lt. Pierce drive the car up the ramp!

Despite labelling this scenario the most 'attractive' in terms of how Jack Ruby gained entry to City Hall basement, that was as far as the HSCA went in 1978. But we will go into much greater detail when we hypothesise exactly what took place when and who was involved to what capacity in a later chapter. One final note on this point. What most become stuck on is how Ruby would have known when to time his entry to the basement and shoot Oswald – presuming that it was premeditated on his part. Some have suggested that he was signaled to from someone up on one of the windows of the Annex Building. It's possible but would it not have been far simpler to start Oswald's transfer when it was seen that Jack Ruby was approaching?

The Transfer of Jack Ruby

Depending on who was asked, for the remainder of Ruby's time in DPD custody at City Hall he was even-tempered. But the ironies of ironies were handed out by the DPD in terms of how well they facilitated Ruby's transfer to the County Jail at 11am on Monday November 25th. Detective Jim Leavelle provided extensive detail about it in his testimony to the

Warren Commission. Needless to say, that it is a shame he was not so detailed with aspects of Oswald's incarceration, intended transfer and slaying and indeed, that the DPD weren't so careful with Oswald's transfer either. Let's refer directly to Leavelle's testimony to WC Counsel, Leon Hubert because paraphrasing it would not do justice to the irony:

Hubert: Did you transfer Ruby?

Leavelle: Yes, I did.

Hubert: It was done at an unannounced hour?

Leavelle: Well, sir; it was so unannounced that the chief didn't know about it and neither did Sheriff Decker. I don't know whether they will admit that or not, but no one knew it but Captain Fritz and myself and three or four officers directly involved.

Hubert: You all just decided to do it, and that was it?

Leavelle: Well, the captain called me and asked me about it and told me what he was thinking about doing and he wanted to know if I thought it would work and I said, "Yes, I think it will the way it has been set up," and he said, "I haven't asked the chief about it," and I said, "All you can do is get a bawling out, but a bawling out is better than losing a prisoner."

Hubert: Did you get bawled out about it?

Leavelle: I didn't. I did not know whether he did or not. I doubt it. Because I am sure the chief was relieved to be rid of the responsibility.

Hubert: How was Ruby removed, then, just for the record?

Leavelle: Well, this would be on Monday morning, I guess, the next Monday morning around 11, around the same hour that Oswald was transferred. The captain had not showed up and I-- he called on the telephone and asked for me and his secretary called me to the phone, and I was in the squad room where several officers were, and asked me if I was in a position where I could talk, and I said, "No, not really," and he said, "Well--" told me to go into his office and take the phone in there, which I did, and he said, "I am down at the Greyhound Bus Station, and I have Officers Graves and Montgomery with me."
He had run into them on the street.
(Fritz) Said, "We have cased the jail and it looks clear. I am going to make a suggestion to you, and if you don't think it will work I want you to tell me."
Said--he said, "We'll pull through the basement of the city hall," said, "You go get Ruby out of the jail anyway you want to, on a "tempo" or whatever you think best, and bring him down to me, down in the elevator and we'll pull through the basement at some given time, and we'll load him up and whisk him right on down and let another squad follow us and we will take him right on down to the county jail."
Said, "The sheriff--I haven't called Decker or the chief about it, either." Said, "Do you think it will work?"
I said, "Yes." Said, "How many men--got enough there to help you with him?"
I said, "Yes, there is three or four here I can get."

"Don't tell anybody where you are going. Just get them like you are going after coffee and get downstairs or somewhere and tell them what you are going to do."

So, I went into the squad room (Captain Fritz had called) Lieutenant Wells, and told him not to let the officers out of the office because he wanted us when he got in there so I just walked out and motioned to Mr. Brown and Dhority and Mr. Beck and told them to follow me, and didn't say a word to anyone, and walked downstairs, and, of course, they are curious, and when I got downstairs I outlined the deal to them and told Beck and Brown to get the car--get the other car in the basement and have it in position to go out, and Dhority and I went up and got the prisoner and brought him down.

Hubert: Brought him down the jail elevator?

Leavelle: Down the jail elevator.

Hubert: Were any newsmen down in the station?

Leavelle: Beg your pardon?

Hubert: Were there any newsmen down in the basement?

Leavelle: In fact, when I walked out one of the newspapermen asked me when we were going to transfer Ruby and I said, "Oh, I don't know." And just like that, and walked on.

Hubert: You had Ruby with you?

Leavelle: You mean--oh, no; the officers and I walking down. When we brought Ruby down in the jail elevator, that elevator is never in view of the public. It is an inside elevator.

259

Never in view of the public, so, anyway, after talking to the captain, I set my watch with his and said, "Be there at exactly 11:15."

So, he set his watch with mine and we brought Ruby down. That is the reason--I got down there about a minute and a half, 2 minutes early to the basement and told the lieutenant on duty, told everybody not to ring for the elevator that we would have it tied up, just held him in the elevator.

Hubert: Kept Ruby in the elevator?

Leavelle: Kept Ruby in the elevator. Mr. Brown standing outside of the jail office, Mr. Beck had his car, his motor running in the parking basement, and Mr. Brown was standing there talking to one of the men in the jail office just as though he was passing the time of day, and he was to give me the nod as soon as the captain's car pulled in on the ramp, which he did.

Hubert: Which side did he pull in on?

Leavelle: Just came off the Main Street ramp and parked across the opening and when he saw him pull in, gave me the high sign and we took Ruby and told him, I said, "I don't want to have to push you or shove you. I want you to move." Of course, Ruby was scared, so, he almost outran me to the car. He ran and got in the back seat of the car with Graves, who was already in the back seat, and Montgomery was driving and Mr. Beck, Dhority, and Brown got to the other car and followed us. We proceeded directly to the county jail.

Hubert: Up Commerce?

Leavelle: We went up Commerce to the expressway and cut back on the expressway to Main Street and came down Main Street to Houston Street where the jail is located, and around the corner on Houston Street, to the entrance of the county jail.

Hubert: Did you have any trouble with the traffic going down Main Street?

Leavelle: We caught every light green going down. Didn't have to stop.

Hubert: Did you have the sirens going?

Leavelle: No, we did not. We drove through there at a good little step faster than normal, but so happened we caught every light. I don't think we even missed a light. When we reached the jail, the officers in the car behind us bailed out and covered the entrance to the jail, and we were (sic) had him inside in a matter of 20 seconds, from the time the car stopped.

If only we could tell if Leavelle ever strayed away from keeping a straight face when he was talking at such length about how secretive yet competently the DPD were able to safely effect the transfer of Jack Ruby. But the irony would be beyond laughable if the consequences for the DPD's mishandling of Lee Oswald's transfer were not so tragic and dire in the scheme of things. It is also telling to note that the key to its success was leaving Curry and Decker out of the loop. Considering how parochial both were in their statements to the press over that weekend, it is understandable. However, it was still somewhat of a risk to not have Decker advised in case the County Jail wasn't prepared to receive Ruby.

But the convoy amounted to two squad cars that, without any escort, still had an unimpeded journey along the same route intended for the Oswald convoy the day before.

CHAPTER THIRTEEN

RUBY ON TRIAL

With Ruby in the safe confines of Dallas County Jail, we can begin to examine the topsy turvy journey up to and then beyond his trial for the murder of Lee Oswald.

The first lawyer, as we know, to represent Jack Ruby was Tom Howard. Despite being in the vicinity only a few seconds prior to Ruby shooting Oswald, it is not clear how or why Howard took it upon himself to offer his services for Ruby's defense. According to Secret Service Agent, Forrest Sorrels' statement to the Warren Commission, when speaking with Ruby on November 24, he also asked Ruby if he had an attorney. Ruby said he did and that it was Stanley Kaufman, a civil attorney. Kaufman's name can be seen in Sorrel's notes. However, it was Tom Howard who was taken up to see Ruby while Agent Hall had been speaking with him.

In any event, it's evident that Howard accessed Ruby within a couple of hours of the shooting and Ruby would continue to convey a sense of grief for the Kennedy family as his prime motive for killing Oswald. This would have more than likely occurred to Ruby before shooting Oswald and encouraged by Howard after the fact because in Texas, at the time, any crime found to be committed as an act of 'passion' would attract a comparably smaller sentence. However, on November 27, Jack Ruby was indicted for murdering Oswald, not as an act of passion but as one of malice which was the equivalent of premeditation and liable to attract a death sentence.

We know that the first person to visit Ruby at the County Jail was local mob boss, Joseph Campisi on November 30. He would tell the HSCA that Ruby was feeling sorry for himself about the whole affair but would catch himself and say it was President Kennedy's kids that he really felt sorry for.[1]

In the meantime, Jack Ruby's brother, Earl, stepped in to help sure up Jack's defense. According to his own testimony to the Warren Commission, when he learned more about Tom Howard's reputation as being an attorney / bondsman, he began to worry about his ability to represent his brother.[2] He said that Jack had also demurred on Howard because he would contradict himself. Ruby's civil lawyer, Stanley Kaufman, was engaged to find reinforcements but people such as Percy Foreman were too expensive or in the case of Fred Brunner, too connected to the DA's office. Jack Ruby's first application for bail would be denied on December 23rd and come the following January, Tom Howard would be replaced by high-profile, Californian attorney, Melvin Belli – who agreed to represent Jack Ruby pro-bono. Fellow prolific attorney, Joe Tonahill would also join Ruby's defense team.

Jack Ruby stood trial for Lee Oswald's murder between March 4 and 14th 1964. He would be found to be sane and guilty of murder with malice and sentenced to death. An appeal was launched immediately and across the following month, Ruby's defense would lodge a motion for a new trial on the grounds of new evidence being allowed to be used and in another jurisdiction on the grounds of prejudice against Ruby in Dallas. This related particularly on the weight of Patrick Dean's testimony that indicated premeditation on Ruby's part for shooting Oswald.[3] Judge Joe B. Brown, who presided over Ruby's trial, overruled the motion and would do so once more. In doing so, he refused to hear corroborative testimony from witnesses for the defense proving the need to Ruby's team for a new trial. Brown also overruled a new bid from the defense for Ruby to be hospitalised on the grounds that it could be proven that he was insane.*

Ruby's defense team would continue the pattern of appealing against Judge Brown's verdicts until the following year, when, in June, Brown himself, requested that the District Court remove him from any further participation in the 'State of Texas vs. Jack Rubenstein' case.

The ensuing years saw Jack Ruby's mental state both deteriorate as he made multiple attempts to commit suicide while being held at the Dallas County Jail.[4] But eventually, in 1966, his 1964 conviction was overturned by the Texas Court of Criminal Appeals due to a technicality regarding

---

*Ruby's defense used an affidavit provided by psychiatrist, Dr. Louis Jolley-West, stating that 'Jack Ruby was insane, and highly susceptible to delusions and suspicions, and a complete paranoid.' Jolley-West had proven connections to the CIA's MKULTRA program and its pioneering of hallucinogenic substances to control people's minds alongside practices of hypnotherapy. This makes his interactions with Jack Ruby worthy of suspicion. For further insight, I recommend Tom O'Neil's 'Chaos'[5] which is an epic investigative book that charts the connections between U.S. Intelligence, domestic operations and the advent of Charles Manson and his 'family'.

how Ruby spoke of premeditation for murder of Oswald in DPD custody that violated Texas criminal law. The defense was also successful in having a retrial ruled to take place in Wichita Falls, Kansas.

However, during a stay in Parkland Hospital for the treatment of pneumonia-like symptoms and blood clots in December 1966, Jack Ruby was diagnosed with cancer. He died of a pulmonary embolism, essentially a blockage of an artery in his lungs, in January 3rd, 1967.

What was the truth regarding Jack Ruby and his knowledge about President Kennedy's assassination and his level of involvement and complicity in that and the murder of Lee Oswald? His proven ties to organised crime are firmly entrenched in his legacy and therefore had created a firm link between the outfit to Lee Oswald's murder lending the whole episode a convenient footnote. Could it actually have been as simple as a mob-linked nut killing another nut or even the mob sending one of their own, whom they had clear links to, to do the job? The fact that Ruby was an informant for the FBI,[6] adds another layer to Ruby, the walking quagmire. We will speculate further in a later chapter but for now, let us refer to the statements he made to the Warren Commission and the Texas District Court. They may provide further insight into his legend.

While the Warren Commission was carrying out its investigation in 1964, Jack Ruby persistently asked to testify and on June 7th, '64, he was able to do so and directly to members of its panel including Chief Justice Earl Warren himself. It is worth reading the testimony that his appearance concluded on:

Ruby: I am in a tough spot, and I don't know what the solution can be to save me. And I know our wonderful President, Lyndon Johnson, as soon as he was the President of his country, he appointed you as head of this group. But through certain falsehoods that have been said about me to other people, the John Birch Society, I am as good as guilty as the accused assassin of President Kennedy. How can you remedy that, Mr. Warren? Do any of your men have any ways of remedying that? Mr. Bill Decker said be a man and speak up. I am making a statement now that I may not live the next hour when I walk out of this room.

Now it is the most fantastic story you have ever heard in a lifetime. I did something out of the goodness of my heart. Unfortunately, Chief Earl Warren, had you been around 5 or 6 months ago, and I know your hands were tied, you couldn't do it, and immediately the President would have gotten ahold of my true story, or whatever would have been said about me, a certain organization wouldn't have so completely formed now, so powerfully, to use me because I am of the Jewish extraction, Jewish faith, to commit the most dastardly crime that has ever been committed. Can you understand now in visualizing what happened, what powers, what momentum has been carried on to create this feeling of mass feeling against my people, against certain people that were against them prior to their power? That goes over your head, doesn't it?

Warren: Well, I don't quite get the full significance of it, Mr. Ruby. I know what you feel about the John Birch Society.
Ruby: Very powerful.
Warren: I think it is powerful, yes I do. Of course, I don't have all the information that you feel you have on that subject.
Ruby: Unfortunately, you don't have, because it is too late. And I wish that our beloved President, Lyndon Johnson, would have delved deeper into the situation, hear me, not to accept just circumstantial facts about my guilt or innocence, and would have questioned to find out the truth about me before he relinquished certain powers to these certain people.
Warren: Well, I am afraid I don't know what power you believe he relinquished to them. I think that it is difficult to understand what you have to say.
Ruby: I want to say this to you. The Jewish people are being exterminated at this moment. Consequently, a whole new form of government is going to take over our country, and I know I won't live to see you another time. Do I sound sort of screwy--in telling you these things?

Ruby was sounding every bit the kook at this point – ascribing himself and his cause with the John Birch Society and the Jewish faith and people. Was he pleading for mercy on the grounds of insanity? Let's continue:

Warren: No; I think that is what you believe, or you wouldn't tell it under your oath.

Ruby: But it is a very serious situation. I guess it is too late to stop it, isn't it?

All right, I want to ask you this. All you men have been chosen by the President for this committee, is that correct?

Warren: Representative Ford and I are the only members of the Commission that are here. Mr. Rankin of the Commission is employed as our chief counsel. Mr. Rankin employed Mr. Specter and Mr. Ball as members of the staff. You know who the other gentlemen here are. You know that Mr. Moore* is a member of the Secret Service, and he has been a liaison officer with our staff since the Commission was formed.

Ford: Are there any questions that ought to be asked to help clarify the situation that you described?

Ruby: There is only one thing. If you don't take me back to Washington tonight to give me a chance to prove to the President that I am not guilty, then you will see the most tragic thing that will ever happen. And if you don't have the power to take me back, I won't be around to be able to prove my innocence or guilt. Now up to this moment, I have been talking with you for how long?

Warren: I would say for the better part of 3 hours.

---

*Secret Service Agent Elmer Moore was incredibly busy across the weekend of the assassination. Included in his endeavours was pressuring Dr. Malcolm Perry to recant on his statements that President Kennedy was likely shot from the front.[7]

Ruby: All right, wouldn't it be ridiculous for me to speak sensibly all this time and give you this climactic talk that I have? Maybe something can be saved, something can be done. What have you got to answer to that, Chief Justice Warren?

Warren: Well, I don't how that can be done, Mr. Ruby, because I don't know what you anticipate we will encounter. Representative Ford. Is there anything more you can tell us if you went back to Washington?

Ruby: Yes; are you sincere in wanting to take me back?

Ford: We are most interested in all the information you have.

Ruby: All I know is maybe something can be saved. Because right now, I want to tell you this, I am used as a scapegoat, and there is no greater weapon that you can use to create some falsehood about some of the Jewish faith, especially at the terrible heinous crime such as the killing of President Kennedy. Now maybe something can be saved. It may not be too late, whatever happens, if our President, Lyndon Johnson, knew the truth from me. But if I am eliminated, there won't be any way of knowing. Right now, when I leave your presence now, I am the only one that can bring out the truth to our President, who believes in righteousness and justice. But he has been told, I am certain, that I was part of a plot to assassinate the President. I know your hands are tied; you are helpless.

Warren: Mr. Ruby, I think I can say this to you, that if he has been told any such thing, there is no indication of any kind that he believes it.

Ruby: I am sorry, Chief Justice Warren, I thought I would be very effective in telling you what I have said here. But in all fairness to everyone, maybe all I want to do is beg that if they found out I was telling the truth, maybe they can succeed in what their motives are, but maybe my people won't be tortured and mutilated.

Warren: Well, you may be sure that the President and his whole Commission will do anything that is necessary to see that your people are not tortured.

Ruby: No.

Warren: You may be sure of that.

Ruby: No; the only way you can do it is if he knows the truth, that I am telling the truth, and why I was down in that basement Sunday morning, and maybe some sense of decency will come out and they can still fulfill their plan, as I stated before, without my people going through torture and mutilation.

Warren: The President will know everything that you have said.

Ruby: But I won't be around, Chief Justice. I won't be around to verify these things you are going to tell the President.

Tonahill: Who do you think is going to eliminate you, Jack?

Ruby: I have been used for a purpose, and there will be a certain tragic occurrence happening if you don't take my testimony and somehow vindicate me, so my people don't suffer because of what I have done.

Warren: But we have taken your testimony. We have it here. It will be in permanent form for the President of the United States and for the Congress of the United States, and for the courts of the United States, and for the people of the entire world. It is there. It will be recorded for all to see. That is the purpose of our coming here today. We feel that you are entitled to have your story told.

Ruby: You have lost me though. You have lost me, Chief Justice Warren.

Warren: Lost you in what sense?

Ruby: I won't be around for you to come and question me again.

Warren: Well, it is very hard for me to believe that. I am sure that everybody would want to protect you to the very limit.

Ruby: All I want is a lie detector test, and you refuse to give it to me. Because as it stands now---and the truth serum, and any other--Pentothal--how do you pronounce it, whatever it is. And they will not give it to me, because I want to tell the truth. And then I want to leave this world. But I don't want my people to be blamed for something that is untrue, that they claim has happened.

Warren: Mr. Ruby, I promise you that you will be able to take such a test.

Ruby: When?

Warren: You will have to let me see when we can figure that out. But I assure you, it won't be delayed, because our desire is to terminate the work of the Commission and make our report to the public just as soon as possible, so there won't be any misunderstanding caused by all of these rumors or stories that have been put out that are not consistent with the evidence in the case. But it will not be unnecessarily delayed, and we will do it on behalf of the Commission, I promise you.

If nothing else, time would indicate that Jack Ruby was not spirited away to Washington but he was given a lie detector test a month after his plea to the Warren Commission. Perhaps consequentially, present were Arlen Specter on behalf of the WC, Clayton Fowler & Joe Tonahill – Ruby's attorneys, William R. Beavers – Ruby's psychiatrist, FBI Special Agent James Woods & Agent Bell Herndon, Chief Jailer E.L. Holmes, court reporter Odell Oliver, assistant district attorney William Alexander.

The polygraph started at 2:30pm and finished at approximately 9pm and it consisted of one hundred and one questions across thirteen tests (*see the appendices for a list of the questions and answers*). By all reports, Jack Ruby was lucid and calm throughout the whole session. A few weeks later, on July 28 1964, the FBI's Bell Herndon, who administered Ruby's test, sat before the Warren Commission and was questioned about his impressions.[8] He stated that ordinarily the time that had passed between when this test was administered and when the events that Ruby was questioned about would 'tend to detract or negate any specific or definite conclusion that could be rendered with regard to the polygraph examination.' In short, because so much time had passed, Ruby's making an effort to recall what he was being asked about would likely have a bearing on the readings and skew them. Herndon also noted that it was not common practice to have so many people in the room watching proceedings but to him, it seemed like Ruby did not mind. The Warren Commission would state in its report that the results of Ruby's polygraph had no bearing on any of its findings. It also inferred in no uncertain terms that the test was 'merely granted' because Ruby requested it. The HSCA analysed the polygraph in 1977 using a panel of experts.[9] They concluded there were four leading factors that affected the integrity of the test:

- 'the time that elapsed since the shooting,'
- 'Ruby's extensive prior interrogation,'
- 'the many people present during the examination,' and
- 'the great number of relevant questions asked.'

Interestingly, the HSCA panel referred to the primary source at the time regarding polygraph examinations, the textbook titled, 'Lie Detection and Criminal Interrogation' by Fred E. Inbau and John E. Reid.[11] In it, the recommended number of relevant questions to ask a subject is … three because the longer a person is tested, the more galvanised they are and less reactive to questions. The panel also took issue to polygrapher, Bell Herndon regarding the:

- wording of control questions (used to gain a baseline of truth through the asking of a simple question) and interrogation questions (to detect truth or lies on pertinent matters),
- use of the polygraph machine which seemed like it was not properly adjusted or was defective,
- and poor analysis of Ruby's answers.

In the end, the panel of experts did not have enough good data to provide any kind of analysis on whether Ruby's polygraph test in 1964 accurately recorded him telling the truth or not.

On March 18, 1965, Ruby's defense team launched an appeal to have him taken into Federal custody. He took the opportunity to speak on his own behalf and address the court. He started his address by accusing his attorney, Joe Tonahill of lying and being party to a conspiracy to 'convince the public' that he was insane. Below is his full statement:

> Now, your Honor, you have had many a person appear before you pleading their case. If I am a person who sounds insane at this time, then the rest of the world is crazy. I say this with choking in my heart and tears in my eyes.
> The most tragic thing happened that Sunday morning when I went down that ramp. I happened to be there for a purpose which is going to be the most tragic thing that ever happened in this world. . . . At 10:15, I left my apartment, and the story was out that this person (Oswald) was supposed to leave the jail at ten am. I

received a call from a young girl who wanted some money. I went to the Western Union, which was coincidental, and prior to that, I will admit (I'd read) a letter (that) was written to Caroline [Kennedy] which broke my heart. This letter was written to Caroline telling her how awfully sorry I was for her. And another situation [in another article], there was something about a trial. Don't ask me what took place, and that triggered me off that Sunday morning.

I accepted the call at 10:15 and went down to the Western Union and parked my car across the street and took off to transact my business. . . . At 11:17 I walked, I don't say it was premeditated, but never prior to Sunday morning, I never made up my mind what to do.

From 11:17 until later, I was guilty of a homicide. Which must be the most perfect conspiracy in the history of the world that a man was going to accept a call and came from his apartment down to the Western Union. If it had been three seconds later, I would have missed this particular person (Oswald). I guess God was against me. I left the Western Union, and it took about three and a half minutes to go to the bottom of the ramp. I didn't conspire or sneak in to do these things, I am telling you. If they had said, 'Jack, are you going down now?' that would make some conspiracy on me. I left the Western Union, and it was a fraction of a second until that tragic act happened.

Now, it seems all these circumstances were against me. I had a great emotional feeling for our beloved President and Mrs.

Kennedy, or I never would have been involved in this tragic crime, that was completely reverse from what my emotional feeling was.

As far as Joe Tonahill is concerned, he doesn't care what happens to me, nor does Phil Burleson, and I am not saying this just to make the headlines, I am not remembering this from rehearsal, I am speaking word-for-word, that I know what took place. And I am like the stupid idiot, that loved this country so much, and I felt so sorry for Mrs. Kennedy when she was standing on that plane with blood on her dress, and they were bringing the casket back with our beloved President, and now I am going to [go] down in history as the despicable person that ever lived.

If I am able to use this little oratory on you, as I am doing, if I have that capability, looking at you and telling this courtroom a slight fraction of a lie then I am a genius. Thank you.

How and why did Jack Ruby come to be involved in Lee Harvey Oswald's murder? The analysis of his movements that weekend indicate that he was someone who was at least on the periphery of what transpired on November 22nd and scrambling to be seen in different lights thereafter – as the grieving Jewish business owner and the 'news groupie' wanting to be around the centre of the action. What is clear is that his ties to organised crime, intelligence and gunrunning would emerge and make him a hot potato that nobody wanted to claim. But the implications by association remained with his links to the mob being used to state that the Oswald shooting had the markings of an 'organised crime' style hit.

Could it have been as simple as that or, like most things in the orbit we're exploring, be too obvious to be true? We will speculate on this in the remaining chapters of this book.

There is one more point to highlight the mystery, turbulence and conflict that surrounded Jack Ruby. On the night of November 24, 1963, Ruby's roommate, George Senator hosted a meeting of sorts at the apartment he shared with Ruby. Joining him were Ruby's attorney, Tom Howard and another attorney, Jim H. Martin.

Arriving soon after at the apartment were two reporters, Dallas local Jim Koethe and Bill Hunter. Both had worked with each other and they had been told about the meeting by local attorney, C.A. Droby. One report says that George Senator allowed Hunter and Koethe to attend so they could search among Ruby's possessions. What was discussed at the meeting, what was found and how long it went for is not known. However, it lingers as a source of much curiosity among researchers because of the five men that were present, three would die unexpectedly in the space of seventeen months:

- Bill Hunter was shot in a Long Beach Police station on April 23, 1964 (the very day that George Senator had testified for the WC in Washington D.C) by a police officer who, at first said he dropped his gun and it fired when he tried picking it up. But when that was disproven, he confessed to playing quick draw with his colleague, who was facing the other way.
- Jim Koethe, who had begun writing a book on the Kennedy assassination, was killed by a lethal blow, a karate chop, to his throat by an intruder in his apartment on September 21, 1964

- And Tom Howard who died suddenly from a heart attack aged 48 on March 27, 1964.

Senator and Martin would go on to live comparably much longer lives but neither would ever divulge what took place in Senator and Ruby's apartment in the evening of November 24, 1963. Hunter, Koethe and Howard's deaths remain an early yardstick for the mysterious deaths aspect to people associated with the events over the weekend of November 22nd. To prove just how small a world Dallas was at the time, Jim H. Martin owned a string of Six Flags motels and it was in one of his establishments just outside of Fort Wort that Lee Oswald's wife, Marina, her two daughters and his mother, Marguerite, were taken to and kept under Secret Service protection for three weeks.

If that wasn't coincidental enough, Martin, who was an associate of Jack Ruby and his defense team would become Marina Oswald's business manager by assisting with the negotiation of deals with LIFE magazine for photographs of her husband and an advance for an autobiography. Marina and her daughters would eventually move in with Martin and his family and the two allegedly struck up an affair.

PART FOUR

ANALYSIS & HYPOTHESIS

CHAPTER FOURTEEN

CONSOLIDATION

We have now come to the point where we have done the work of assembling the pieces of the puzzle in terms of the numerous narratives and threads of evidence regarding Lee Oswald's shooting and its aftermath. In doing so, we have uncovered some untruths that have escaped scrutiny ever since the crime. And consistently, clear questions have emerged. This is important of course because answers cannot be established without questions. What we are building to is establishing the most comprehensive scenario of what took place that culminated in Lee Harvey Oswald's death in Dallas Police custody. Before we do this, however, we will consolidate, in chronological order, the numerous aspects we have covered so far in this book for context:

Alleged assassin of President Kennedy and killer of Dallas police officer, J.D. Tippit, Lee Harvey Oswald, was held in police custody at Dallas City Hall from approximately 2:00pm Friday November 22 1963. Later that evening, he was charged for Tippit's slaying and allegedly charged for President Kennedy's shooting just after midnight Saturday November 23.

Later on, Saturday, at approximately 4:00pm, Police Chief Jesse Curry asked Captain of Homicide and Robbery, J.W. Fritz, if Oswald could be transferred to the County Jail that afternoon. Fritz said that he wouldn't be so Curry announced to the press at 6:00pm that the transfer would take place at 10:00am the following morning. The statement was made without a definitive decision being made as to whether the Sheriff's Department would conduct Oswald's transfer, per common practice, or that the DPD would in light of extenuating circumstances.

Local nightclub owner / mob affiliate / former gunrunner and FBI informant Jack Ruby charted a chaotic itinerary of movements between President Kennedy's assassination and up until the morning of November 24. For instance, Ruby was allegedly seen at Parkland Hospital just prior to the announcement of the president's death, at the Texas Theater when Lee Oswald was apprehended, busying himself with closing his nightclubs out of respect for Kennedy's passing and ensuring everyone he encountered knew as much and blending in with the chaos at Dallas City Hall when Oswald was detained there.

Early Sunday November 24 Captain Frazier was contacted by the Sheriff's Department and the FBI separately, alerting him to threats from a committee threatening to kill Oswald while he was being transferred to the County Jail. Despite these threats, Oswald's transfer was not brought forward to avoid any attack.

Having relieved Captain Frazier on the night shift and with Oswald's transfer approaching, Capt. Cecil E. Talbert took the initiative by delegating responsibility of security for the City Hall basement to Sergeant Patrick T. Dean and having patrol officers called into City Hall so they could be assigned at intersections between City Hall and the County Jail – despite not being told exactly what route the convoy would take by his superiors.

At the same point in time, an armoured truck was called upon by Captain Charles Batchelor from a local business, 'Armored Motor Car Services' to transport Oswald. Just prior to doing this, Chief Curry would be heard speaking on the phone with Sheriff Bill Decker about whether his DPD or Decker's Sheriff Dept. would transfer Oswald. The exchange ended with Curry saying, 'if you want us to, we will.'

Security of the basement started with reserve officers Brock, Worley and patrol officers Vaughn, Nelson and Patterson being designated entry points to stand guard at and not let anyone in other than police and credentialled media personnel. Approximately a dozen reserve officers, led by Reserve Capt. Arnett assisted Dean in searching across the basement car park. Members of the media witnessed the entirety of the search including a group of City Hall workers being asked to leave by the DPD. The search included parked cars, cavities around air conditioning and piping along the ceiling. The search did not include the sub-basement level which spanned under all of the old City Hall building and half of the newer Annex and included the locker room that had direct street access. The Annex building appears to have been presumed as being locked as it was kept that way on weekends. There is no evidence it was checked as part of the search – despite it too having a direct avenue of access to and from outside.

Two of the displaced City Hall workers, Harold Fuqua and Alfreadia Riggs, went to the sub-basement locker room to try and watch Oswald's transfer on the TV down there. Instead, they encountered a man they believed to be a DPD officer in the locker room telling them the transfer wouldn't be shown live so they may as well leave.

Acting Detective William J. 'Blackie' Harrison and Detective Louis Miller left the Third Floor of City Hall where they had just arrived for work at approximately 8:30am to walk to the Delux Diner, nearby on Commerce Street, to get a coffee. There, Harrison would spend time on the diner's payphone. Harrison and Miller both said it was because someone had called after them there telling them to come back. Both walked back but others in the Juvenile Bureau, which Harrison was working in, said the next time they would see him was when he was walking up from the sub-basement locker room just after 11am and claiming to have bought some cigars down there.

At 10:20am, Chief Curry told the assembled press exactly how the DPD would be moving Oswald from the Third Floor to the basement using the jail elevator to get the transfer underway. He also admitted that Oswald would have been transferred overnight because of 'threats' that had been phoned in but he did not want to go back on his word to the press about when Oswald would be transferred.

Between 10:45am and 11:00am, reserves Brock and Worley were reassigned from their posts in the eastern side of the basement car park to traffic duty on intersections along the convoy route. This left the stairway down from the Annex Building unguarded.

11:08am saw the arrival of two armoured cars from the 'Armored Motor Car Services' company. One (No. 46) was large enough to accommodate multiple people in its rear compartment and was intended as the one to provide the DPD for its transfer of Oswald. The other that accompanied it, was smaller and strictly there as a backup in case the larger had trouble starting – as it had earlier that morning. Both cars arrived at the Commerce Street ramp exit and No. 46 only stayed at the top of the ramp as the driver was concerned about hill starting it. When Capt. Fritz received word of an armoured truck being used to affect Oswald's transfer, he recommended against it as, if there was an attack of some kind, a large cumbersome vehicle like that would be limited in its maneuverability. Plans were changed to still use the armoured car in the convoy but as a decoy instead and have Oswald ride in an unmarked squad car behind it.

Jack Ruby walked into the Western Union office on Main Street, east on the same block as the City Hall complex at approximately 11:15am. He transferred $25.00 to Carousel Club dancer, Karen Carlin who was in Fort Worth. The receipt for the transaction was stamped by attending Western Union supervisor, Doyle Lane at 11:17am.

At 11:18am, Sgt. Rio S. Pierce, on orders from Chief Curry and Capt. Stevenson, acquired an unmarked squad car to drive it from the basement car park around to the Commerce Street ramp exit to be the lead car in the convoy. Lt. Pierce and Maxey were assigned by Sgt. Dean to ride with him. To achieve this, Pierce drove the car up to the Main Street ramp where Officer Vaughn ensured he was able to pull out.

Upwards of *forty six* members of the media stood amongst *forty six* members of the DPD in the area outside the jail office, the corridor to the basement car park ramp and along the foot of the Commerce Street ramp. That represents a ratio of one DPD officer to every member of the media present. To highlight the lack of regard for security even more, of members of the media who gave statements for the investigations and were asked if they were required to present identification / credentials to enter the basement that morning, there is a similar ratio between those who were and those who were not.

Lee Oswald, with his hands cuffed together and his right handcuffed to Detective Leavelle, was escorted by him, Detectives Graves (who was holding Oswald's left arm), and Montgomery as well as Lieutenant Swain and Captain Fritz from the Third Floor in the jail elevator to the jail office. After a momentary pause, Oswald was brought out to a cordon of DPD detectives, the end of which had four reporters and two reserve officers before the majority of media personnel and cameras.

Detective Doherty reversed an unmarked squad car to meet Oswald and his escorts. Oswald was within six feet of the car when a man, instantly identified by some as Jack Ruby, sprung out from behind a detective to Oswald's left and shot him in the abdomen from point blank range.

The scene erupted into chaos with up to a dozen surrounding DPD personnel swarming over Ruby to subdue and disarm him. In amongst this was one detective who covered Ruby's head with some kind of garment in the melee. Oswald was tended to by only Det. Leavelle, who was handcuffed to him, and Det. Combest who was standing to Leavelle's immediate right rear when the shooting occurred. Oswald was removed from the scene within seconds and taken to the jail office as was Ruby, a few moments later.

In the jail office, Ruby was lying face down on the floor while he was briefly searched. The jacket he was wearing was removed and he was then handcuffed and taken by a group of DPD personnel in the elevator to the Fifth Floor jail. Oswald showed signs of consciousness to some witnesses in the jail office but by the time the City Hall First Aid Attendant, Fred Bieberdorf arrived, he could not detect signs of life so he began administering manual CPR to revive Oswald. In the meantime, an ambulance had been called.

Four and a half minutes after the shooting, an O'Neal ambulance arrived and Oswald was brought back out from the jail office on a stretcher and loaded into it. Detectives Leavelle, Dhority, Graves and First Aid

Attendant Bieberdorf would also ride in the ambulance to Parkland Hospital. There, he would undergo surgery to save his life but Lee Oswald would be pronounced dead at 1:07pm.

Jack Ruby was detained up on the Fifth Floor jail from the time he was taken there in the minutes after the shooting until approximately 3:00pm. On the Fifth Floor he would be interviewed briefly by the local head of Secret Service, Forest V. Sorrels before a break of up to one hour where he was monitored by Detectives McMillon, Clardy and Archer and Sgt. Dean (Dean, only for part of that time). During the time that Sorrels was present and before FBI Agent C. Ray Hall arrived to question Ruby at 12:40pm, it was alleged by Dean that Jack Ruby admitted to how he entered the basement to shoot Oswald. But the detectives did not include this in their first reports about that day. However, Ruby would tell Captain Fritz, with Sorrels present, of how he entered the basement down the Main Street ramp.

Sgt. Dean spoke to Dallas Times Herald reporter, David Hughes, back down in the basement. Dean gave his account of what happened when the shooting took place including seeing Jack Ruby walk down the Main Street ramp. When the article came out, Dean vehemently denied saying that he saw Ruby come down the ramp.

Jack Ruby was witnessed in several states of mind. Some said he was calm, others said he was grief stricken and / or dazed and confused. When he was being restrained on the jail office floor, he called out 'I'm Jack

Ruby. You all know me.' After he was visited by his first lawyer, he started to refer to his motivations for shooting Oswald as being out of grief for President Kennedy.

On November 25, almost twenty-four hours to the minute after Oswald's shooting, Ruby was transferred to the Dallas County Jail by the DPD. The transfer was not announced to the press, although some were present to report and photograph it. The transfer was also not divulged to Chief Curry or Sheriff Decker yet it was carried out the same as Oswald's was apparently intended – with Ruby being brought down from the jail and through the basement office and into a waiting car at the ramp. The transfer went smoothly and without incident the whole way along.

On November 27, 1963, Jack Ruby was indicted for the charge of murdering Lee Oswald with malice. Before his trial would commence, he would have a new legal team led by Melvin Belli. On March 14, 1964, Ruby would be found guilty and sentenced to death. Ruby's legal team would ultimately be successful in having this conviction overturned and a new trial, to be held interstate, was scheduled. Before he could stand in his retrial, Jack Ruby died.

Key Figures

As we have examined the evidence regarding all facets from before, during and after Oswald's shooting, several figures have emerged who warrant further scrutiny. Some were clearly acting suspiciously and others had elements of their testimony that went completely against everybody else's. All are listed as well as the key reasons why. I am not alleging that these people were conspirators directly involved in some kind of master plot to murder Lee Oswald. At this point, they are just the largest grains left in the sieve. In the next chapter, I will refer to some in further context when laying out a comprehensive scenario of what took place across that weekend.

Detectives Don Ray Archer, Barnard S. Clardy, Thomas D. McMillon:
- Archer claimed to hear Ruby exclaim 'You son of a bitch' as he stepped forward to shoot Oswald when others much closer and all visual and audio records do not corroborate him doing so.
- Archer claimed Oswald yell 'Oh no' when being shot when, again, when others much closer and all visual and audio records do not corroborate him doing so.
- McMillon claimed to hear Jack Ruby yell 'You rat son of a bitch, you shot the president' as he lunged out to shoot Oswald. While McMillon was comparatively closer than Archer, none of the records of the shooting captured Ruby getting such a mouthful out while he shot Oswald.
- all were present on the Fifth Floor when, barely a few minutes after the shooting, Ruby allegedly spoke of his entering the basement down the Main Street ramp. Yet none of them reported Ruby making such a statement in their initial DPD reports.
- Archer and Clardy admitted to knowing Ruby prior to the shooting while McMillon would only ever admit to 'knowing of' and speaking with him a few times.

Lieutenant George Butler:
- according to reporter Thayer Waldo, Butler was the go-to member of the DPD for all updates regarding Oswald in custody across that weekend. Butler was calm at all times but in the moments prior to Oswald's shooting, Waldo noted that he was sweating profusely and his lips were trembling.
- Butler was Sgt. Dean's superior officer.

Detective Billy H. Combest:
- he testified, to the FBI, of hearing Ruby, whom he knew for several years, cursing before shooting Oswald. Combest also said that he yelled, 'Jack Ruby, you son of a bitch, don't do it' when no one else nor the visual and audio records corroborate this.

Reserve Sergeant Kenneth S. Croy:
- it is not clear where Croy was from the time he clocked on November 24 because his testimony is incredibly vague*. It amounts to his being in the assembly room mainly but fellow reserve Barney Merrell, who was also in the assembly room and verified as such by others, does not mention anyone, Croy or otherwise, helping him with assigning officers.
- Croy knew Jack Ruby for three years and was standing precisely in the location he emerged from when he lunged out to shoot Oswald.

---

*Croy's affidavit for the DPD's investigation is incredibly hard to read so there is a copy of it produced in the appendices for this book.

Police Chief Jesse Curry:
- prioritised the needs of the media over the protection of Lee Oswald by letting the press crowd City Hall over the weekend and announcing details of Oswald's transfer in advance.
- failed to act by bringing Oswald's transfer forward in response to threats being received on his life.
- did not delegate overall responsibility of the transfer to ensure all boxes were checked in the overall planning.
- was who instigated the transfer when he came into Fritz's office and told him that the cars for the convoy were in place in the basement, when they were not.

Detectives Wilbur Jay Cutchshaw, L.C. Graves, James K. Ramsey:
- all testified to seeing events take place in the minutes after Oswald's shooting that do not correlate with visual records or the testimony of anyone else:
    - Graves', unsigned and undated, DPD statement had him saying that Oswald was loaded straight into an ambulance immediately after the shooting.
    - Cutchshaw said that Oswald was brought into the jail office on a stretcher.
    - Ramsey said he helped get Ruby into the jail office and then came back out to see Oswald still laying on the ground where he had been shot. So, he said that he helped him onto a stretcher into the ambulance that had just arrived.

Sergeant Patrick T. Dean:

- knew Jack Ruby for twelve years.
- despite being responsible for overall security of the basement, the search he oversaw was confined to only the basement car park. It did not include the sub-basement level which could be accessed from Commerce Street (locker room).
- under his watch, the basement was not sealed the entire morning prior to the shooting. Aside from the sub-basement level per the last point, the basement would be further compromised when the two reserve officers guarding the eastern end of the car park under the Annex Building were reassigned within forty minutes prior to Oswald's shooting - on Dean's orders.
- while still in charge of security of the basement, in the minutes after the shooting, Dean sought out seeing Jack Ruby on the Third Floor before encountering him on the Fifth Floor. From there, the account of Ruby telling him and other DPD officers of how he entered down the Main Street ramp emerged.
- his own account of where he was at the time of the shooting contradicts another statement he made to a reporter of seeing Ruby walk down the Main Street map. If his stated position, the back of the armoured car, was to be believed, because of how low the ceiling was, Dean couldn't have possibly seen all the way up to the ramp to see Ruby enter.

Captain J.W. Fritz:
- was part of Oswald's escort from the Third Floor to the basement. As such, he was in the front position of the formation in the basement and left a gap of at least five feet between himself and Oswald resulting in a clear opening for Ruby to take his shot.

Acting Detective William J. 'Blackie' Harrison:
- knew Jack Ruby for eleven years.
- used the payphone at the Delux Diner whilst getting a coffee with Detective Miller after 8am on November 24.
- was not seen again by his colleagues until he was coming up from the locker room at around 11am having bought cigars from the vending machine down there.
- was who Ruby stepped around to shoot Oswald.

Tom Howard:
- was able to access the basement in the minutes prior to Oswald's shooting and was present to see him being brought out of the jail office elevator and hear being shot.
- quipped that he'd seen all he needed to as he walked back the way he came toward the Harwood Street entrance.
- presented himself as Ruby's attorney in the jail office after the shooting and was able to meet with him soon after.
- it was only after Ruby spoke with Howard that he (Ruby) stated that he entered the basement down the Main Street ramp.

Reserve William J. Newman:
- was stationed in the basement car park for the two hours leading up to Oswald's shooting
- gave incredibly garbled accounts of seeing a man wearing a suit but not wearing a hat coming down the ramp and climbing through the railing but flip-flopped on it taking place before or after the shooting.
- was tentatively identified by fellow reserve, Harold Holly as being the reserve officer who told him at Parkland that it was Jack Ruby who shot Oswald and he was able to do so by using a press pass to enter the basement. Newman vehemently denied this claim.

Jerry O'Leary, Ike Pappas & Maurice Carroll:
- their accounts of racing Oswald in the elevator down from the Third Floor down a flight of stairs could not have happened – regardless of the inconsistencies across their individual accounts – because the stairs did not lead directly down to the basement.
- at least Carroll and Pappas' movements in the basement could be traced in pre-shooting footage. Jerry O'Leary, on the other hand, was never visible despite his testifying that he was standing at the bottom of the Main Street ramp.

Patrolman Harry Olsen:
- met with Jack Ruby, who he was friends with for three years prior, in the early hours of November 23rd and discussed the assassination. The details of the conversation remained vague.

- o Ruby sought to not divulge what was discussed, even to his attorney during his trial.

George Senator:
- was Ruby's alibi at their apartment on the morning November 24 during which time Ruby took a call from Karen Carlin asking for money to be transferred to her.
- when it was announced that Oswald had been shot, Senator contacted attorney Jim Martin and told him that Jack Ruby would need an attorney. He allegedly made this call *before* it had been announced that Jack Ruby was the shooter.

FBI Agent Milt Newsom:
- notified the Sheriff about threats they (the FBI) had received from a committee against Oswald's life in the early hours of November 24 and instructed Sheriff Deputy McCoy to notify the DPD about them as well.
- took the statements of both key persons at the Sheriff and Police Department (McCoy and Frazier) related to the handling of the threats that night.
  - o Frazier confirmed that the references to his speaking of Oswald's transfer plans were false and McCoy's, much more detailed, report to Sheriff Decker completely contradicts the statement attributed to him by Newsom.
- Newsom's actions infer FBI overall control of the 'Threats' narrative and laying the blame for Oswald's shooting on the DPD.

CHAPTER FIFTEEN

SUSTAINED SPECULATION

In 'peeling the onion', layer by layer, by examining the evidence, we have substantiated, well and truly, that the shooting of Lee Harvey Oswald was not the spur of the moment, opportunistic crime of another lone nut. It was a planned event that was orchestrated by design and opportunity. Using what we have gathered and organised across the previous chapters, I will now propose how Oswald's shooting most likely took place. Hypothesising is a vital piece of any investigation. It is its own process to corroborate and consolidate as much data as reasonably as possible and explore all possible meanings and outcomes with it. By doing so, new or previously discarded evidence may come into relevance.

Along the way we have uncovered several facets to the case:
- all of Dallas City Hall's Annex Building, basement and sub-basement was not actually sealed, searched and secured,
- the potential for the 'committee' threats to Oswald's life being a fabrication that Police Chief Curry and the DPD failed to respond promptly to anyway,
- how few members of the media were asked to provide their credentials to enter the basement on November 24,
- the even ratio of DPD to media personnel at the scene,

- and that Ruby did not enter the basement down the Main Street ramp.

It must be acknowledged that while there were some one hundred people across the basement, from inside the jail office and out to the car park and along the ramps, not all witness statements have been referred to in this book. This is because many did not see the shooting nor anything or anyone that seemed out of place. And we gathered from the witnesses that were within the immediate vicinity of Oswald's shooting how little they saw, or told they saw.

So, to quote Kevin Costner's Jim Garrison in 'JFK'… "Let's just for a moment speculate, shall we?"

November 22nd

I will concede that my focus has been mostly zeroed in on Oswald's slaying on November 24 – from its lead up, to its occurrence and aftermath. But I am confident with the contention that there were clear linkages between President Kennedy's death and that of Lee Oswald.

Firstly, I believe that Oswald was marked for death the moment President Kennedy's limousine had sped out of Dealey Plaza to Parkland Hospital. The plotters who had orchestrated the assassination would have made it part of their plans for that day. And all plans would have had contingencies.

Some have written that perhaps Oswald, regardless of how he left Dealey Plaza, was to be flown out of the country by the plotters and that Officer Tippit was his ride to Red Bird Airport where the escape flight was alleged to depart from. But why go to so much trouble to accommodate their scapegoat when so much work had been done to incriminate him before the fact? If Oswald was somehow spirited out of the country, apart from his wife and two daughters, what was their guarantee that he would not divulge how much he knew? Before November 22nd, Lee Oswald's legend had well and truly been established by his pro and anti-Castro provocateur work, his intelligence background and the numerous accounts of his being impersonated. All said, his framing for President Kennedy's murder was covered on a variety of angles, so why bother keeping him alive?

If Lee Oswald was marked for death from the outset, when and how was it to take place? As conveyed in an earlier chapter, I think that it was not intended that Oswald be at the top of the steps of the Book Depository's main entrance along with other building employees when the motorcade passed. If he was inside as intended, or somehow guided or instructed to be by a benefactor, then it would have been very easy for the first Dallas police officer on the scene, in this case Marrion Baker, to shoot and kill Oswald with no witnesses around. From there, a small incriminating firearm could be planted on him and it just be said that he was fleeing. But Oswald was on the steps and this very well could be why Officer Baker can be seen in cameraman, Dave Wiegman's footage, veering suddenly to the right as he is running to the Book Depository entrance because shooting one of many spectators for no apparent reason would simply not wash.

And Bart Kamp's 'Prayer Man – More Than a Fuzzy Picture' demonstrates that TSBD superintendent, Roy Truly and Baker likely entered the building separately according to witness statements.[1]

With Oswald surviving the initial minutes after the assassination, the plotters would have to of reverted to a backup plan – the question being when and what was it? Could someone have reached Oswald in the TSBD and given him instructions? It's very possible and would have been something along the lines of 'we're blown or something's happened and you're not safe, you need to get to the rendezvous point etc..' or words to this effect. This would have seen Oswald either walk down through Dealey Plaza and get into the station wagon or leave to take public transport. Compellingly and relevant to this facet is the work of, researcher John Armstrong, that posits that two plain clothed policemen stormed the same bus that Oswald was alleged to have boarded. Bus passenger Mary Bledsoe corroborated this in her WC testimony as well.[3] Only they did so after the man thought to be Oswald, alighted it. If this is true, why did two members of the DPD pick that bus, that was stuck in traffic, to search? Who were they looking for? Apparently, they did not say as they too quickly left the bus without saying a word. No record of this event exists in DPD records either.

I personally believe that the weight of evidence (independent witness corroboration including the credibility of Roger Craig) makes it more likely that Oswald left Dealey Plaza in the station wagon and taken directly to the Texas Theater. So, if that was the case, why? An obvious answer is because the plotters would have needed time to build another cause to incriminate him further to justify his being killed.

Some researchers allege that Officer Tippit, who was friends with Jack Ruby, had a role that day in the assassination. If so, as a designated driver for anyone involved in the shooting in Dealey Plaza seems plausible. However, his role could have easily changed to that of the sacrificial lamb to be killed by someone doubling for Oswald. Then it was a matter of leading a trail to the Texas Theater, where the real Oswald had been designated and had most likely been there since around the same time that Tippit was shot.

At the Texas Theater, Lee Oswald was likely waiting to be contacted by someone about what was going on and / or what to do next. As long as he stayed there, the shooting of Officer Tippit could be carried out and police could be led there to apprehend him. Was the theater where the next attempt to kill Oswald would be made? If so, it could have been by one of the police subduing him during the scuffle when apprehending him. But Oswald was heard by most in the theater yelling 'I am not resisting arrest!' Did he sense what could have happened therefore yelled out what he did to nullify any cause for him to be killed? If so, through his own wits, just like by standing with other witnesses at the time of Kennedy's shooting, he evaded another attempt on his life.

In any event, Oswald was arrested and he was taken into police custody. By all accounts, from that point on Oswald kept his calm and was relatively composed, particularly when in public view, but he must have seen from early on that he had been or was being set up. Among the few times he expressed frustration at his situation was when he was being placed in lineups with people that did not look like him, when presented with a photograph of himself that he thought was doctored depicting him holding a rifle and communist literature and when reporter Bill Mercer told him he had been charged with President Kennedy's murder. Oswald was also alleged to have pleaded for Ruth Paine to be 'left out of all of this' as a result of Roger Craig identifying him as the man who got into a station wagon (which is the same type of car that Paine owned and drove). Oswald allegedly then lamented that 'now everyone will know who I am...'

Jack Ruby and President Kennedy's Assassination

What was Ruby's involvement in President Kennedy's assassination? According to Julia Ann Mercer's testimony, he transported a man and his rifle to the scene of the crime earlier that same day. And there was the implication of his foreknowledge about the shooting when he invited a friend to 'watch the fireworks'. This last point relies on the testimony of a convicted felon who was operating as an informant at the time. And conceptually, Ruby could have innocently been referring to the festivities of the motorcade itself as it drove through the city of Dallas.

On the face of it, Jack Ruby was a local mob connected night club owner with many cops for friends who was an FBI informant and went way back with gunrunning into Cuba. This puts him in the same orbit as a great many people and factions suspected as being involved in the president's removal. The alleged sightings of him accommodating another person that is strongly alleged to have been involved in the Kennedy assassination, David Ferrie, at his nightclub in the weeks prior to November 22nd is compelling. Also, equally compelling, are reports of Lee

Oswald meeting Jack Ruby at the Carousel Club within weeks of the assassination.[2]

Foundations of the Shooting

We have touched on the motive to kill Lee Oswald but to re-emphasise the point, the stakes were incredibly high to, not only eliminate him before he could take relative haven in maximum security conditions at the County Jail but do so in such a way that the plotters would evade detection. If it was not successful or those behind Oswald's killing were detected and brought to justice, the connections to those responsible for President Kennedy's assassination would been vulnerable to being exposed.

Is it such a fait accompli that Oswald and Kennedy's murders were linked? I am sure they were when the alternatives are weighed up – that Oswald's elimination was an isolated event. The point to consider here is what would the motive be for anyone within the DPD to take justice into their own hands and let Oswald be killed? And do so in a way that would be of the highest embarrassment to the entire organisation. Vengeance for their colleague, J.D. Tippit's murder perhaps? This is a stretch because, shocking as it was, Tippit was not the first, nor would he be the last, Dallas police officer to be killed in the line of duty. And Texas law at the time placed the sentence of execution for anyone found guilty of premeditated murder. No, it would have been smarter and easier to let the system sentence Oswald accordingly – provided they felt there was enough evidence to convict. In this instance, the DPD had so much more to lose than gain so the notion of their orchestrating Oswald's shooting of their own volition can be excluded.

So, what were the depths of the DPD's culpability in Lee Oswald's shooting? From a planning perspective, I think it was very narrow. After all, the principles of compartmentalisation dictate that the less people know about something, i.e. a plan and a clear objective in this case, the higher the chance is of keeping it contained therefore succeeding.

To begin with, by having in custody the man who was alleged to have killed one of their own and committed the crime of the century, that commanded the focus of the entire world, what did the DPD do? They left the door wide open for local, interstate and foreign members of the press to pack their corridors at City Hall – in the name of transparency. With this came an environment of barely controlled chaos. Lee Oswald was led through the throngs of people by police between interrogations, lineups, to and from stints in his jail cell and even a press conference environment. It is a wonder that someone didn't attack him earlier that weekend. Or was someone, as in Jack Ruby, meant to but did not pull it off?

With this factored in, the plotters had the circumstances of when to silence Oswald decided for them – in view of the media and therefore publicly. Killing Oswald behind closed doors would also never have washed because he always presented as being calm and composed. Therefore, trying to justify killing him, say, in the name of self-defense against some kind of 'frenzy' on his part would never have been tenable. And the DPD would never have been able to live it down. Adding to the planning was the fact that the clock was ticking because, as mentioned earlier in this book, Oswald technically could have been transferred to the County Jail as early as the evening of Friday November 22nd.

The only publicly stated, reason he hadn't been was because Capt. Fritz wanted Oswald at City Hall for the interrogations and witness lineups he felt he needed for his investigation. Does this point make Fritz an accessory to the plot? Perhaps, although I have not found any basis for that contention. I think it most likely that Fritz knew something was going to happen and that's why he left so much space between him and Oswald in the basement.

Jumping back, the next thing that ought to have caused Oswald to be abruptly moved to the County Jail were the alleged threats in the early hours of November 24. But, as also examined earlier in this book, the one person who could have made that call was **Chief Jesse Curry**. And we know that, at first, he could not be reached by phone at his home to be told of the threat and therefore make a decision.

Does this make Curry a willing participant of the plot? We will never know for sure but I would say so – this and the fact that he was so forthcoming about the specifics of the transfer plans with the media. This is not to say that Curry would have known all of the details of the planning. I don't think that was the case. Just as long as he stayed so true to form and character in terms of his lack of leadership and delegation & adoration for the media, that would have been more than enough. All he needed to be told was 'something is going to happen to Oswald before he gets to the County Jail. It's for the sake of national security... keep him at City Hall for as long as possible... we'll tell you when we're ready...' And as long as no members of the DPD would get hurt and stay protected, he would have gone along with it.

Setting the Scene

With clear knowledge of when Oswald's transfer would take place (courtesy of Chief Curry), ensuring control over where the assault on Oswald would take place would be another priority. Given that all the TV cameras had moved down to the basement earlier that morning, it would have been made clear that this would be where the shooting would need to take place. Enter **Sgt. Patrick T. Dean.**

Whether Dean volunteered or was handed responsibility of security of the basement, I think he was an insider on the plot so he knew to what outcome he was operating to. And even if he had not been given responsibility of security of the basement, he would have been resourceful and respected enough to pull the strings he needed to that morning. But he was delegated overall responsibility so firstly, he coordinated a search of the basement that we can conclude was nothing more than a PR exercise to convey that the DPD was carrying out security measures. We know that the search did not extend beyond the immediate vicinity of the basement car park and as such, the Annex Building and sub-basement levels were not searched or sealed.

Dean also knew what he was doing when he assigned two lowly reserve officers, not regular officers, Worley and Brock, to stand guard at the eastern end of the car park underneath the Annex Building. He did so because the intent was to always have them reassigned from there prior to when Oswald was brought out. Doing so would not stir any waves because they were just volunteering reserves, essentially auxiliaries that had no accountability. And the City Hall workers were ordered to leave so as to ensure that they were not around to see someone enter the basement from the stairway and testify how they could have done so. It is remarkable that there was not one line uttered by anyone for any of the investigations justifying why utility workers, some of whom were long-term employed, were deemed such a risk to security that they were told to leave – yet the media was allowed to stream in and largely do so unchecked.

Setting the Shooter

With Dean keeping control of where the shooting was to take place, someone would have needed to have been keeping in contact with Jack Ruby – be it directly with him or through a benefactor. **Acting Detective William J. 'Blackie' Harrison**, who until recently, was a patrolman in the Patrol Division that Dean was sergeant for, made it his priority to be away from his desk and colleagues that morning and instead be near payphones at the Delux Diner and down in the locker room. I am sure that Harrison was the man that porters Harold Fuqua and Alfreadia Riggs encountered down there and who told them to leave. It's reasonable to conclude that both men may have not wished to identify who the person in the locker room actually was nor state the degree of the warning from them for the fear of theirs and their family's safety. Regardless, Blackie Harrison would have been using the payphones at the diner and the locker room to either give updates and / or directions to Ruby or a handler of his. The phones in the locker room would have served to also make and take calls across City Hall. What's to say Sgt. Dean didn't use the phone in the First Aid office that Fred Bieberdorf was vacated from to give and receive updates to Harrison over in the locker room or any other related reason. Harrison would have likely been acting as the conduit between Ruby, the basement and the movements of the Third Floor in terms of when things were looking like wrapping up with Oswald. And it's likely he only came up to the basement when he knew Jack Ruby was on his way to the vicinity of the City Hall.

Jack Ruby spent the morning of November 24 at his apartment. According to his roommate, **George Senator,** Ruby had risen from bed just after 9am. Senator was doing washing that morning so he was in and out of the apartment. He would testify to Ruby eating scrambled eggs for breakfast, watching television and reading through a newspaper. At around quarter past ten, Ruby received a call from his employee, Karen Carlin / Little Lynn asking for $25.00. This was allegedly because of the loss of earnings from Ruby closing his clubs that weekend. Because Senator was doing his laundry, he was in and out of the apartment and might not have known of any other calls that Ruby might have received – perhaps from Blackie Harrison telling him that Oswald was going to be transferred soon and to get moving. In any event, Senator would notice Ruby pacing around the apartment after he had gotten dressed and ready to go into Dallas to transfer Little Lynn her money. Was Ruby pacing out of anxiousness because of the other objective he now had to complete – shooting Lee Oswald at City Hall. Still with Senator's WC testimony, he said that Ruby left saying he was taking his dog 'Sheba' to the club but did not say when he would be coming back.

The topic of Karen Carlin / Little Lynn's call to Ruby that compelled him to go to the Western Union (which happened to be on the same block as the City Hall complex) remains contentious. The need for money was a prevailing theme for her that weekend so Carlin and her husband, Bruce, arranged to meet Ruby at the Carousel Club on the Saturday so he could give her some money. According to Carlin's testimony to the WC, Ruby didn't show up to the meeting so when she reached him by phone, he asked her to call him back the next day to tell him how much she needed. When Carlin did, it was Ruby who suggested he get it to her by transferring it through Western Union. By his own design, Ruby now had his reason for being in the vicinity of City Hall. From this point, it is not a stretch to speculate that even if Carlin hadn't called, he still would have gone to the Western Union to transfer the money. Then he could have just called Harrison at City Hall and updated him of his intended movements as a heads up. By transferring money, having his dog in the car etc... Ruby laid the foundations for his shooting Oswald as a spontaneous act.

How George Senator may fit into the scheme of things is interesting. Is his testimony that Ruby was in bed before 9am on November 24 reliable? I think so considering that the sightings of Ruby outside City Hall at the same time rely on people that did not know him personally. There are some inconsistencies in the men in the news truck, Richey, Walker and Smith's statements which are likely indicative of vague recollections being used to implicate Ruby as a stalker of Oswald. One description had Ruby as though he was wearing clothes that were crumpled as if he slept in them. By all reports, Ruby was always meticulous with his appearance. And Ruby's suit certainly didn't look crumpled when he shot Oswald later that morning. Could the man the TV truck workers saw have been on hand to impersonate Ruby or was it just someone who generally resembled him. And the same regarding the preacher who thought he shared an elevator with Ruby that morning at City Hall too? I think the latter is most likely but am not tethered to this notion when we consider how much Oswald was impersonated.

Regardless, George Senator's call to Jim Martin telling him that Ruby would need an attorney for shooting Oswald *before* it had been announced that Ruby was the shooter is compelling and implies foreknowledge on his part - at the very least. If he knew what Ruby was about to do, did he try to stop him? He never testified to this and understandably so as it would've made him culpable and infer premeditation on Ruby's part. Presuming that he didn't try to stop him, did Senator have some kind of inside knowledge about Ruby's objective? Either from Ruby himself or from the plotters to ensure Ruby wouldn't renege on going through with it. Either way, his call to Martin could have been what triggered Tom Howard, a friend of both Senator and Martin, to present at the jail, before or after the shooting, as Ruby's attorney.

Ruby parked his car on Main Street across the road from the Western Union office. In it, he left his dog, identification and hundreds of dollars of bills in it. I think this was done to signify the lack of premeditation for what he was about to do. As is clear in the Google Maps view of Main Street, it is evident that windows of the Annex Building provide a view directly towards where the Western Union was. This was also the case in 1963. I think one of the plotters stood lookout at one of these windows for Ruby. They would have seen him enter then exit the Western Union office and this would have triggered the start of Oswald's transfer. Some have concluded the opposite – that Ruby was signaled by a person from a window up on the Annex Building to make his way to the basement. I think this was too complex – it's perfectly plausible to consider that Ruby's arrival at the Western Union is what got Oswald's transfer in motion. And who was it that entered room 317 and asked Fritz if Oswald was ready to be transferred? Chief Curry. I think he did and he did so having been told by someone who had been serving as the lookout over in the Annex Building.

The Shooting

Ruby transferring money was something he would do regularly at the Western Union. To this, the supervisor tending to him that morning, Doyle Lane, claimed to recognise him as a repeat customer. As was the process, Lane noted the time of the transfer on a receipt – which for Ruby on November 24 was 11:17am. When he left the Western Union, Ruby walked along Main Street but only as far as the alleyway. From there, he went down to the outer door that Fuqua and Riggs had exited out of, and locked behind them, a bit earlier. He was likely able to open it and enter because Dean, or someone acting on his orders, would have made sure it was unlocked. On this point, conceivably it's very possible that Patrick Dean may not have known Ruby was the shooter because his (Dean's) sole purpose could have just been to have the scene ready. I say this because in the interview he was filmed giving in the basement just after the ambulance had taken Oswald to the hospital, Dean looks and sounds rattled as he's talking to reporters. This is down to interpretation, of course.

Once inside the Annex Building, Ruby would have used the fire escape stairway to access the service elevator and come out of it on the First Floor. From there, all he needed to do was walk to the stairwell and down one flight to the basement door, which did not lock as it was an emergency exit. From there, Ruby could have simply walked across the car park himself. It's likely, however, that he was met by someone like **Reserve Sergeant Kenneth Croy**, who was dressed in police uniform. Either way, it was then just a case of having to climb through the ramp railing and get into position in front of Croy and behind Blackie Harrison. See the below diagram charting Ruby's route from the Western Union to his final position in the basement:

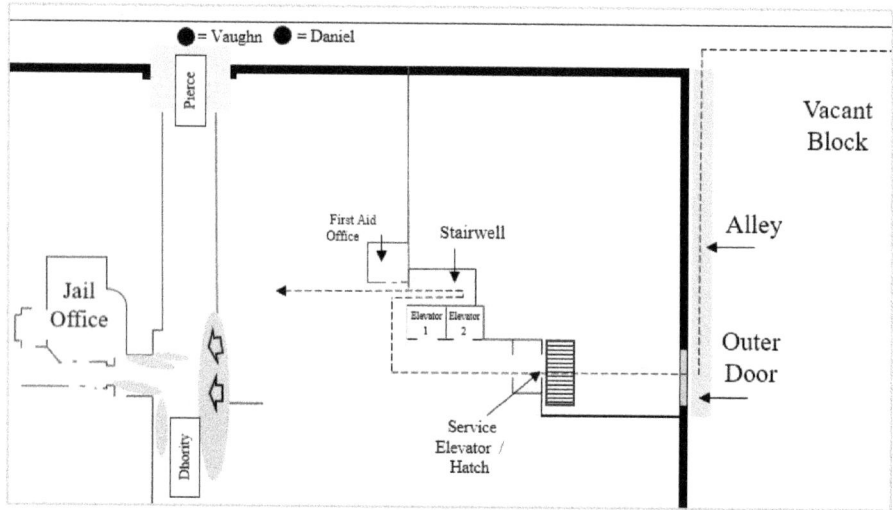

Copyright Paul Abbott

Four minutes for Ruby to walk from the Western Union to that point without any obstacle is incredibly plausible. But what if there was some kind of delay with Ruby on his path? I don't see that there could have been one because all doors were literally left open for him. Conceptually, he could have been stopped on Main Street by someone he knew or recognised by a member of the press in the basement. The latter possibility is probably why Kenneth Croy would have escorted him across the basement car park. He may have even met him at the outer door.

Shielded by Harrison, I think Ruby was in a good enough position to judge when to leap out and take his shot at Oswald. Much has been made of the two car horns sounding as if they were some kind of signal to him. I don't think this was the case. The timing makes it a compelling notion but I think the crowd of both DPD and media personnel out of position, was just that thick to necessitate Dhority needing to use the horn to make sure no one was in his way while reversing into position. If they were a signal for the shooting, Dhority would have had to have been in on the plot and alternatively, at least one could have been to signify Ruby was in position. It's also been speculated that the horns were to signal Capt. Fritz that Ruby was in place. This is more likely however, because when he walked out from the jail office, Fritz surveyed the scene including where Ruby was. Was this to see for himself that he was in place?

Regardless, Ruby simply had to aim at Oswald's abdomen at near point-blank range and fire. The entire plan did not hinge on how good a shot Ruby was. It hinged on how the DPD responded to Oswald being wounded. And what did we conclude on that front? That they were incredibly slow and clumsy with their response. To begin with, Oswald was not put straight into any vehicle and rushed to hospital as he ought to have been. He was moved back to the jail office and away from the eyes and cameras of the media. Once in there it is anybody's guess as to what might have happened to Oswald before First Aider, Fred Bieberdorf could arrive.. or was allowed to arrive. Recall Bieberdorf let slip in 2007 that Oswald was shot in the jail office. Accounts from the DPD present are muddled so it is anybody's guess. Rough treatment could have been given to Oswald including applying chest compressions to exacerbate internal wounds before Bieberdorf arrived. And what's to say that someone didn't strong-arm Bieberdorf into doing the same as well, which surely must have been counter to his medical training up to that point. The ambulance would arrive a few minutes later but once Oswald was loaded into the back, its departure out of the basement up the Commerce Street ramp was delayed by the armoured truck failing to move. This delay, forty seconds, was never accounted for or attributed to anyone or any valid reason yet is clear to see in raw post-shooting footage. Could this have just been bad luck for Oswald i.e. the truck had trouble starting again or had something else happened to cause the delay? Such as a person or persons blocking its path?

With a wound such as the one that Oswald had suffered, every second he was without proper treatment was critical. But he would have to wait twenty-three minutes from when he was shot until he started receiving adequate treatment. Incompetence certainly played a large part in the delay of treating Oswald but key decisions to not rush him to hospital straightaway and the potential mistreatment and exacerbation of his wounds contributed toward the outcome of the plot.

While only two detectives tended to Oswald, including Leavelle who had no choice on account of his being handcuffed to him, approximately a dozen DPD personnel swarmed over Jack Ruby. This included Louis Miller, who stepped forward and, as clearly visible in slowed down footage, covered Ruby's head with a garment – to conceal his identity.

Some DPD testified to Ruby being stunned by all of the attention when he was being subdued. In the jail office, Don Ray Archer said he heard Ruby say, 'You all know me. I'm Jack Ruby.' Could it be presumed that as the shooter, Ruby may not have been expecting such a violent and heavy-handed response? I would say this is most likely. Clearly in Davidson's footage, Ruby had his jacket removed (which nobody testified to), then handcuffed and taken to the Fifth Floor jail.

Patrick Dean made it a priority to get to Ruby. I think this was purely so he could be present to 'hear Ruby admit how he entered the basement down the Main Street ramp' and therefore testify as much. But we know that Ruby almost certainly did not say any such thing. Why? Because he did not enter that way therefore not be able to be so specific and he was protecting his confederates in the DPD. Instead, he stayed close-lipped on the matter by providing no comment until after his visit from Tom Howard.

Dean, however, apparently returned to the basement in time to quiz the officers at the entrances (those he did not have moved) and give an interview to a journalist who wasn't present at the shooting, David Hughes. If this did take place, I think Dean used the opportunity to continue with the story of Ruby admitting coming down the Main Street ramp to start covering his tracks. That's if he spoke with Hughes at all. Given the date of Hughes' statement to the DPD, his piece could have even been an exercise devised a couple of weeks after the fact when the heat on Dean was building. And Dean would pile on the deflections in the coming months. In a report to Chief Curry in February 1964, he added the detail that Ruby also said up on the Fifth Floor, along with his declarations of how he entered the basement, that he first got the idea to shoot Oswald when he saw a sarcastic look on his face during the press conference earlier that weekend.

Billy Grammer's story of his 'friend' Jack Ruby ringing the DPD the night before the shooting to warn of an attack on Oswald would have been a neat bow on the growing narrative of premeditation on Ruby's part. If this was the case, perhaps he is another example of someone perhaps playing a role within the plot without knowing the full picture.

What I have presented is perhaps the most straightforward hypothesis of how Jack Ruby came to shoot Lee Oswald and who was involved in the DPD. In this scenario, it is an incredibly contained conspiracy that relied on two central characters, Patrick Dean and Blackie Harrison as its point men. Louis Miller could have been more of a peripheral player as it is possible that he was just with Harrison at the Delux Diner to provide an alibi for something he didn't know anything about and to just be ready to cloak the man who shot Oswald.

Chief Curry would have known something was going to happen but did not need to have any of the details. And I think Fritz's part was as much as leaving space for Oswald to be shot in the basement. Remember, **Lieutenant George Butler**, an experienced member of the DPD, and Sgt. Dean's former superior, was showing indications of being incredibly tense and nervous in the moments prior to Oswald emerging. Did he have some foreknowledge? It is hard to be sure as there is nothing else, other than his demeanour, to suspect him with. Reporter Seth Kantor interviewed Butler in the late 70's for his book 'The Ruby Cover-up'.[3] In it, he said that Butler told him he was nervous at the time Waldo indicated. However, he said it was because he knew security that morning was not adequate enough. That's well and good to say years after the fact but it is not clear in any of the records that Butler sought to improve the security of the basement at the time.

Mastermind

I contend that this was the DPD's **Captain of Personnel, William R. Westbrook**. This is a name that has hardly been mentioned in this book and this is because Westbrook had no visible part in Oswald's transfer that day. It is not even known if he was on duty either. Essentially the DPD's head of 'HR', Westbrook technically did not need to have had anything to do with it either. But as researcher, John Armstrong deftly posits, this did not stop Westbrook from being involved in events out in the field immediately after President Kennedy's assassination and Lee Oswald's apprehension. Recall that I referred to two police officers who boarded the bus that Oswald was alleged to have just left? Researcher John Armstrong makes a very good case for the two DPD officers as being Capt. Westbrook... and Reserve Sergeant Kenneth Croy.

At this point, I will happily refer anyone to John Armstrong's website, harveyandlee.net for his incredibly in-depth account of Westbrook and Croy's movements that day, so I will just summarise them here. Essentially, despite having no official business of being a part of the DPD's response to the shooting in Dealey Plaza, Westbrook and Croy are claimed to have been on their own mission that day that involved:
- boarding and searching the bus that Oswald, or a double, just got off from,
- guiding Officer Tippit to Tenth & Patton,
- being, at least, present there by sitting in an unmarked squad car that was parked back in the driveway that Tippit had stopped in front of,
- Croy remaining at the scene and disguising his uniform while Westbrook laid a jacket that was supposedly Lee Oswald's in a car park between where Tippit was shot and the Texas Theater,
- a wallet including identification of Oswald being planted at the Tippit murder scene,
- and the car that Oswald was taken away from the theater in was the car that Westbrook had been driving.

Neither could give credible accounts of their movements that afternoon. Croy told the WC that he was sitting in his car in the basement of City Hall at the time of the president's shooting and that he got caught in congestion when he was trying to get to the scene to assist. Whereas Westbrook said he *walked* to Dealey Plaza from City Hall, a twelve block journey, yet nobody witnessed him doing so nor did he have any business going there in the first place. Giving up because of the congestion, Croy said that he decided to have lunch with his estranged wife. And that he happened to be nearby in his own car when he heard word of Tippit's shooting so he drove there. This despite the exact location of Tippit's shooting not being broadcast. John Armstrong's theory regarding Westbrook and Croy is incredibly compelling when we consider the circumstances of Oswald's shooting.

Perhaps Westbrook and Croy's mission commenced when Oswald needed to be set up and killed after leaving the Book Depository. When that failed, both had to see the job through with another plot based at City Hall. William Westbrook as the plot's mastermind fits. As the head of personnel for the DPD, he would have known of every officer (reserve and regular) on the force and been privy to how they conducted themselves and perhaps most importantly, who had worked with whom. Potentially enough so to either build the plot around Jack Ruby by involving officers that were friends or acquainted with him. Who knows when we consider the history between Dean, Harrison and Miller. Dean had been Harrison's sergeant in the Patrol Division and Harrison and Miller had both just been transferred to the Juvenile Bureau, which George Butler was the Lieutenant of. Westbrook's position to literally know who and which strings to pull really does make him the most likely 'Operations Manager' behind the November 24 shooting. Even more so when we recall that Captain Westbrook was part of the DPD's investigation into Lee Oswald's shooting therefore in a perfect position to ensure it did not open any of the 'wrong doors.'*

We can use the benefit of time to track Westbrook's fate after the events of Dallas in 1963 which may give an indication of his involvement then. He assisted with the DPD investigation and, most relevantly, told the HSCA in 1978 that nobody checked if the outer door on the eastern side of the Annex Building was locked on the morning of November 24.[4] Westbrook left the DPD in 1966 to take up a job with the Office for Public Safety in Vietnam. The 'OPS' was alleged to have direct links to the CIA. Could such a posting have been recognition for his contribution over the weekend of November 22nd 1963?

Detecting Guilt and Innocence

While it is true that no one other than Jack Ruby was held to account for Lee Oswald's murder, elements within the DPD and Warren Commission had their suspicions. In later years, the HSCA would pick the thread back up to a degree. From the DPD point of view, those listed below were given lie detector tests:

- Roy Vaughn: as where he was posted was where Ruby was alleged to have entered,
- Blackie Harrison: because, according to DPD investigator Jack Revill, Harrison looked over his left shoulder when Ruby was standing to the left of his shoulder,[5]

---

*Allen Dulles arguably held a similar role as part of the Warren Commission. By far the most active member of the panel, it too is not too much of a stretch to consider that he was in such a position to steer the WC from getting too close to focusing on incriminating evidence and interviewing compelling witnesses.

- and Napoleon Daniels: was standing near to Vaughn but gave a conflicting account to him.
  o Daniels did not pass the test and it was not followed up on.

Harrison took tranquilisers to get through his, in early December '63, and apparently after a couple of attempts he was deemed as telling the truth when he said that he did not see Jack Ruby enter the basement, that he only recognised him at the time of the shooting and he had not seen him anywhere in the basement before the shooting.

Patrick Dean's testimony to the Warren Commission in April '64 was fraught with clear lies and attempts at deflection – we have already referred to these regarding Sorrels with Ruby and the basement stairwell. So much so that WC counsel, Burt Griffin approached him during a break and told him, off the record, as much. Griffin recounted the conversation to his superior, General Counsel J. Lee Rankin, in a memo a few days later. The below is an excerpt of it as laid out in Griffin's 2023 book, 'JFK, Oswald and Ruby: Politics, Prejudice and Truth':[6]

'... I told him that in the two or three hours that he and I had been talking I found him to be a likeable and personable individual, and that I believed he was a capable and honest police officer. I tried to approach him on a basis of respect and friendship... I then stressed that this investigation... was of extreme importance to the National Security and that ... if there was some way that he could be induced to come forward with a more forthright statement without injuring himself, the Commission

would probably be willing to explore a means to afford him the protection that was necessary... I pointed out to him that if he had any such inclination to change his story it would probably be best that he not approach us directly but that he secure an attorney so the problem that he faced could be worked out without committing himself to anything on the record.

... I told him what I was particularly concerned with what Ruby told him about how he got into the basement. I explained that although he might not see the significance of that inquiry, he would have to accept my statement that... it was extremely important to the national security to learn how Ruby entered the basement.'

After Dean concluded his testimony that day, two chains of events would take place that would become the perfect symbol of the larger powers at the time.

Dean's response to Griffin was to lodge a complaint with DA Henry Wade. This triggered a chain of events that would see Burt Griffin recalled to Washington D.C. and not be allowed to return to Dallas when other members of counsel returned for further hearings. Griffin, despite his best efforts to assuage his superiors that he was not heavy-handed with Dean, had clearly cottoned on to how guilty he looked and was wandering out of bounds with his thinking and approach to him.

Also, after that WC testimony, Dean requested Chief Curry that he be allowed to sit a lie detector test. This was granted and Dean would be allowed to take the test and write his own questions. The Warren Commission was never made aware of the fact that Dean sat a lie detector test therefore been given the results of, or at least the list of questions he had been asked. By the time the HSCA had Dean in their sights for its investigation, no record of his lie detector test in 1964 could be found.

The final word on this was from Dean himself when he admitted to an investigator for the HSCA in 1978, long after he left the DPD, that, he actually failed the lie detector test. He ignored all correspondence from the HSCA from then on but was still not subpoenaed to testify for them.

Herein lies an agonising and frustrating aspect of the JFK assassination. Someone who was clearly suspect was, both at the time and more so in later years, had come so close to being exposed only to have higher powers step in and intervene.

Officer Roy Vaughn sat for his lie detector test in the weeks after the Oswald shooting like Harrison. But unlike him and Dean, Vaughn did not write his own questions, he only needed to answer the questions once and without the use of drugs to calm himself. The results for Vaughn showed that he had answered all questions truthfully indicating that he did not let Jack Ruby enter down the ramp or at least see or talk with him on November 24. This appeared to be the end of the suspicion on Vaughn as others on the DPD who witnessed where he was posted had leapt to his defense including Rio Pierce and Don Flusche.

What we can strongly speculate is that Patrick Dean, Blackie Harrison and Louis Miller (to a lesser degree) were willing participants in a plan to eliminate Lee Oswald using a mobbed up, intelligence asset in Jack Ruby and it appears that they got away with it. To this, I'll note a couple more important and telling points. Everybody that was called to testify before the Warren Commission, whether it was in Washington D.C. or Dallas, were entitled to have an attorney present with them as they would be required to testify under oath. Only a very small group of people in Dallas chose to have a lawyer present when testifying that included ... Patrick Dean and William J. 'Blackie' Harrison.* What were they so worried about? Were two seasoned DPD personnel at risk of wilting under the pressure? And Louis Miller actually had his time in front of the WC deferred by a day when he refused to be sworn in. However, the next day he did agree to it after he had was told that the alternative would involve him being subpoenaed to testify to the full Warren Committee in Washington D.C.

If **Police Chief Jesse Curry** and **Captain J.W. Fritz** were largely accessories before the fact, we must consider who may have been accessories after Oswald's shooting. I think it is very clear that **Detectives Don Ray Archer, Barnard Clardy** and **Thomas McMillon** were, as it is obvious that they did not initially corroborate Dean's statement that Ruby divulged how he entered the basement down Main Street. They only did so in subsequent statements and testimonies. If they were willing conspirators, they would have come out singing from the same hymn sheet as Dean was regarding Ruby's alleged admissions in the Fifth Floor jail.

---

*The Carlins also insisted on having a lawyer present when providing their testimonies to the Warren Commission.

How many witnesses to the shooting saw more than they testified? We will never know. All that is clear from the record is that a great many witnessed very little and many were never asked to testify at all.

What is almost certain is that when the mysterious deaths related to the assassination of President Kennedy began to materialise, the silence of many that shrouded the murder of Lee Oswald continued.

Jack Ruby and the Mob

You may have noted that there is minimal reference to Jack Ruby's ties to organised crime in this book. This is because it is beyond any doubt that Jack Ruby had links to organised crime that span back to his formative years in Chicago.[7] Without wanting to sound glib, I did not feel the need to divert from the topic of Lee Oswald's shooting to substantiate what so many other researchers and authors have already established. In essence it's a foregone conclusion that Ruby was tied to organised crime but where I think this comes into things regarding Oswald's murder is its part in his 'eligibility' to kill Oswald.

When we break the whole plot down, Jack Ruby was the perfect candidate on a few fronts regardless of who planned Oswald's execution. Ruby probably thought he was in the good graces of DPD personnel of all ranks at the time. To most, he would have been lively and generous company as the owner of two nightclubs around Dallas. Capt. Fritz was known to spend time there. Ruby was even the boss of some police officer's girlfriends or wives.

We have seen in testimonies and statements that members of the DPD even acknowledged having friendships or acquaintances with Ruby after he shot Oswald.

Conversely, Ruby would have been a source of information on local crime elements - likely on matters further afield. Drugs, gambling, gunrunning and he may have been more of a source or informant. Given the allegations of corruption through the DPD at the time, might Ruby have been a partner to some DPD on these fronts even?

Speaking of crime elements, Ruby's ties to organised crime would have surely been known to people in the DPD. If the plan to remove Oswald was planned and orchestrated by elements within the DPD, as I have proposed in this scenario, the fact that he was tied to the mob would have come into their thinking. Similarly to Oswald's framing, it is also perfectly credible for the plotters to have enlisted Ruby as the mob associate that he was. Guilt through association on that front would have drawn in arguably the most complex and present boogey men around - the mob. Thus, deftly deflecting any suspicion of the DPD beyond judgement of incompetence. To me, both instances are two sides of the same coin.

Could the mob/mafia have facilitated Oswald's murder by using one of their own? It's possible ... in less than extraordinary circumstances other than those of the weekend of November 22nd. The resources and contacts were likely there for mob elements to draw on within the ranks of the DPD to be able to initiate or collaborate on such a plot. But the stakes were astronomically high and the amount of planning to ensure an all-points cover-up from within the DPD alone rules it out, in my mind. Plus, what would have been in it for the mob to stick their necks out like that? I suppose it really depends on if or how much they might have been involved in President Kennedy's murder and any ties to Oswald to necessitate them carrying out the plan to silence him.

With all considered, I think the most plausible explanation is that Jack Ruby was enlisted by elements of the DPD to kill Oswald because either way, mob backing or not, he had help to access the basement on November 24. Who, when and what the pitch might have been to Ruby to shoot Oswald?

Given how close he clearly felt to the DPD, it could have been put to him that he would be their hero for either a) doing them a favour by getting rid of Oswald, b) avenging their colleague, Tippit or c) be the hero of the nation for avenging President Kennedy.

Or he could have simply been told to do it because either someone in the DPD or higher leaned on him or a benefactor in or out of the mob to make sure he killed Oswald. Whether his arm was twisted or not, Ruby would have likely been reminded that a crime of passion carried a lighter sentence and that he would only have to serve a few years in prison. And when he was released, any debts he had would have been paid. Further to this, recall that Ruby was allegedly told off by teller Bill Cox at the Merchant Bank on the afternoon of November 22nd for carrying $7,000 in cash. Was this his payment in advance for killing Oswald?

From the DPD angle, I think that the meeting Ruby had with **Officer Harry Olsen** in the early hours of Saturday November 23 warrants consideration as to when a message might have been conveyed to Ruby. In subsequent months, Ruby's attorney, Joe Tonahill would be made aware of this conversation but Ruby would never divulge what was discussed. Only that it was a light-natured sharing of impressions type conversation that included Olsen saying that the DPD wished to cut Oswald into threads for killing Tippit. Was it so Olsen could give Ruby instructions for the first time or reinforce them because he (Ruby) missed an opportunity to kill Oswald at the midnight press conference? There is evidence that Ruby was trying to get close to Oswald in police custody across that weekend, and he did admit to the FBI that he had his loaded revolver on him at the time. Was Ruby really meant to have killed Oswald much sooner than he ultimately would? I think this is very possible. If opportunities were missed overnight of Friday and Saturday, the plotters could have regrouped and set the wheels in motion for the basement attack. Regardless, publicly, Ruby would attribute his shooting Oswald, who he said he had never met, out of anger and grief for the president's assassination.

The scenario I have laid out in this chapter is incredibly simple. I devised it as such because the more complications are woven into any plan, the greater the chance there is for it to be detected and fail. And with Oswald's successful murder, it did not fail and no one, other than Ruby, was brought to justice for a part in it.

I did not set out writing this book with a scenario in mind and therefore cherry-picked conducive evidence to frame it around. I have simply followed the evidence and drawn questions and conclusions. However, other key questions and curiosities uncovered in this book do not correlate with the scenario that I have just laid out. Oddities which may or may not be significant such as:

- the three reporters totally implausible account of racing an elevator down from the Third Floor.
- numerous instances of media personnel not being acknowledged or accounted for at the scene of the shooting.
- DPD and other media personnel testifying to hear Ruby and Oswald exclaim, say and yell things just before, during and after the shooting that nobody else did nor was captured in audio or film records.
- inexplicable accounts by members of the DPD that totally ran counter to the record of Oswald being taken back to the jail office after the shooting and when he was loaded into the ambulance.
- the fact that George Phenix's microphone can be seen hanging over Pappas, Carroll and Pettit in the Beers photograph, plus the Bleckman and Davidson footage, but is not visible in the Bob Jackson photograph.

Despite my intentions of bringing clarity to a historic event that has largely been shadowed by the assassination of President John F. Kennedy, digging deeply into the shooting of Lee Harvey Oswald was always going to present unanswered tangents. For me, I see this merely as the price of admission for bringing the case further into the light.

Look far enough on the internet though and you will see in-depth theories that Oswald was shot by a man (with a different neck hairline to Ruby's) only to switch with the real, drugged and / or hypnotised Jack Ruby. Or how Oswald was actually shot with a blank before being fatally shot out of the view of the media to ensure his death.

The marginalisation of such theories by the broader research community is evident but I would not be true to my questions-followed-by-answers approach in this book if I did not at least acknowledge these. What are the explanations for these oddities and other things related to Oswald's shooting?

Hopefully I have shined a strong enough light on the topic and removed the veil of 'presumed truths' to enable people to cut straight to the chase when it comes to any remaining unsolved aspects. Remember, there were similar instances in the assassinations of John F. Kennedy and Robert F. Kennedy. Both were the subject of early speculation from 'kooks' that became more and more plausible over the passage of time. Who were the first people to contend that Lee Oswald was a government informant and that Sirhan Sirhan was in a hypnotic state at the time of RFK's shooting? These and many other contentions would have seemed beyond belief at the time but now, through the tireless work of many, these are completely acceptable and credible narratives.

Ultimately, what I have presented in this chapter is merely an example of a plausible scenario using the most compelling evidence regarding Lee Oswald's shooting. So, to take another quote from 'JFK', 'don't take my word for it, don't believe me. Do your own work, your own thinking...'

Events as complex as assassination really ought to be treated with a scientific perspective. I don't mean just the physical science related to the scene of the crime but in terms of the true definition of science – to build and organise knowledge in the form of testable hypotheses and predictions. I interpret this as science being something that we do. It is a process that builds upon itself with the aim of reviewing and testing evidence to keep moving toward final and absolute proof – whatever it may be. Science, however, should not be manipulated for some preordained outcome. Nor should it be disregarded if it does not suit baked in orthodoxies and presumptions.

Perhaps we have all been guilty of setting a course based on presumptions when it comes to this line of research. The Kennedy, Tippit, and, as now demonstrated, the Oswald killing, are immensely complicated subjects. It is easy to not see the wood for the trees. And just because an author or a researcher has a different premise to their work than others, does that mean that all of their work to come to that point must be wrong therefore ought to be discredited? Not in my eyes. I'll refer to John Armstrong again to make the point. His work on the concept that there were two Oswalds is far from most JFK assassination research orthodoxies. But regardless of whether you see any merit to this point, the weight of research and insight he has provided to support this contention has included casting the likes of Westbrook and Croy fairly into the spotlight.

It goes to the point that the assassination of President Kennedy and the murders of Officer J.D. Tippit and Lee Harvey Oswald form one giant puzzle. And it's up to us to continue searching for and connecting the puzzle pieces to form the clearest picture of what took place on that weekend in November 1963.

CHAPTER SIXTEEN

CONCLUSION

Lee Oswald's death was the final bookend to a weekend that time will never forget. If President Kennedy's murder marked the end of an era of innocence, I think the inhumane execution of his alleged assassin marked the beginning of an era of awakening & cynicism. From that moment on, minute cracks in the armour of official narratives, that were most likely always there, started to become visible, arguably ushering in skepticism and critical thinking. Many atrocities on human rights and dignity have no doubt taken place in police custody for as long as there have been jail cells but what happened to a defenseless man in Oswald, who should have at least had the benefit of police protection and the presumption of innocence until proven guilty, is a blight on modern humanity. And the general blind acceptance of the established narrative regarding it is another failing of ours.

What have I learned from my examination into Oswald's murder? Aside from how so many presumed-as-true aspects to it were anything but, I would say that it pays to think critically. And to do so is not taking a blanketed pessimism to anything and everything but being prepared to follow up on a hunch. Before setting out on my work to compile the Garrison Files index and this investigation into Oswald's shooting, I was skeptical about the value of any JFK assassination-related documents that remain to be released by the United States government. But I have well and truly had it confirmed since that the smallest piece of evidence can be vital when correlated with other items and contexts. This gives me hope for when or if any more documents are released.

The question of what if Lee Oswald lived to stand trial is an intriguing one and thankfully, at least has been the subject of books and TV movies. Most recently the outstanding 'JFK Assassination Chokeholds' book established, beyond all doubt, the lack of evidence that Lee Oswald committed President Kennedy's murder.[1] Even Police Chief Jesse Curry would allegedly come to admit as much in his later years. The concept of Oswald living to stand trial was clearly a two-pronged threat for those responsible for President Kennedy's assassination because in the process of Oswald's innocence being assured, their fingerprints all over him would have been exposed. The same could be speculated about Jack Ruby. What if he had lived to be retried for Oswald's shooting? What might he have revealed about the event given the weight of DPD personnel testimony that saw him sentenced to death in 1964. And what is perhaps the most frightening and haunting aspect of all is what would have happened in the mid-1960's if the truth about President Kennedy's assassination emerged. In July and September 2024, the United States faced a new 'what if?' scenario with two assassination attempts made on Donald Trump in Butler, Pennsylvania and West Palm Beach, Florida respectively. Take or leave Trump, if he was killed either day, it would have been the lighting of a tinder box full of tension and polarisation that would have led to civil war across the United States. Even for an Australian, it is a truly frightening concept.

'Death to Justice – The Shooting of Lee Harvey Oswald' may be the first book focused on dissecting all aspects of Oswald's murder. I certainly hope it is not the last because we have well and truly penetrated the surface to at least conclude that much of the event has been sitting in obscurity. The Dallas Police Department were culpable but to what extent should remain an ongoing question. We know that they could never have been trusted to carry out a full and honest investigation on its own structure, system, hierarchy and personnel. Time pressure aside, the outcome of such an extensive investigation ought to have seen heads roll for such a high profile killing happen on their watch, on their premises. In the absence of a full investigation, it is incredibly insightful to read back over their report and see the literal side-stepping of land mines in it. To me, it smacks of a larger apparatus at play that kicked in almost instantly that weekend to control as much of the narrative as possible. As stated in this book, it could well have been for genuine motives related to the threat of literal war breaking out. Ensuring Lyndon Johnson's re-election was no doubt crucial and beyond that perhaps trying to preserve as much faith from the American people in its government and beyond that, the world's. Those responsible for the killings of Kennedy, Oswald, and Tippit to a lesser degree, clearly leveraged off these factors to ensure a multi-faceted cover-up and I think that it is highly plausible to say that they factored all of this in with their planning and execution of each.

The 'apparatus' that I refer to materialised very quickly was the Warren Commission and the FBI. The two, whether the FBI liked it or not, would combine with the WC incorporating the investigative work that the FBI commenced almost straightaway after the weekend of November 22nd. Reading the statements that the FBI took from witnesses of the Oswald shooting, it is clear that there was an agenda to only dig so deep that included holding the Dallas Police Department to only so much account. And it would appear that this would continue with the Warren Commission. However, in an interesting sidenote, come well into 1964, and FBI Director J. Edgar Hoover was bristling at the fact that the Warren Commission were not, in his eyes, leveraging off of the investigative work of his FBI. According to Seth Kantor's 'The Ruby Cover-up', he attempted to 'out' consulting professor to the WC, Norman Redlich, as a communist.[2] To further demonstrate that the Warren Commission wasn't the well-oiled machine of misinformation that it has largely been purported to be, we should recall Burt Griffin's detection of Patrick Dean not being truthful in his testimonies and his attempt to correct this. However, Griffin and fellow WC counsel, Leon Hubert (both of whom led the Ruby aspect of the investigation) did raise the alarm to the commission advising that there was much more to Jack Ruby than perhaps any of them had bargained on. Griffin and Hubert went as far as submitting a chapter to be included in the final Warren Report titled 'The Killing of Lee Harvey Oswald' or included as a sub-chapter.[3] The chapter attempts to chart Ruby's movements from Thursday November 21 through to after Oswald's shooting on Sunday November 24 before acknowledging the discrepancies of Ruby's statements during and just after the shooting. The document openly acknowledges the DPD's Dean, Archer, McMillon, Clardy, Harrison and

Miller and lingering questions around them. Imagine if this had been part of the final Warren Report. Each could have been led to the precipice of accountability and from there, who knows what would have happened in terms of exposing the truth of Lee Oswald's shooting and perhaps more.

Instead, the chapter was not included and these people along with others plus suspicious and unanswered aspects of the case were protected for those crucial first years after the fact. The apparatus had ensured it.

Fifteen years after the fact and with a lot of the initial politicking and threat of conflict left behind, the House Select Committee for Assassinations would provide the most thorough analysis to Oswald's shooting but it too clearly had its limitations. But with this book, light has been shed on all facets of Lee Oswald's shooting that were covered over. The fate of the Warren Commission and the HSCA I think says a lot about how much of the truth has been withheld or cut off in mid-pursuit. 'Why?' is the question that must continue to be asked. If for no other reason than to ensure that the governments that are instilled with serving the people continue to do just that – and not the other way around.

In presenting this book, and resources within the appendices, I hope it will cast a new lens on Lee Oswald's murder and prompt others to take an interest that will see more questions asked and answered. I do not, and never will, profess to having all of the answers regarding Lee Oswald's shooting. If anything, I have drawn upon the research efforts of others to help make sense of the evidence amounting to thousands of pages. And by doing so, I have organised it all into a book to promote it as a topic worthy of research. However much of the truth went with Lee Oswald and Jack

Ruby to their graves regarding their actions on the weekend of November 22nd 1963 will remain impossible to know. There are plenty of other works to help you come to your own conclusions on that front. But whatever you think about him, Oswald's murder in police custody should not have happened. Period. Let alone the disturbingly equal ratio of media to police personnel that it took place in front of. We're all the poorer for Lee Oswald not having the chance to stand trial but spare a thought for his family, especially his two daughters, and what they would have to of grown up hearing about their father.

My final hope for 'Death to Justice' is that it is proof that time need not be an overruling factor when it comes to our being able to uncover evidence so many years after that weekend in 1963. It's why I set out to complete the Garrison Files Index and I can reaffirm this having uncovered what I was able to for this book regarding the Oswald shooting. With the advent of technology and the potential for the declassification of more JFK Assassination-related documents, who knows what more can be uncovered. Will it enable Lee Oswald and Jack Ruby to be stood fairly in the face of justice? No. Will it bring back President Kennedy, Malcolm X, Martin Luther King and Robert F. Kennedy, who's legacies are so entwined with their untimely demises? No, of course not. But continued research and interest in them and their murders really may ensure that the perpetrators behind the assassinations have not fully gotten away with it. And that somehow at least Lee Harvey Oswald and Jack Ruby will also continue to be figures for sensible and productive scrutiny.

- **Paul Abbott**

ACKNOWLEDGEMENTS

This book, and I imagine countless other works, would simply not have been possible if it weren't for the Mary Ferrell Foundation website. It is a seemingly endless depository of information that is easy to access. Anyone that is interested in modern history should at least be a paid member of this website.

I owe a tremendous amount of credit to people that I will sadly never have the chance to meet as they have been lost to time. Col. L. Fletcher Prouty, Mark Lane, District Attorney Jim Garrison, Harold Weisberg, Vincent Salandria, Sylvia Meagher, Mary Ferrell and Dr. Cyril Wecht remain giants in the research community who led the way, while at great risk to themselves, to shed light on the assassination of President Kennedy. They devoted significant aspects of their lives and careers to ensure the path to the truth was always clear and present for future researchers to follow and maintain.

I owe a great deal to the many current researchers that continue to provide valuable research and commentary on all political assassinations of the 1960's. I have benefitted from their work over the years so I figured that when I finally had something worthwhile to contribute, it would be out of respect to them. People such as James DiEugenio, Lisa Pease, Robert Groden, Bill Simpich, Vince Palamara, Bart Kamp, David Talbot, Dick Russell, Gary Hill, Johnny Cairns, Larry Hancock, John Armstrong, Jefferson Morley and more. While his research was devoted to another topic, David Whelan, who authored 'The Assassination of John Lennon'[1] has also been a source of inspiration. His insightful work on Lennon's murder pushes back against ingrained orthodoxies on the case so in that instance, its similarity to the case of Lee Oswald's murder and its own under-coverage was not lost on me.

I must acknowledge Paul Bleau in particular. The foreword that he provided for this book truly humbles me. It was actually Paul's outstanding work for JFK research in general and his approachability that ultimately gave me the confidence to contribute to the cause by indexing the Garrison Files – from which the impetus for this book emerged. There is a chance for all of us to take a leaf out of his book when it comes to the meaning of positive collaboration with others in the name of forwarding research. His co-authoring of 'JFK Assassination Chokeholds' with James DiEugenio, Matt Crumpton, Andrew A. Iler and Mark Adamczyk in 2023 is evidence of this.

Long form conversations in the format of podcasts have become an invaluable resource of information for topics as complex as President Kennedy's assassination. Some podcasts that I recommend for excellent listening are Black Op Radio, Out of the Blank, Solving JFK and William Ramsey Investigates.

Being an Australian, the Kennedy assassination and its many facets is a fairly lonely topic to be interested in. While it is not directly part of our experience as a country, the effects of President Kennedy's death were felt, particularly regarding the war in Vietnam when Australia's role increased with its escalation – arguably an outcome of Kennedy's assassination. Yet, the subject has provided me with 30 years of interest so far and I do not foresee a time when I will still not stop in a bookstore to see if there are any books on the shelf related to the topic. They were certainly few and far between when I was growing up! Any time I could strike up a conversation with someone about the topic, I had to learn very early to measure my enthusiasm by picking up on a person's level of understanding and not necessarily their leanings of beliefs, to really contextualise the conversation. And to a degree, I formatted this book the same way. To allow context to be the north star and not cut to the chase straight away. Anyway, thank you to those who showed interest ... or even just feigned it!

Finally, and most importantly, my partner in life, Sara. She has listened to me voice thoughts and theories on the topic over many years. She has sat through watching documentaries and films with me and been a fantastic sounding board when it came to my writing this book and wanting it to make sense. Above all, the hours upon hours over the years where I have been reading and writing with 100% concentration is only because of her love, support, tolerance and understanding. Simply put, writing this book was also only possible because of her. I know and am thankful that this will be the case for anything I work on in the future. No word count is large enough to express my love and gratitude to her.

REFERENCES

- All photographs in this book are courtesy of University of North Texas Libraries, The Portal to Texas History, https://texashistory.unt.edu; Dallas Municipal Archives
- For ease of locating referenced materials;
  - all FBI materials were sourced from the Mary Ferrell Foundation website and are mostly contained in the 'Documents' category,
  - Dallas Police Department Investigation materials were sourced from archive.org
  - Warren Commission Hearings transcripts were sourced from jfk.assassination.eu but are available at numerous other websites
  - Film Clips as listed on YouTube were current at the time of publication of this book.
  - Extended and multi-character website addresses have been condensed as 'tinyurl'

Chapter One:

1. https://www.presidency.ucsb.edu/documents/executive-order-11063-equal-opportunity-housing
2. https://history.state.gov/historicaldocuments/frus1961-63v11/d272
3. Manchester, 'Death of a President', p 39
4. https://22november1963.org.uk/jfk-assassination-grassy-knoll-witnesses
5. Warren Commission Hearings: Vol. VII - Page 535
6. Warren Commission Hearings: Vol. VI - Page 312
7. https://spartacus-educational.com/JFKtippet.htm
8. https://harveyandlee.net/Tippit/Tippit.html
9. McBride, 'Into the Nightmare' p 448

Chapter Two:

1. https://archive.org/details/OrleansParishGrandJuryTestimonyOfRuthHydePaine18Apr1968
2. Warren Commission Hearings: Vol. II - Page 247
3. Warren Commission Hearings: Vol. XI - Page 480 - 481
4. Warren Commission Hearings: Vol. XI - Page 38
5. https://ia902804.us.archive.org/22/items/McAdams_JFK/siegel1.htm
6. https://www.pbs.org/wgbh/frontline/article/8-things-you-may-not-know-about-lee-harvey-oswald/
7. Warren Commission Hearings: Vol. I - Page 326
8. https://www.maryferrell.org/showDoc.html?docId=43068#relPageId=18
9. https://www.csmonitor.com/2001/0824/p11s1-cods.html
10. Hill, 'The Other Oswald'
11. https://archive.nytimes.com/www.nytimes.com/times-insider/2015/07/29/1959-lee-harvey-oswald-in-moscow/

12	Poulgrain, 'JFK vs. Allen Dulles – Battleground Indonesia' pp 49 - 50
13	https://www.kennedysandking.com/john-f-kennedy-articles/oswald-and-the-shot-at-walker-redressing-the-balance
14	Armstrong, 'Harvey and Lee'

Chapter Three:

1	https://ratical.org/ratville/JFK/PG/PGchp7.html#fn5
2	Warren Commission Hearings: Vol. VI - Page 400
3	Warren Commission Hearings: Vol. II - Page 291
4	Warren Commission Hearings: Vol. II - Page 294
5	https://aarclibrary.org/publib/jfk/wc/wcvols/wh25/pdf/WH25_CE_2641.pdf
6	https://www.maryferrell.org/showDoc.html?docId=233493#relPageId=3&search=marvin_robinson
7	FBI Memorandum by Special Agent Earle Haley on Interview with Roy Cooper, November 23, 1963, Reproduced in Harvey and Lee by John Armstrong.
8	Douglass, JFK and the Unspeakable', Pp 277 - 278
9	Warren Commission Hearings, Volume VI - Page 266
10	Roger Craig, 'When They Kill a President'
11	Russell, 'The Man Who Knew Too Much' Pp 287 - 288
12	Warren Commission Hearings, Volume XI - Pp 386 - 389
13	https://jfk-online.com/alicelho.html
14	Warren Commission Hearings: Vol. X - Page 353
15	https://www.maryferrell.org/showDoc.html?docId=95645#relPageId=121&search=jiffy_store
16	Warren Commission Report - Pp 164 - 166
17	Warren Commission Hearings: Vol. VI - Page 443
18	Douglass, 'JFK and the Unspeakable', p 290
19	Marrs, 'Crossfire', p 354
20	Douglass, JFK and the Unspeakable', p 293
21	Johnston & Roe, 'Flight from Dallas'
22	https://archive.org/details/Rockefeller-commission-report-to-the-president-by-the-commission-on-cia-activities
23	https://www.aarclibrary.org/publib/church/reports/contents.htm
24	https://www.archives.gov/research/jfk/select-committee-report
25	https://www.archives.gov/research/jfk/review-board/report

Interlude:

1	Kamp, 'Prayer Man - More Than a Fuzzy Picture'

Chapter Four:

1	Warren Commission Hearings, Volume XV - page 588
2	Crenshaw with Hansen and Shaw 'Conspiracy of Silence' p 190
3	http://oswald-has-been-shot.blogspot.com/ (WFAA-TV)

4	https://www.youtube.com/watch?v=orJ1AGAn4OQ
5	http://oswald-has-been-shot.blogspot.com/ (NBC-TV)
6	https://www.youtube.com/watch?v=yzAZ0o5_2yE
7	https://www.youtube.com/watch?v=EuH20bCFB1Y
8	https://www.youtube.com/watch?v=H_xJjedgWsY
9	https://tinyurl.com/3xjzdu52

Chapter Five:

1	Manchester, 'Death of a President', p 726
2	Press Raps Dallas Police' The Associated Press
3	Press Raps Dallas Police' The Associated Press
4	Warren Commission Report Current Section: Appendix XI. Reports Relating to the Interrogation of Lee Harvey Oswald at the Dallas Police Department - Pp 599 - 611
5	Kamp, 'Prayer Man - More Than a Fuzzy Picture', page 175
6	https://www.maryferrell.org/pages/JFK_Assassination.html
7	https://tinyurl.com/43f3dwvr
8	https://tinyurl.com/cbuaza2s
9	https://tinyurl.com/mr36x6k5
10	https://tinyurl.com/4vjypjyf
11	https://archive.org/details/WARREN_COMMISSION_VOLUMES/WARREN%20COMMISSION%20REPORT/page/n7/mode/2up
12	Warren Commission Hearings: Vol. XIII - Page 135
13	https://www.maryferrell.org/pages/JFK_Assassination_Quotes_by_Government_Officials.html
14	https://www.maryferrell.org/pages/JFK_Assassination_Quotes_by_Government_Officials.html
15	Meagher, 'Accessories After the Fact'
16	McKnight, 'Breach of Trust'
17	Brown, 'The Warren Omission'
18	https://tinyurl.com/mk8xdtef

Chapter Six:

1	Warren Commission Hearings: Vol. XII - Page 45
2	Kamp, 'Prayer Man - More Than a Fuzzy Picture', p 319
3	https://www.youtube.com/watch?v=UxvxgODFxEo
4	https://www.maryferrell.org/showDoc.html?docId=1136#relPageId=424&search=jesse_curry%20fbi
5	Warren Commission Hearings: Vol. XII - Page 35
6	Warren Commission Hearings: Vol. XII - Page 46
7	https://tinyurl.com/musszm9r
8	Warren Commission Hearings, Volume XII, page 57
9	https://tinyurl.com/mvwfbut7
10	Warren Commission Hearings: Vol. XV - Page 183
11	Warren Commission Hearings: Vol. XII - Page 7

12 Warren Commission Hearings: Vol. XII - Page 103
13 Warren Commission Hearings, Volume XXI, page 2

Chapter Seven:

1   https://tinyurl.com/4nr3rcxc
2   https://tinyurl.com/3nk6ue9t
3   Warren Commission Hearings, Volume XIII, page 150
4   Warren Commission Hearings: Vol. XIII - Page 143
5   Warren Commission Hearings: Vol. XIII - Page 171
6   Warren Commission Hearings: Vol. XII - Page 363
7   https://tinyurl.com/yc5s3rnf
8   https://tinyurl.com/2rkh7m5t
9   https://tinyurl.com/2th7usrt
10 https://tinyurl.com/4pa3nwsc
11 https://tinyurl.com/5exy27k3
12 https://tinyurl.com/4kxtspbm
13 https://tinyurl.com/mpe35aw8
14 https://tinyurl.com/43r2knr2
15 https://tinyurl.com/59p6mw9d

Chapter 8

1   Warren Commission Hearings: Vol. XV - Page 592
2   Warren Commission Report, page 225
3   https://tinyurl.com/mr2d259s
4   https://tinyurl.com/mr3mbkv5
5   Carroll, 'Accidental Assassin'
6   https://tinyurl.com/vpnm7aax
7   https://tinyurl.com/3n5bcyd5
8   https://tinyurl.com/bdp3y9rb
9   https://tinyurl.com/bdzyerme
10 https://tinyurl.com/2e5u6ujz
11 https://tinyurl.com/bp9vybyr
12 https://www.carlbernstein.com/the-cia-and-the-media-rolling-stone-10-20-1977
13 https://tinyurl.com/2jcwyvp6
14 https://tinyurl.com/35h3hshh
15 https://tinyurl.com/bdfku6ze
16 https://tinyurl.com/2uzmjvye
17 https://tinyurl.com/mr2h975j
18 https://tinyurl.com/58k9pfa9
19 https://tinyurl.com/4vsrb729
20 http://oswald-has-been-shot.blogspot.com/

21	https://tinyurl.com/35dxkvan
22	https://tinyurl.com/yprr4m2u
23	https://tinyurl.com/4nmj77n6
24	https://tinyurl.com/359yh74h
25	https://tinyurl.com/4psvfnan
26	https://tinyurl.com/ykumhxcc
27	https://tinyurl.com/3d5v22h5
28	https://tinyurl.com/373w2are
29	https://tinyurl.com/ycx7pxfn
30	http://www.davidnewland.com/2009/11/eyewitness-to-oswalds-shooting.html
31	https://tinyurl.com/yrxexj38
32	https://tinyurl.com/srpsnd64
33	https://tinyurl.com/yc4vrw25
34	https://www.c-span.org/video/?309244-1/memories-lee-harvey-oswald-shooting
35	https://tinyurl.com/bdzxf3wd
36	https://jfkassassinationfiles.wordpress.com/2024/01/
37	https://tinyurl.com/58zjpyzn
38	https://tinyurl.com/4hzsdnkc
39	https://documents.latimes.com/eyewitness-account-oswald-shooting/
40	https://tinyurl.com/f3skbz49
41	https://tinyurl.com/2amyrcsy
42	Warren Commission Hearings: Vol. XV - Page 680
43	https://tinyurl.com/3h227nxm
44	https://tinyurl.com/52wnernh
45	https://tinyurl.com/3wkzuj9r
46	https://tinyurl.com/47vrnbc2
47	https://kenlevine.blogspot.com/2013/11/amazing-first-person-account-of.html
48	https://stevenwarranresearch.blogspot.com/2013/11/schematic-diagram-of-basement-parking.htm
49	Stone & Sklar, 'JFK: The Book of the Film'

Chapter Nine:

1	https://tinyurl.com/2khnr22a
2	Warren Commission Hearings: Vol. XV - Page 163
3	Warren Commission Hearings: Vol. XII - Page 111
4	https://tinyurl.com/bdzxf3wd
5	https://tinyurl.com/yrxexj38
6	https://tinyurl.com/5n7wrymp
7	Huffaker 'When the News Went Live: Dallas 1963'
8	https://tinyurl.com/4p5v4twv
9	https://tinyurl.com/3uemnnjz
10	https://tinyurl.com/84vdc93y

11	Warren Commission Hearings: Vol. XII - Page 238
12	Warren Commission Hearings: Vol. XII - Page 305
13	Warren Commission Hearings: Vol. XII - Page 208
14	Warren Commission Hearings: Vol. XII - Page 273
15	https://tinyurl.com/4chm54tf

Chapter Ten:

1	https://tinyurl.com/nhdf444b
2	Warren Commission Hearings: Vol. XII - Page 175
3	Warren Commission Hearings: Vol. XII - Page 385
4	https://tinyurl.com/2tdsrcve
5	https://tinyurl.com/bddu954r
6	https://tinyurl.com/yyvaftz7
7	https://tinyurl.com/cbuaza2s
8	https://tinyurl.com/2jadvd52
9	https://tinyurl.com/yc44bwmf
10	Warren Commission Hearings: Vol. XV - Page 117
11	https://tinyurl.com/5fy4kudv
12	Warren Commission Hearings: Vol. XII - Page 339
13	https://tinyurl.com/4rwacvp8
14	https://tinyurl.com/2edceh7k
15	https://tinyurl.com/yxxyuwrn
16	Warren Commission Hearings: Vol. XII - Page 226
17	Warren Commission Hearings: Vol. XV - Page 680
18	HSCA Report, Volume IV, page 588
19	https://tinyurl.com/zfxr3ce
20	https://tinyurl.com/2d22bs54
21	https://tinyurl.com/mrxnksnn
22	https://tinyurl.com/22dpzuhu
23	https://tinyurl.com/5exy27k3
24	https://tinyurl.com/tvh7bmds
25	Warren Commission Hearings: Vol. XII - Page 325
26	https://tinyurl.com/vbystvn6
27	Warren Commission Hearings: Vol. XIII - Page 4
28	Warren Commission Hearings: Vol. XII - Page 16

Chapter Eleven

1	https://tinyurl.com/mryan6hd
2	https://tinyurl.com/ywvrkp6r
3	https://tinyurl.com/3fss6bd8
4	https://tinyurl.com/35dxkvan

5	Warren Commission Hearings: Vol. XIII - Page 47
6	https://tinyurl.com/3s5m45w7
7	https://tinyurl.com/mr3xdsw6
8	https://tinyurl.com/mr2npn28
9	https://tinyurl.com/7mckxvrp
10	https://tinyurl.com/akwxnykx
11	https://tinyurl.com/bdfyapvm
12	https://tinyurl.com/mu4m9rkt
13	https://tinyurl.com/3udwrrku
14	https://tinyurl.com/49k7zf9s
15	https://tinyurl.com/5n7x6nyt
16	https://tinyurl.com/h27hwwp8
17	https://tinyurl.com/2dja5fk4
18	https://tinyurl.com/bddveypt
19	Ibid.
20	https://tinyurl.com/2hvp7jk6
21	https://texashistory.unt.edu/ark:/67531/metapth337932/
22	https://www.jfkmagazine.org/2023/10/why-did-somebody-put-bag-over-jack.html
23	https://tinyurl.com/42t9ncub
24	https://aarclibrary.org/publib/jfk/wc/wcvols/wh19/pdf/WH19_Bieberdorf_Ex_5123.pdf
25	https://tinyurl.com/msm8rsxa
26	Warren Commission Hearings: Vol. XIII - Page 84
27	https://tinyurl.com/mwe8b6me
28	Warren Commission Hearings: Vol. XIII - Page 116
29	https://tinyurl.com/2xx4a9ty
30	https://tinyurl.com/3w2st8jh
31	Warren Commission Hearings: Vol. XIII - Page 99
32	Crenshaw with Hansen and Shaw, 'Conspiracy of Silence' pp 190 - 191

Chapter Twelve:

1	Warren Commission Hearings: Vol. XII - Page 401
2	https://tinyurl.com/8zpwvhva
3	Warren Commission Hearings: Vol. XIII - Page 63
4	https://tinyurl.com/yrx2ffrz
5	https://tinyurl.com/mrxns7p3
6	https://www.youtube.com/watch?v=6YOcymSKhxE
7	https://tinyurl.com/3hxr4tfa
8	https://tinyurl.com/45fptvfh
9	https://tinyurl.com/5n7bzhmp
10	https://tinyurl.com/4c95dtf2
11	https://tinyurl.com/ht2jvd4t

12	https://tinyurl.com/5n7bzhmp
13	https://tinyurl.com/2hm7a4a3
14	https://tinyurl.com/mr3xdsw6
15	https://tinyurl.com/yupcjyxp
16	https://tinyurl.com/mu8dhfv9
17	https://tinyurl.com/yemtdktu
18	https://tinyurl.com/ypj9ywm6
19	https://tinyurl.com/556mn4xh
20	Warren Commission Hearings: Vol. XV - Page 63
21	Warren Commission Hearings: Vol. XIII - Page 89
22	https://tinyurl.com/yjj26rsu
23	https://tinyurl.com/34vby8ds
24	Warren Commission Hearings: Vol. XV - Page 537
25	Warren Commission Hearings: Vol. XIV - Page 430
26	Kantor, 'The Ruby Cover-up' p 87
27	Warren Commission Hearings: Vol. VII - Page 91
28	https://tinyurl.com/4xxrdzk9
29	https://tinyurl.com/yxzvn2nh
30	Warren Commission Hearings: Vol. XIII - Page 452
31	Kantor, 'The Ruby Cover-up' - page 62
32	https://tinyurl.com/cb59xm9t
33	https://tinyurl.com/2p8xw4hm
34	https://www.jfk-assassination.eu/warren/wch/vol15/page31.php
35	https://tinyurl.com/ycxk9xsp
36	https://tinyurl.com/2x57dp3k
37	https://www.youtube.com/watch?v=xhckLcuEINg
38	Warren Commission Hearings: Vol. XV - Page 483
39	https://www.youtube.com/playlist?list=PL0O5WNzrZqlPwuPUrTqvDryXU5kahDaY5
40	Warren Commission Hearings: Vol. XIV - Page 631
41	Warren Commission Hearings: Vol. V - Page 191
42	Warren Commission Hearings: Vol. XIV - Page 629
43	Warren Commission Hearings: Vol. V - Page 194
44	Warren Commission Hearings: Vol. XIV - Page 218
45	Warren Commission Hearings: Vol. XIII - Page 468
46	Warren Commission Hearings: Vol. XV - Page 355
47	https://tinyurl.com/32jts9x4
48	https://tinyurl.com/39dd2nwy
49	https://tinyurl.com/4xycs5bx
50	Warren Commission Hearings: Vol. XIII - Page 210
51	https://www.jfk-assassination.net/russ/testimony/wall_b.htm
52	Warren Commission Hearings: Vol. XIII - Page 292

53	Warren Commission Hearings: Vol. XIII - Page 279	
54	Warren Commission Hearings: Vol. XIII - Page 257	
55	Warren Commission Hearings: Vol. XIII - Page 230	
56	https://tinyurl.com/mvmk5crc	
57	Warren Commission Hearings: Vol. XIII - Page 211	
58	Warren Commission Hearings: Vol. XIII - Page 221	
59	Warren Commission Hearings: Vol. XIII - Page 180	

Chapter Thirteen:

1	https://tinyurl.com/28vv55zr
2	Warren Commission Hearings: Vol. XIV - Page 397
3	Kantor, 'The Ruby Cover-up' p 242 - 243
4	Kantor, 'The Ruby Cover-up' p 316 - 319
5	O'Neil, 'Chaos - The Truth Behind the Manson Family Murders'
6	https://tinyurl.com/42e43mz3
7	DiEugenio, 'JFK Revisited' p 321 - 326
8	Warren Commission Hearings: Vol. XIV - Page 580
9	https://tinyurl.com/yjv7jxwb
10	Inbau & Reid, 'Lie Detection and Criminal Interrogation'

Chapter Fourteen:
No references

Chapter Fifteen:

1	Kamp, 'Prayer Man - More Than a Fuzzy Picture', p 34 - 35
2	https://texashistory.unt.edu/ark:/67531/metapth340051/m1/1/
3	Kantor, 'The Ruby Cover-up' pp 136 - 137
4	https://tinyurl.com/5n7rete3
5	https://tinyurl.com/4jdcfv62
6	Griffin, 'JFK, Oswald and Ruby: Politics, Prejudice and Truth'
7	DiEugenio, Bleau, Crumpton, Iler, Adamczyk 'The JFK Assassination Chokeholds' p 185

Chapter Sixteen

1	DiEugenio, Bleau, Crumpton, Iler, Adamczyk 'The JFK Assassination Chokeholds'
2	Kantor, 'The Ruby Cover-up' – p 299 - 302
3	https://tinyurl.com/2rywsedn

Acknowledgements:

1	Whelan, 'Mind Games: The Assassination of John Lennon'

APPENDICES

1. Report of Lee Harvey Oswald's arrest at the Texas Theater

November 23, 1963

Captain W. P. Gannaway
Special Service Bureau
Dallas Police Department

Thru:
Lieutenant Jack Revill
Criminal Intelligence Section
Special Service Bureau
Dallas Police Department

SUBJECT: PRESIDENTIAL ASSASSINATION
LEE HARVEY OSWALD

Sir:

The following report is submitted for your information.

On November 22, 1963, Lee Harvey Oswald was arrested in the balcony of the Texas Theater, 231 West Jefferson Blvd and was charged with the murder of President John F. Kennedy and the murder of Officer J. D. Tippit.

Respectfully submitted,

L. D. Stringfellow, Detective
Criminal Intelligence Section

2. Dallas DPD Investigation Schematic Map.

Below is the list of people (in alphabetical order) that the Dallas Police Department accounted for on their schematic of the basement prior to and at the time of Oswald's shooting. DPD personnel are in bold.
All appear within sections of the schematic over the next three pages.

Name & Number	Schematic Section	Name & Number	Schematic Section
Archer – 2	A.	Jackson – 53	A.
Arnett – 3	A.	Johnston - 55	A.
Batchelor – 3A	A.	Jones – 56	A.
Beaty – 4	A.	Kantor – 58	A.
Beck – 5	A.	**King - 60**	A.
Beers – 6	A.	Kriss - 61	A.
Brantley – 7	A.	Leavelle – 63	A.
Brockway – 9	A.	Lewis - 64	A.
Brown – 10	A.	Lowery – 66	A.
Burgess – 11	A.	Lumpkin – 66A	A.
Campbell – 14	A.	Martin - 68	A.
Carroll – 100B	A.	McCoy – 72	A.
Chambers – 16	A.	McGee – 73	A.
Clardy - 17	A.	McMillon – 74	A.
Combest – 18	A.	Merrell – 75	A.
Craig - 20	A.	Miller – 76	A.
Croy – 21	A.	Montgomery – 77	A.
Cutchshaw – 22	A.	Nelson – 78	A.
Davidson – 24	A.	Newton – 80	A.
Dawson – 26	A.	**Pate – 81**	A.
Dhority - 29	A.	Pappas – 80A	A.
English – 30	A.	Pelou – 83	A.
Ferguson – 33	A.	Pettit – 83A	A.
Fenley - 34	A.	Phenix - 84	A.
Fritz – 37	A.	**Ramsey – 87**	A.
Goolsby – 38	A.	**Reynolds – 89**	A.
Graves – 40	A.	Slack – 91	A.
Greeson – 41	A.	Slocum – 92	A.
Hankal – 43	A.	Smart – 93	A.
Harrison (W.) – 45	A.	Smith (D.) – 93A	A.
Huffaker – 50	A.	**Stephens – 95**	A.
Hutchinson – 52	A.	Stevenson – 95A	A.

Suits – 95B	A.	Harrison (O.) – 44	B.
Swain – 96	A.	Hopkins – 49	B.
Talbert – 97	A.	Jez – 54	B.
Tankersley – 97A	A.	McCain – 71	B.
Thornton – 99	A.	Newman – 79	B.
Timmons – 99A	A.	Patterson – 82	B.
Unknown Japanese Reporter – 100A	A.	Richey – 89A	B.
Carroll – 100B	A.	Smith (J.) – 93B	B.
Van Cleave – 101	A.	Taylor – 98	B.
Venso – 102A	A.	Walker – 104A	B.
Wagner – 104	A.	**Watkins – 105**	B.
Watson – 106	A.	Daniels – 23	C.
Wiggins – 107	A.	Maxey – 69	C.
Butler – 13	B.	Pierce – 85	C.
Capps – 15	B.	Putnam – 86	C.
Cox – 19	B.	Vaughn – 102	C.
Dean – 27	B.		

A: Basement Junction & Jail Office:

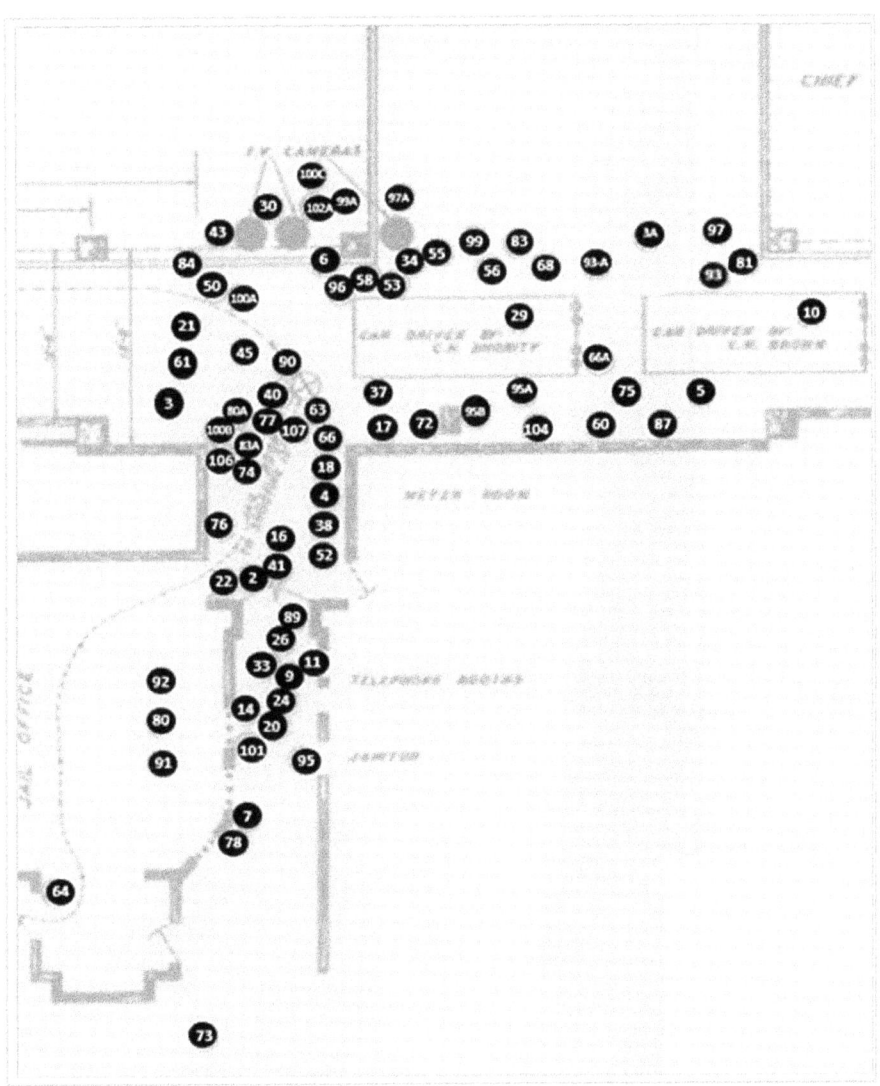

- Figure '90' represents Jack Ruby

B: Commerce Street:

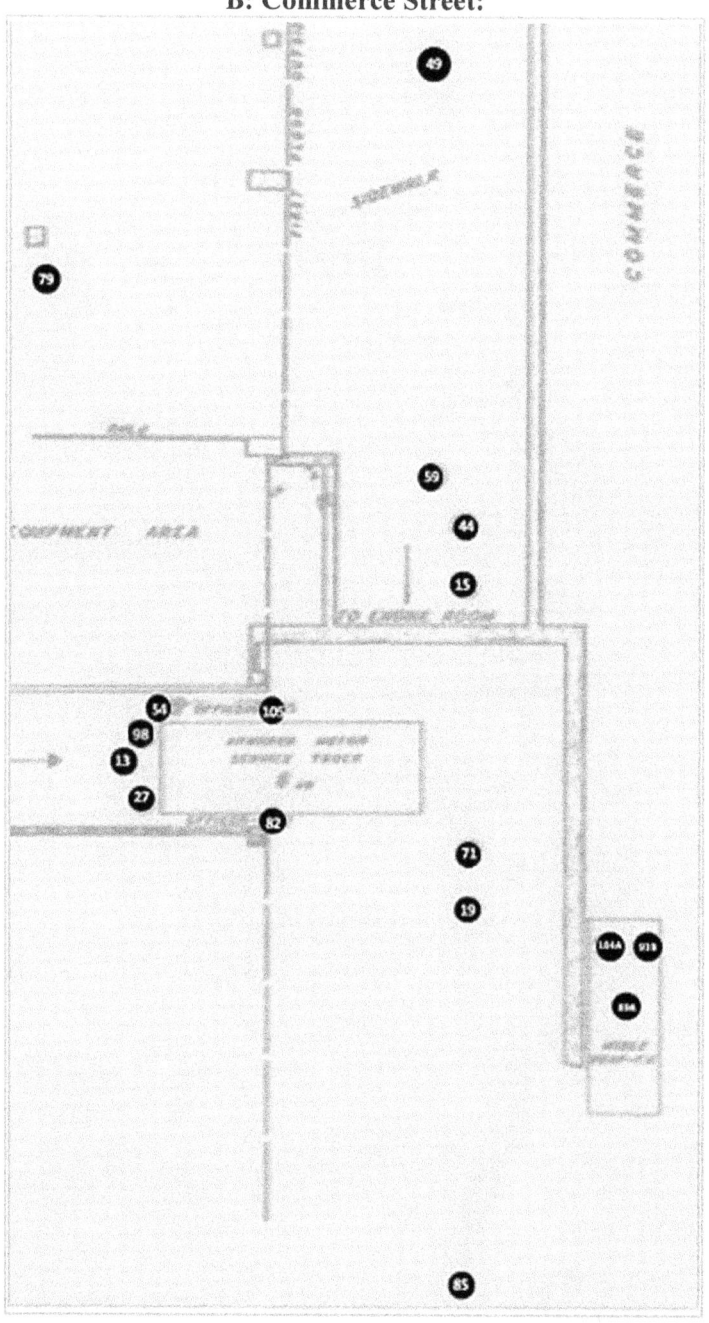

C: Main Street:

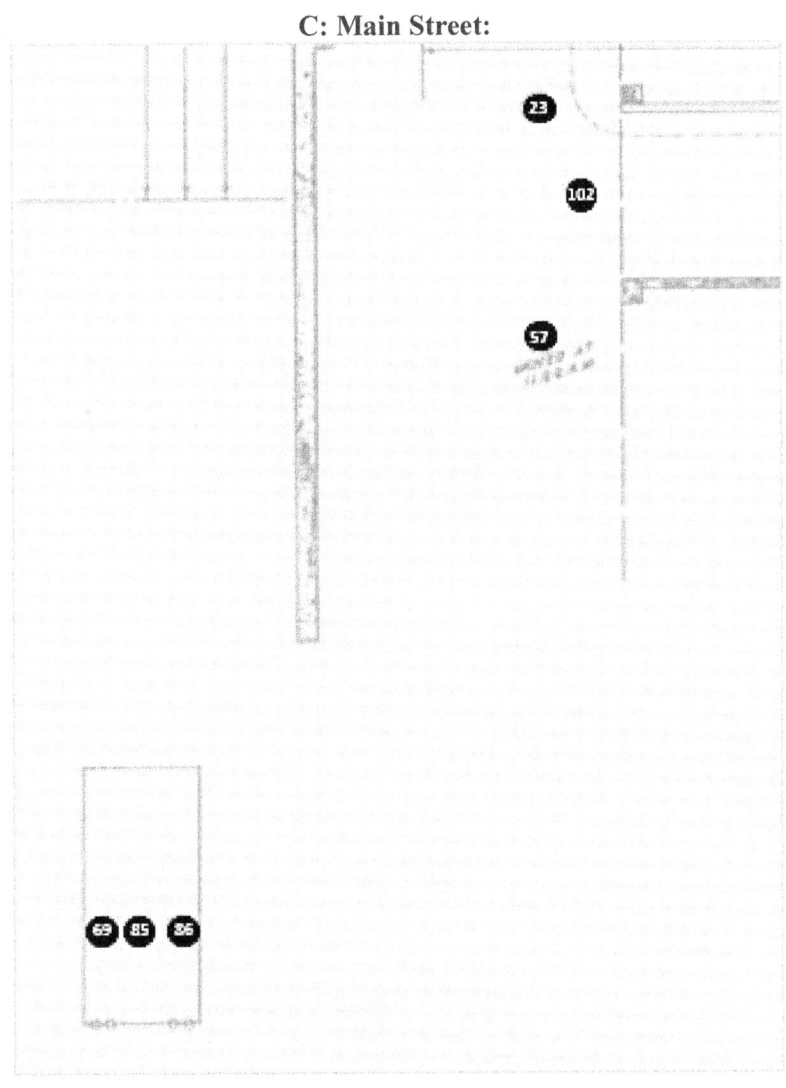

'57' was not named by the DPD in its corresponding schematic list but it was Wilford Ray Jones, noted as being present in this position until 11:00am.

3: Indicative Positionings of Shooting Witnesses:

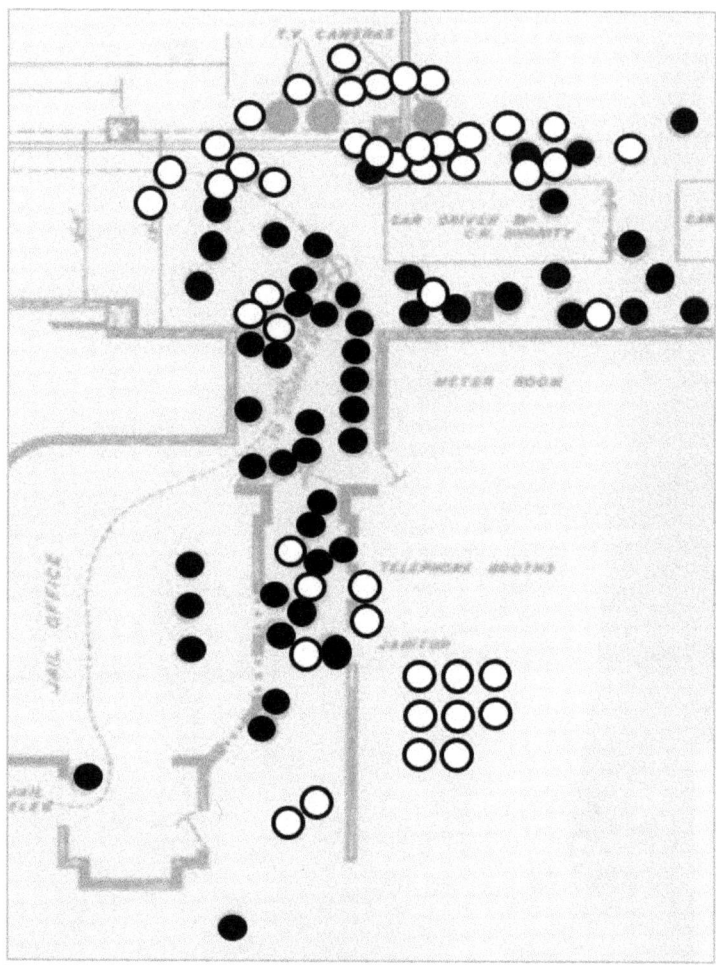

This version of the schematic represents, with the exception of those in the jail office, the concentration of witnesses in the immediate vicinity of Oswald's shooting. The black circles represent DPD personnel and the white circles are media personnel.

Including the 7 media personnel acknowledged as being at the scene but their positions never confirmed, this schematic represents the concentration of **46** members of the DPD and **38** members of the media confirmed as witnesses of the shooting. Porters Fuqua and Riggs are not represented in the above.

4. Assorted Articles Reporting on Oswald Shooting

Police Capture Owner of Club

Sparing Mrs. Kennedy Agony Of Oswald Trial Called Motive

BY ED JOHNSON
Star-Telegram Writer

DALLAS, Nov. 24—Lee Harvey Oswald, assassin of President Kennedy, was shot fatally by a self-appointed executioner Sunday in the basement of Dallas City Hall.

The single bullet that ended the professed Marxist's life was fired at 11:20 a. m. by a man who lurched from a crowd of reporters and lawmen.

Police immediately pounced upon the gunman, Jack Ruby, a quick-tempered strip tease club owner who reportedly has been seething with hatred about Kennedy's assassination.

"I did this because I have a deep sense of responsibility to Mrs. Jacqueline Kennedy," a Dallas policeman quoted Ruby as saying.

"I did it to spare Mrs. Kennedy the agony of a prolonged public trial."

Oswald was slain as he was being escorted to an armored car that was to insure his safety as he was transferred from the city jail to the Dallas County jail.

The former marine died at 1:07 p. m. while undergoing surgery at Parkland Hospital, where Kennedy died Friday.

BODY PUT UNDER GUARD

His body was taken to Fort Worth and placed under police guard after arriving late Sunday at Miller's Funeral Home.

Ruby, born James Rubinstein, was charged with murdering Oswald. The charge was filed before Peace Justice Pierce McBride.

McBride told reporters he advised Ruby of his rights. The prisoner said he would be represented legally by one of several lawyers whose names he mentioned, McBride stated.

"He is very calm," the official said of the 53-year-old Ruby.

No bond was set immediately.

McBride said he had not been asked to conduct an examining trial to determine if Ruby should be released on bail.

However, Attorney Tom Howard told the Star-Telegram he expected to make an attempt to free Ruby on bond. The attorney indicated he would request an examining trial in a few days.

Filing of the murder charge against the club owner had the effect of canceling a habeas corpus hearing that had been scheduled for Ruby Monday morning. Purpose of this hearing would have been to win the prisoner's release from custody.

It was reported that Oswald was seen recently in Ruby's downtown strip house, the Carousel Club.

The slug fired by the club owner apparently ended the state's investigation of the presidential assassination.

"As far as we are concerned, the case of the assassination of the President is closed," said Dallas Detective Capt. Will Fritz. ". . . We are absolutely convinced that Oswald was the assassin and that no one else was involved."

DETECTIVE FORESAW ACT

In Washington, a Justice Department spokesman said, "Very strong evidence points to Oswald as the assassin. The FBI will continue to investigate every lead and every bit of evidence."

(And, in Moscow, a leading radio commentator claimed the killing of Oswald was intended to conceal the truth about the sniper-slaying of Kennedy. He asserted the assassination was not the work of one man but was inspired by a group of people, and then made reference to right-wing activities in Texas.)

Dallas Detective B. H. Combest declared he saw Ruby—whom he knew—an instant before the shooting.

"I knew what he was going to do," the detective said. "I shouted at him, 'Jack, you son of a bitch!'

"I tried to reach over to him but I couldn't get him. He rushed right up to Oswald and put the gun flat against him. And I saw a flash of fire."

Tens of thousands across the nation heard the historic shot.

They heard it and saw it on their television screens—the dramatic event was being shown live by two of the major TV networks.

Ruby apparently jumped from a car as Oswald was brought from the elevator into an enclosed loading ramp.

He leaped a three foot high railing and darted into the mob of reporters and lawmen.

"I saw the man crouch down and then jump up and fire one shot," said Dallas Policeman P. T. Dean.

The manacled Oswald groaned in anguish and slumped over.

Oswald Slain

Policemen dragged him back inside the building while other officers jumped Ruby and took his .38 pistol.

Confusion reigned in the ramp area. Bystanders tried to get into the area.

One man hurrying to the scene carried a baby bottle filled with milk. Another tried to focus a small box camera on the run.

An emergency ambulance soon rolled up. The stretcher bearers darted inside, then appeared seconds later with the dying assassin on their cot.

As the ambulance driver started for the hospital, he found his path blocked by the armored van that was supposed to have protected Oswald, a former Fort Worth resident who had been living in Dallas.

The van was moved and the ambulance lurched forward. As the cot containing Oswald was wheeled into the Parkland Hospital emerecency room at 11:32 a. m., it passed under a sign reading: "Pay your blood debt."

As they had done for Kennedy and Governor Connally Friday, hospital attendants pulled out all stops to save Oswald. But their efforts failed.

The slaying triggered pandemonium in this city.

There were reports of bomb threats. A threat was made against the life of an attorney who had gone to City Hall to inquire about Ruby.

A police security guard swarmed about the ramp area before Oswald was brought downstairs from his cell.

Normally, police drive their cars down the ramp and unload their prisoners at a hallway leading to the basement booking area. From the booking office, the prisoners are taken upstairs to their assigned cells by elevator.

But the armored car slated to transport Oswald could not be backed up to the hallway—the ceiling above the ramp was too low for the van.

Hence the van was backed up to the Commerce St. exit of the ramp.

And so it was that police had planned to march Oswald up the sloping ramp to the awaiting van.

He never made the trip. Oswald was just entering the ramp from the hallway when mortally wounded.

Police announced Saturday night that Oswald would be transferred to the county jail Sunday morning.

Security Measures Criticized

This, combined with Oswald's death, prompted criticism of security measures taken by police.

Later, after being barraged with reporters' questions pertaining to this matter, Dallas Police Chief Jesse Curry stated:

"If I hadn't promised you people I would not take Oswald until this morning, we would have taken him during the night. I told you I wouldn't back down on my pledge."

In Washington, the Associated Press reported, foreign policy officials reacted with shock and dismay to the shooting of Oswald.

With the eyes of the world focused on the United States as a result of the assassination of the President, the officials had hoped the arrest and trial of Oswald would demonstrate the order, fairness and justice which the nation has presented to others as a major virtue of a democracy.

Johnson Orders Inquiry

The Justice Department announced in Washington that President Johnson had ordered the FBI to make a full investigation of Oswald's killing.

Assistant U. S. Attorney General Jack Miller Jr., head of the department's criminal section, flew to Dallas Sunday after the shooting. The only reason given by the department for the mission was that Miller was to confer with U. S. Attorney Barefoot Sanders.

District Attorney Henry Wade of Dallas said Ruby will be prosecuted for murder in an attempt to send him to the electric chair.

Wade revealed at a press conference Sunday night the evidence gathered against the slain Oswald.

Here is the evidence Wade presented:

1. A number of witnesses saw a person on the sixth floor of the Texas School Book Depository with a gun, he said.
2. The killer's palm prints were found on a box near the window from which the fatal shots were fired.
3. The gun was purchased from a mail order house under the assumed name of A. Hidell. The murder weapon was sent to a Dallas postoffice box. Wade said they had found in Oswald's wallet an identification of the assumed name and the postoffice box number.
4. A picture was found showing Oswald with both the rifle
4. A picture was found showing Wade with both the rifle which killed President Kennedy and the pistol, which killed Dallas Policeman J. D. Tippit.
5. Wade said Oswald ordinarily went to Irving, where his wife was living, on Friday night and returned to Dallas on Monday. Last week he went to Irving Thursday night and returned Friday morning with a package which Oswald said was window shades.
6. Mrs. Oswald said her husband had the death gun with him the night before the assassination. Friday, it was missing from the Irving home.

Seen in Building

7. A policeman saw Oswald in the building after the shooting, but let him go when the manager said he was an employe.
8. Oswald was the only person missing from the building when police checked out workers after the shooting.
9. Oswald boarded a bus on Lamar St. and told the driver the President had been shot, and laughed about it.
10. A woman bus passenger asked Oswald how he knew of the shooting and he replied that a man had told him.
11. Oswald left the bus in the Oak Cliff section of Dallas, took a taxi cab to his rooming house, quickly changed clothes and left.
12. Then, traveling on foot, Wade said, Oswald was sighted by a police officer after the ex-marine's description had been broadcast. The officer went up to Oswald and the assassin shot him.
13. Witnesses saw Oswald eject fired cartridges and reload his gun as he crossed a vacant lot to enter the Texas Theater.
14. Oswald tried to shoot Policeman M. N. McDonald when the officer arrested him, but he was subdued.
15. Wade said Oswald's palm prints were found on the metal part of the rifle and paraffin tests on his cheek and hand showed he recently had fired a gun.
16. The DA stated positively that the rifle bearing Oswald's prints was the one that killed the President.
17. Wade added that witnesses had placed Oswald on the sixth floor of the building at noon Friday.

REPORTER GIVES HIS VERSION

Gunman Seen as Brown Blur

By BOB FENLEY
Staff Writer

He was a brown blur, dashing from the group of newsmen straight toward the slender figure of Lee Harvey Oswald.

Crouching, he shoved the pistol against the prisoner's black sweater and there was a flash and the blunted sound of the gun.

Oswald's face contorted in pain.

"Oh no!" someone yelled.

"Jack, you son of a —," shouted a detective.

Leaping, clawing, shoving, shouting policemen in suits and uniforms surged toward the man in the brown hat and brown suit as Oswald crumpled in the arms of the horrified detectives who had been at his side.

BASEMENT BEDLAM

The basement of Dallas City Hall was bedlam.

We rushed forward toward the tangled mass of men which now looked like the pile-on game that school children play.

A policeman leaped on the trunk of a car, ran over its top and down the hood to join the melee.

"Get back! Get them back!" and we were shoved back by other frantic policemen.

Then we couldn't see—either Oswald or the man in brown.

"Seal the entrances. Don't let anybody out."

"Please, please guys, keep back. My God."

It was a scene from a Grade B movie. It was a bad late-late show. There were elbows and hands against my chest and grim, menacing, startled faces before my eyes but I couldn't believe it:

The man who killed President Kennedy had been shot by a short, heavy man in a brown suit and both were down somewhere in that mass of shouting policemen.

TANGLE DISSIPATES

Suddenly the tangle had disappeared inside the booking room and we were shouting questions at the harried line of policemen holding us back. Detectives were dashing in and out of the door.

It was unreal; it was like dozing on a couch and listening to the shouts of a crowd at a football game.

I had been standing with Seth Kantor, a friend and former Times Herald reporter, who now works in Washington for a newspaper chain. I looked around and he was still there in the crush of half a hundred reporters and cameramen and I said, "Good God."

"I don't believe it," he gasped.

Reporters were interviewing reporters. "He was well dressed," one said.

The police line had fallen back almost to the doors and one of the detectives I know came out. He was wiping tears from his eyes.

A SUDDEN FEAR

"Who did it?" He shook his head. "How's Oswald? I don't know."

"Was it one of your own men?" I had a sudden fear that a plainclothes man had gone berserk and had shot Oswald.

..., he said, leaning forward to whisper, "Ruby."
"Ruby what?"
"Jack Ruby, he runs a girlie show." The detective dashed back inside.
"Ambulance! Clear the way. Clear the way," and we moved as the flashing light atop the vehicle whirled down the ramp from Main Street into the basement.
We darted forward. A stretcher careened from the door of the booking room, drawn by running attendants who picked it up and shoved the inert body of Oswald inside.

SEES HEAD ROLL

I could see his head roll limply from side to side and that his mouth was open and that his left arm was over his stomach.
There was no blood, or at least I couldn't see any on that black sweater he still wore.
The ambulance driver hit the siren button but he couldn't move.
"Get that truck out of the way." In the pandemonium, it had been forgotten that the big square armored truck that was to take Oswald to the county jail was still parked in the opening of the Commerce Street entrance, in addition to two police sedans.
The truck's green-glassed doors were still open at the rear and you could see a cot inside.

COMES TO LIFE

The truck sputtered to life and the sedans were gunned up and the ambulance went up the ramp and away.
I had a flashing recollection of a smiling and tan John F. Kennedy stepping off a gleaming jet. Was it Friday?
I had arrived at City Hall about 8:15 a.m. Sunday and had walked by a television truck parked at the Commerce Street entrance, up the stairs and to the elevator. I mashed the third floor button and when the door opened, there were more television cameras in the hall manned by a couple of half-asleep technicians.
There were only a half dozen or so press people about; in the press room a pair who said they had been up all night, thinking Oswald might be transferred to County Jail early.

DRINK BAD COFFEE

But the announcement had been made by Police Chief Curry that the transfer would begin at 10 a.m. We waited, drinking bad coffee and trying to wake up. The press room blackboard said Mrs. Connally would hold a conference at 11 a.m.
I talked to Kantor, who is a White House correspondent for Scripps-Howard, and we mulled over Friday. "I'm drained," he said.
Sometime after 9 a.m., a police official came out and announced that Oswald would not be brought to the third floor—that he would be taken directly from his cell on the fifth floor of the Police Building, down the jail elevator, out the basement booking room to the vehicle which would pick him up in the drive-through parking area.
The basement parking area is a vast room, fairly well lit but with a few dark nooks.

ROOM WAS FILLED

Reporters, photographers, television cameramen and policemen all moved down to the bright booking area where police records are kept and where the only people usually coming around on an early Sunday are those bailing out drunks. But Sunday, it was filled with policemen and reporters.
One officer told a patrolman: "Go look in the hospital room and have those elevators secured." He meant those under City Hall property. Other policemen stood at the drive-through's entrance and exit.
Oswald's route was established: He would emerge from the elevator which is behind the booking desk enclosure, move through a small anteroom, out propped-open doors and onto the drive through ramp which separates the parking area from the booking rooms.
Photographers and reporters milled about the small booking anteroom, hoping to be as near as possible. But 10 a.m. suddenly turned into 10:30 a.m. and no Oswald.
Our photographer, Bob Jackson, had arrived and he said he probably would have to leave soon to photograph Mrs. Connally if Os-

wald weren't brought down. (Mrs. Nellie Connally, wife of the Texas Governor, had scheduled a press conference at 11 a.m. Sunday, her first since the president was assassinated and the governor was shot Friday.) We decided another photographer should be sent and he should wait. He was, in fact, about to take one of the most dramatic news pictures I have ever seen.
It was 11 a.m. and the officers said we would have to clear out of the booking area, that we could stand between two posts at the far side of the drive-through and that Oswald would come right by. Two cars were moved directly across from the booking room door so that live television cameras could be set up there.
We lined up. I was standing about 25 feet away from the booking room door. To my right was one pillar, surrounded by newsmen, and beyond, the television cameras aimed right at the door. There were perhaps more than 30 of us watching and waiting.
At 11:20 a.m. there was a shout: "Here he comes."
Oswald, preceded by a few plainclothesmen, was being walked briskly from the door.
His face was sallow. I could see the small wound above one of those eyes which he seemed to cast about strangely.
And then, somewhere from the clot of press people on my right, the short man in the brown clothes burst across the drive and, about 15 feet away from where we were standing, delivered the shot. It seemed to me, although I could not see the man's face, his eyes must have been riveted on Oswald's heart. He planted the 38 caliber snub-nosed revolver, and there was the shot. It was not too loud. It sounded a bit muffled.
It was a fantastic scene. I still hardly believe it.

(Mount Clipping In Space Below)

INDIGNATION AT OSWALD KILLING

Press Raps Dallas Police

By THE ASSOCIATED PRESS

The nation's newspapers generally expressed shock and dismay at the slaying of Lee Harvey Oswald, accused assassin of President Kennedy.

Some editorials also assailed the authorities of Dallas, charging them with laxity or sensation-seeking.

"The misguided, degraded citizen who fired the shot that killed Lee Oswald . . . has placed a serious blot on the record of American justice," said an editorial in a special edition of the Las Vegas, Nev., Review-Journal.

"Dallas authorities are responsible for the Oswald case," said the Omaha World Herald. "It happened because officials undertook to turn the transfer of a suspected murderer into a Roman circus."

SEES PARADOX

"Here again," said the Portland, Maine, Press Herald, "we have the paradox of America— a country boasting of its unparalleled system of government by law, but with a thread of lawlessness and violence running through its national history. . . ."

"One crime, however monstrous, and however it may shake the nation and the world, cannot justify another crime," said the Milwaukee Sentinel, "even the shooting of an accused, disreputable assassin . . . if we have faith in the law, we must let the law take its own deliberate course."

"Some called Oswald's end deserved," said the Nashville Tennessean. "Some called it irony. Some called it poetic justice. Irony it may have been, but it was not justice under the law . . . it was as misguided, as senseless and as void of 'solving' anything as was the assassin's action in striking down President Kennedy. . . ."

TIMES CRITICAL

The New York Times charged that "the Dallas authorities, abetted and encouraged by the newspaper, TV and radio press, trampled on every principle of justice in their handling of Lee H. Oswald. . . .

"After two days of . . . prejudgings of guilt, in the electrically emotional atmosphere of a city angered by the President's assassination and not too many decades removed from the vigilante tradition of the old frontier, the jail transfer was made at high noon and with the widest possible advance announcement . . . it was an outrageous breach of police responsibility."

The New York Herald Tribune said Oswald's killing "has served only to compound a heinous crime. . . .

"Those who applaud the killer on the ground that he gave the suspected assassin his due must share in the disgrace. They do no honor to our late President, to the nation or to the institutions which President Kennedy fought to uphold."

York Daily News, "a Dallas

"Yesterday," said the New Citizen climaxed a ghastly week and in U.S. history by assassinating Oswald.

"You can understand the act. Many of us are convinced that the only good murderer is a dead murderer and the only good Communist a dead Communist.

"Communist murderers in this country, however, like other murderers, should be made dead only by due process of law...."

"NEGATES JUSTICE"

The Long Beach, Calif., Independent, Press-Telegram declared that the shot from a revolver wielded by nightclub proprietor Jack Ruby, which took Oswald's life, "has negated the whole theory of American justice, which requires that those suspected of crimes be tried in courts of law rather than by the vigilance committee."

"Justice is thwarted," added the editorial.

The Miami Herald declared Oswald's death as "another incredible blunder of security—a blunder so fantastic that it almost seemed contrived...."

The Herald added that with Oswald "dies the motive of a murder that has staggered the world. With him goes a story which well may have had complications grave for the national security, made even more serious now by an eternal silence."

The editorial called it an "unthinkable decision to transfer him (Oswald) from one jail to another as reporters and photographers and loiterers milled around the scene."

The Albuquerque Journal said that "whether every precaution possible was taken to protect the President's life as he rode through Dallas downtown in an open car may never be satisfactorily answered.

"But," the Journal added, "certainly there can be no excuse for the lack of security which resulted in the shooting to death of the President's alleged slayer...."

"Dallas is not to be shamed as a city, but certainly shame falls upon the few people who carried the responsibility for what happened."

"EXAMINE CONSCIENCE"

"Let us Americans conduct a national examination of conscience," said the Providence Journal. "In the last 72 hours, the world has witnessed in shock a display of horrid savagery that shames the greatest free nation in the world...

"In these two murders... is frightening evidence of the spread of the canker of disrespect of law and of the readiness to resort to violence against those with whom we disagree."

The Baltimore Sun called it "shame heaped upon shame that the man accused of the murder of Mr. Kennedy should himself have been murdered, and that his guilt, or his innocence, should not have been determined by the orderly processes of the law...

"The immediate blame rests with a municipal police force which could not protect a prisoner on its own premises, and which incredibly violated one of the first rules of police custody, the rule that says the moving of a controversial prisoner must not be told in advance to the public.

"But a deeper fault, a fault we cannot in honesty and decency fail to face, lies in a diseased spot of hate somewhere in our society."

"ADDS TO TRAGEDY"

The St. Louis Globe-Democrat said that the killing of Oswald "only adds to the bitterly shameful tragedy.

"Even though Oswald was guilty, as seemed evident, he was entitled to a speedy trial and swift punishment, if convicted. Only a further blot is added by his street slaying, and Dallas police protection should be investigated."

Ruby, said the Rochester N.Y., Democrat and Chronicle, "denied America the chance to show the world that this is a nation of law and justice and order....

"If it gives more force to the claim upon all of us to reflect on our own actions and our own angers, to re-examine our own lives and our associations, to remind us how close we walk to anarchy and how we must always guard against it, then even this footnote has a value."

"HORRIBLE CRIME"

The Cleveland Plain Dealer said Oswald's murder "has compounded a horrible crime and undoubtedly has delayed or permanently impaired — the pursuit of justice....

"There is almost no question but what he was the assassin who killed President John F. Kennedy," said the Plain Dealer. "But did he have accomplices? ... what was behind the shooting of our president? ... Oswald alive was a valuable link to the infamous Kennedy crime ... Jack Ruby should be hailed as our national fool."

"Senseless and futile," said the Arizona Republic of Phoenix. "It would have been the last thing President Kennedy would have wanted."

"The Dallas police will be accused, with no justification of course," of having branded the prime suspect in President Kennedy's death as a Communist and then having engineered his murder."

EXPRESSES HOPE

The Las Vegas Review-Journal expressed the hope that "somehow, perhaps in the trial of Oswald's own killer, the evidence against the man charged with taking the President's life will be unveiled by authorities in Dallas and responsible federal officials. The public is entitled to know everything possible about why our great leader has been taken from us."

The Kansas City Star said the deaths in Dallas "symbolize as dramatically the kind of atmosphere that has been created, at home and abroad, in the market ing hatred of but a few men and a few groups bending beneath the world's tensions.... a man accused of the most heinous crime is entitled to a fair trial. He was not to receive it and this fact, to the degree that it symbolizes the atmosphere of the nation, is a fact of shame."

CALLED LYNCHING

"In effect," said the Detroit Free Press, "Oswald was lynched by a man whose motives also are obscure.... the sequel to the Kennedy assassination is thus a chain reaction of terrible proportions. When do men cease to take the law into their own hands? When does this orgy of hate and fear and suspicion and violence come to an end? Until it does, America must hang its head in shame as well as remorse before the civilized world."

The Utica, N.Y., Daily Press said that "no matter what Americans thought of this professed Communist, murdering him was no answer... the shooting... darkened the picture that so many in the world have of the United States and only added weight to the impression that we are a lawless, bitter nation.

Millions of Eyewitnesses Watch Oswald Shooting

An eyewitness in a shooting death is considered a rare windfall for a prosecutor, but there were millions of witnesses to the slaying of Lee Harvey Oswald.

Horrified Sunday morning television viewers saw the shooting from coast to coast via live television.

Both CBS and NBC cameras telecast the scene live from the basement of the Dallas City Hall.

In addition, film cameramen shot pictures of the event. George Phenix of KRLD-TV, The Times Herald station, had film showing the gunman waiting in the crowd with reporters as they brought Oswald down from the city jail.

The film shows Jack Ruby peering around reporters at Oswald on Oswald's left. He stepped forward and took a good look at Oswald. Then he stepped back, possibly to draw his gun. Then he started to move forward.

As he did so, Oswald turned his head to look at Ruby, who crouched and wheeled into the open pathway, firing as he did.

As a city detective said, he was bootlegging the pistol on his hip like a quarterback with a football.

Detectives immediately pounced on Ruby. Capt. Will Fritz, head of the Homicide and Robbery Bureau, had just walked ahead of the spot of the action. He turned and rushed to Oswald. A uniformed officer grabbed Ruby's hand which held the gun and pointed it toward the floor.

A police captain in uniform yelled to the mob, "He's been shot."

Detectives then blocked the doorway and rushed Oswald and Ruby back into the main police building, keeping reporters out in the underground area until an ambulance came.

George Underwood, a KRLD TV announcer, became the press counselor of Mrs. Eva Grant, Ruby's sister. Mr. Underwood was the first reporter at the woman's house and she recognized him from his TV appearances. She invited him into the house and asked him to help her. She insisted that Mr. Underwood accompany her when she went to police headquarters to talk with Capt. Fritz and to see her brother.

Weekend of Terror Spawns Wild Rumors

The murder of President Kennedy and the slaying of his accused killer brought a nightmarish finish to the most terror-filled weekend in Dallas history.

Strangely enough other crimes dipped sharply during the 66-hour span which followed the President's assassination here Friday.

"We were lucky that we didn't have an outbreak of other crimes," an officer said Monday morning in the silent wake of a weekend of fear and uncertainty.

There was the usual number of aggravated assaults and petty thefts and rhubarbs.

Traffic officers—especially those assigned to the automobile clogged downtown section—were extremely busy.

Crank telephone calls into police headquarters kept officers and workers in the dispatcher's office flooded with work. Many of the callers were drunks.

Rumors ran rampant during the hours after the President was fatally shot and again Sunday when his alleged slayer, Lee Harvey Oswald, was gunned down in the basement of the police station.

Rumors of every description buzzed through the city Sunday afternoon and night. They continued coming in Monday.

There was one report that circulated through Dallas during the night that Dist. Atty. Henry Wade had been killed by a sniper. Another rumor spread that a caravan was converging on Dallas to storm the city.

Neither was right.

Sunday night a thief used a screw driver to pry open a door at the Ross Avenue Baptist Church at 5301 Ross Ave. and stole 13 purses from women members of the church choir.

A memorial service for the dead President was being held.

Later Sunday night a gunman and accomplice struck at Cabell's Minit Market, 2910 N. Haskell, and fled with an undetermined amount of cash after forcing Paul Barefoot, an employe, to sack up the money for them.

5. Sheriff Deputy C.C. McCoy's Report to Sheriff Decker Regarding Threats Received Against Oswald

FORM 114 SUP. INV.

COUNTY OF DALLAS
SHERIFF'S DEPARTMENT

SUPPLEMENTARY INVESTIGATION REPORT

Name of Complainant   Serial No.

Offense

RE: LEE HARVEY OSWALD W/M- IN CITY JAIL

DETAILS OF OFFENSE, PROGRESS OF INVESTIGATION, ETC.:
(Investigating Officer must sign)

Date NOVEMBER 24, 1963.

MR. DECKER,

I HAD RECEIVED SEVERAL LONG DISTANCE CALLS FROM PEOPLE ALL OVER THE UNITED STATES - THE SAME PERSON CALLED THREE TIMES FROM NEW JERSEY. I MIGHT ADD THAT HE SOUNDED TO BE QUITE DRUNK, AND STATED THAT HE HAD BEEN TO TEXAS DURING WORLD WAR TWO AND HE STATED THAT HE THOUGHT A LOT OF THE PEOPLE HERE AND HE WANTED TO LET US KNOW THAT HE FELT VERY SORRY FOR ALL OF US. ONE LADY CALLED FROM CALIFORNIA AND SHE LET ME KNOW WHAT SHE THOUGHT OF THE WHOLE STATE OF TEXAS AND THE PEOPLE WHO LIVED HERE. ONE MAN CALLED FROM PENNSYLVANIA AND STATED THAT HE HAD HEARD WHAT KIND OF PEOPLE WE WERE AND THAT HE WAS A LEADER OF 14,000 NEGROES AND THAT THEY WERE ALL COMING TO TEXAS AND GET THIS BUNCH OF BARBARIANS STRAIGHTENED OUT. HOWEVER, THE MAJORITY OF PEOPLE WERE VERY NICE AND JUST WANTED US TO KNOW THAT THEY FELT SORRY FOR US AND WANTED TO KNOW IF THE OFFICERS WERE SURE THAT THEY HAD THE RIGHT MAN.

WHEN YOU CALLED THE OFFICE AT 2:00 AM., I HAD NOT RECEIVED ANY THREATS ON THE LIFE OF OSWALD BUT AT THAT TIME YOU MENTIONED THE FACT THAT YOU THOUGHT THAT OSWALD SHOULD BE TRANSFERRED FROM THE CITY JAIL WHILE IT WAS STILL DARK AND YOU WANTED TO KNOW ABOUT WHAT TIME THAT IT WAS DAY LIGHT, AND I TOLD YOU THAT IT WAS DAY LIGHT AT APPROX. 6:30 AM. OR 6:45 AM. AND YOU ASKED ME TO CALL YOU AT 6:00 AM. AND YOU WOULD SEE ABOUT GETTING OSWALD TRANSFERRED WHILE IT WAS STILL DARK.

AT APPROX. 2:15 AM. I RECEIVED A CALL FROM A PERSON THAT TALKED LIKE A W/M AND HE STATED THAT HE WAS A MEMBER OF A GROUP OF ONE HUNDRED AND THAT HE WANTED THE SHERIFF'S OFFICE TO KNOW THAT THEY HAD VOTED ONE HUNDRED PER CENT TO KILL OSWALD WHILE HE WAS IN THE PROCESS OF BEING TRANSFERRED TO THE COUNTY JAIL

I recommend this case be declared Unfounded / Inactive (not cleared) / Cleared by Arrest   Case declared Inactive (not cleared) / Unfounded   (CONT'D)

Signed _____   Signed _____

DECKER EXHIBIT No. 5323—Continued

FORM 114 SUP. INV.

COUNTY OF DALLAS
SHERIFF'S DEPARTMENT
SUPPLEMENTARY INVESTIGATION REPORT

Name of Complainant _____ Serial No. _____

Offense _____

DETAILS OF OFFENSE, PROGRESS OF INVESTIGATION, ETC.:
(Investigating Officer must sign)

Date _____ 19___

PAGE 2

AND THAT HE WANTED THIS DEPARTMENT TO HAVE THE INFORMATION SO THAT NONE OF THE DEPUTIES WOULD GET HURT. THE VOICE WAS DEEP AND COURSE AND SOUNDED VERY SINCERE AND TALKED WITH EASE. THE PERSON DID NOT SEEM EXCITED LIKE SOME OF THE CALLS THAT WE HAD RECEIVED RUNNING DOWN THIS DEPARTMENT, THE POLICE DEPARTMENT AND THE STATE OF TEXAS AND HE SEEMED VERY CALM ABOUT THE WHOLE MATTER. VIRGIL AND ALSO LISTENED TO PART OF THE CONVERSATION. A SHORT TIME LATER, MR. NEWSOME, FROM THE FBI OFFICE CALLED AND WANTED TO KNOW IF WE HAD RECEIVED ANY CALLS ON THE LIFE OF OSWALD AND I PASSED ON THE ABOVE INFORMATION AND HE ASKED ME TO CALL THE POLICE DEPARTMENT AND GIVE THEM THE SAME INFORMATION. I CALLED THE CITY HALL AND TALKED TO SOMEONE IN CAPTAIN FRITZS OFFICE. I DID NOT GET HIS NAME. THE OFFICER MADE SOME SLIGHT REMARK AND SAID THAT THEY HAD NOT RECEIVED ANY SUCH CALLS AS YET.

I RECEIVED ONE OTHER CALL REGARDING THE TRANSFER OS OSWALD AND WHEN I ANS-WERED THE TELEPHONE, A MALE VOICE ASKED IF THIS IS THE SHERIFF'S OFFICE AND I SAID THAT IT WAS, HE SAID JUST A MINUTE AND THEN ANOTHER MALE VOICE STATED THAT OSWALD WOULD NEVER MAKE THE TRIP TO THE COUNTY JAIL. I COULD NOT DETERMINE WHETHER OR NOT THIS WAS THE SAME VOICE THAT HAD CALLED EARLIER.

AS YOU KNOW, WHEN I CALLED YOU AT 6:00 A.M., YOU WANTED TO KNOW WHO WAS THERE AT THE OFFICE AND I TOLD YOU THAT KENNEDY, VIRGIL, WATKINS AND ONE OR TWO OTHERS AND YOU ASKED ME TO CALL BOCKEMEHL AND HAVE HIM CALL YOU AT HOME AND THEN YOU ASKED ME IF I THOUGHT THAT KENNEDY AND I COULD TRANSFER OSWALD FROM THE CITY JAIL WITHOUT CAUSING MUCH OF A SCENE BY HAND CUFFING OSWALD TO ME AND BY KEEPING OSWALD IN THE FLOOR BOARD OF THE CAR SO THAT HE COULD NOT BE SEEN. I TOLD YOU

(CONT'D)

FORM 114 SUP. INV.

COUNTY OF DALLAS
SHERIFF'S DEPARTMENT

SUPPLEMENTARY INVESTIGATION REPORT

Name of Complainant   Serial No.

Offense

DETAILS OF OFFENSE, PROGRESS OF INVESTIGATION, ETC.:
(Investigating Officer must sign)

Date _____ 19____

PAGE 3

THAT WE WOULD GIVE IT A TRY AND YOU ADVISED TO HOLD UP UNTIL YOU TALKED TO FRITZ A SHORT TIME LATER, AN OFFICER CALLED FROM THE POLICE DEPARTMENT, I BELIEVE HE WAS CAPTAIN TOLBERT, AND HE WANTED TO TALK TO YOU AND I TOLD HIM THAT YOU COULD BE REACHED AT HOME AND I GAVE HIM YOUR NUMBER. A SHORT TIME LATER YOU CALLED BACK AND TOLD ME THAT YOU HAD BEEN UNABLE TO REACH FRITZ BUT TO HOLD UP AND ALSO TO HOLD THE LATE NIGHT SQUADS AT THE OFFICE FOR A WHILE. A SHORT TIME LATER CAPTAIN FRAZIER CALLED, FROM THE POLICE DEPARTMENT, AND STATED THAT HE HAD BEEN TRYING TO CONTACT CHIEF CURRY BUT COULD NOT GET AN ANSWER ON THE TELEPHONE AND I BELIEVE THAT HE STATED THAT HE WAS GOING TO SEND A SQUAD BY THE CHIEF'S HOME. I ASKED CAPTAIN FRAZIER TO CALL YOU AT HOME AND GIVE THAT INFORMATION TO YOU. ALL OF THE LATE NIGHT SHIFT STAYED AT THE STATION AND WAS HERE WHEN YOU CALLED BACK AT ABOUT 7:50 A.M. AND YOU STATED THAT THEY WERE NOT GO FOR MAKING THE TRANSFER AT THIS TIME (FROM THE CITY JAIL TO THE COUNTY JAIL) AND TOLD US TO GO ON HOME AND GET SOME SLEEP.

McCOY

I recommend this case be declared { Unfounded / Inactive (not cleared) / Cleared by Arrest }   Case declared { Inactive (not cleared) / Unfounded }

Signed _____   Signed _____
            Investigating Officer   Commanding Officer

DECKER EXHIBIT No. 5323—Continued

6. Capt. William B. Frazier's FBI Statement Regarding Threats Received Against Oswald

```
FD-302 (Rev. 1-1-59)            FEDERAL BUREAU OF INVESTIGATION

1                                              Date   11/25/63

        Captain W. B. FRAZIER, man in charge, Dallas Police
Department, at 3:20 AM was advised of information received
from an unknown caller by Security Patrol Clerk VERNON R.
GLOSSUP at the Dallas FBI office, as follows:  "I represent
a committee that is neither right nor left wing, and tonight,
tomorrow morning, or tomorrow night, we are going to kill the
man that killed the President. There will be no excitement
and we will kill him. We wanted to be sure and tell the FBI,
Police Department, and Sheriff's Office and we will be there
and we will kill him."

        FRAZIER said the Police Department has not received
any calls of this type to his knowledge, but he advised he
would check other bureau heads in the Police Department to see
if a call of this type had been received. He stated he would
advise the Dallas office of this information. He said he would
give this information to Chief of Police JESSE E. CURRY immediately.
He was advised that the Dallas Sheriff's Office received a similar
call.

        FRAZIER said that plans to transfer OSWALD to the
County Jail may be changed in view of this threat, and the
Dallas Police Department will keep the FBI advised.

        FRAZIER stated that OSWALD's planned transfer had
been publicized primarily as a form of cooperation with the
press and news agencies of the press, and other news agencies.




                                    DL File 44-1639
on  11/24/63  at  Dallas, Texas           DL. File # 89-43
by Special Agent  MILTON L. NEWSOM/mfr           Date dictated  11/24/63

                                            FRAZIER,W.    Deposition
                                              Dallas      3-25-64

            FRAZIER EXHIBIT NO. 5087
```

Note the notations of 'Incorrect' next to the paragraphs that Frazier stated he did not say. If Sheriff Deputy McCoy had been able to testify before the Warren Commission, what might he have said about the statement attributed to him by Agent Newsom also?

7. Reproduction of Reserve Sergeant Kenneth S. Croy's Affidavit for the DPD Investigation

1 December 1963

I am a Reserve Police Sergeant with the Dallas Police Reserve. On November 24, 1963 I reported to the office Assembly Room at approximately 8:35 a.m. to Lieutenant Merrell who was making assignments. I then took over making assignments from him. I wrote the men up on the roster at the time they arrived and made assignments to them until approximately 10:00 a.m.

At that time (sic) I went to the basement and worked from the basement of the City Hall, assigning reserve officers who were late arriving, and also checking on where my ... has been assigned. Prior to Oswald's appearance into the basement of the City Hall I stationed myself at the foot of the north end of the ramp in the basement. I was there for quite some time watching the reporters. Someone had made the remark to watch the reporters and to move them back against the rail. There were several reporters in front of me. Captain Arnett was standing to the right of me. I was approximately in the middle of the ramp between the wall and the rail. Someone in authority gave instructions to move the press back against the rail.

At that time (sic) I turned and told two me standing to my left to move back against the rail. One of those men had a motion picture camera, the other was wearing a dark marron coat with black thread woven into it. He was wearing a brown hat. (My father has a coat something similar to the one the man was wearing that I spoke to) I then turned my attention back to the reporters which were standing in front of me. I believe this man that I spoke to have been Jack Ruby. The man with the motion picture camera got up on the rail. The man with the dark maroon coat stepped back a little. I turned back around (sic) and one or two officers came out of the jail office and then Captain Fritz, and then they brought Oswald out. He was handcuffed to one of the officers and there was a man on each side of his holding his arm. There was a reporter standing there with a microphone in his hand. The reporters then converged on Oswald. The report with the microphone stuck it up in Oswald's face and asked him, "Do you have any comment?'

At this time (sic) I observed a blur come from my left side. I was off balance. I saw a man running into the crowd in a crouch. At that moment I reached for this individual and touched his coat tail attempting to stop him. I saw him run right up to Oswald and I heard a shot.

At the time I heard the shot, there were several officers who swarmed him and wrestled him to the pavement. I also tried to grab hold of his gun, but there were too many men there for me to be effective. At that point an officer did disarm him and took him out. I didn't to see the man were wrestling to the floor because too many officers swarmed him.

At this point orders were given to seal the basement. I ran approximately half way (sic) up the north ramp and stopped reporters trying to leave the basement. During the interview with Lieutenant Jack Revill and Lieutenant and F.I. Cornwall something was mentioned about an automobile leaving the basement via the north ramp to the Main Street. I recall an automobile driving out, but I can't recall the time (sic) nor can I recall how many men were in the automobile. I seem to recall this automobile as being a light blue squad car.

8. Transcript of Jack Ruby's Polygraph Test – July 18 1964 (conducted over a period of six hours):

Q. Did you know Oswald before November 22, 1963?
A. No.
Q. Did you assist Oswald in the assassination?
A. No.
Q. Are you now a member of the Communist Party?
A. No.
Q. Have you ever been a member of the Communist Party?
A. No.
Q. Are you now a member of any group that advocates the violent overthrow of the United States Government?
A. No.
Q. Have you ever been a member of any group that advocates violent overthrow of the United States Government?
A. No.
Q. Between the assassination and the shooting, did anybody you know tell you they knew Oswald?
A. No.
Q. Aside from anything you said to George Senator on Sunday morning, did you ever tell anyone else that you intended to shoot Oswald?
A. No.
Q. Did you shoot Oswald in order to silence him?
A. No.
Q. Did you first decide to shoot Oswald on Friday night?
A. No.
Q. Did you first decide to shoot Oswald on Saturday morning?
A. No.
Q. Did you first decide to shoot Oswald on Saturday night?
A. No.
Q. Did you first decide to shoot Oswald on Sunday Morning?
A. Yes.
Q. Were you on the sidewalk at the time Lieutenant Pierce's car stopped on the ramp exit?
A. Yes.
Q. Did you enter the jail by walking through an alleyway?
A. No.

Q. Did you walk past the guard at the time Lieutenant Pierce's car was parked on the ramp exit?
A. Yes.
Q. Did you talk with any Dallas police officers on Sunday, November 24, prior to the shooting of Oswald ?
A No.
Q. Did you see the armored car before it entered the basement?
A. No.
Q. Did you enter the police department through a door at the rear of the east side of the jail
A. No.
Q. After talking to Little Lynn did you hear any announcement that Oswald was about to be moved?
A. No.
Q. Before you left your apartment. Sunday morning, did anyone tell you the armored car was on the way to the police department?
A. No.
Q. Did you get a Wall Street Journal at the Southwestern Drug Store during the week before he assassination?
A. No.
Q. Do you have any knowledge of the Wall Street Journal addressed to Mr. d. E. Bradshaw?
A. No.
Q. To your knowledge, did any of your friends or did you telephone the FBI in Dallas between 2 or 3 a.m. Sunday morning?
A No.
Q. Did you or any of your friends to your knowledge telephone the sheriff's office between 2 or 3 a.m. Sunday morning?
A. No.
Q. Did you go to the Dallas police station at any time on Friday, November 22, 1963, before you went to the synagogue?
A. No.
Q. Did you go to the synagogue that Friday night?
A. Yes.
Q. Did you see Oswald in the Dallas jail on Friday night?
A. Yes.
Q. Did you have a gun with you when you went to the Friday midnight press conference at the jail?
A. No.

375

Q. Is everything you told the Warren Commission the entire Truth?
A. Yes.
Q. Have you ever knowingly attended any meetings of the Communist Party or any other group that advocates violent, overthrow of the Government?
A. No.
Q. Is any member of your immediate family or any close friend, a member of the Communist Party?
A. No.
Q. Is any member of your immediate family or any close friend a member of any group that. advocates the violent overthrow of the Government?
A. No.
Q. Did any close friend or any member of your immediate family ever attend a meeting of the Communist Party?
A. No.
Q. Did any close friend or any member of your immediate family ever attend a meeting of any group that advocates the violent. overthrow of the Government?
A. No.
Q. Did you ever meet Oswald at your post office box?
A. No.
&. Did you use your post office mailbox to do any business with Mexico or Cuba?
A. No.
Q. Did you do business with Castro-Cuba?
A. No.
Q. Was your trip to Cuba solely for pleasure?
A. Yes."
Q. Have you now told us the truth concerning why you carried $2,200 in cash on you?
A. Yes.
Q. Did any foreign influence cause you to shoot Oswald 1
A. No.
Q. Did you shoot Oswald because of any influence of the underworld?
A. No.
Q. Did you shoot Oswald because of a labor union influence?

A. No.
Q. Did any long-distance telephone calls which you made before the assassination of the President have anything to do with the assassination?
A. No.
Q. 'Did any of your long-distance telephone calls concern the shooting of Oswald?
A. No.
Q. Did you shoot Oswald in order to save Mrs. Kennedy the ordeal of a trial?
A. Yes
Q. Did you know the Tippit that was killed?
A. No.
Q. Did you tell the truth about relaying the message to Ray Brantley to get McWillie a few guns?
A. Yes.
Q. Did you go to the assembly room on Friday night to get the telephone number of KLIF ?
a. Yes.
Q. Did you ever meet with Oswald and Officer Tippit at your Club?
A. No.
Q. Were you at the Parkland Hospital at any time on Friday?
a. No.
Q. Did you say anything when you shot Oswald other than what you've testified about?
A. No.
Q. Have members of your family been physically harmed because of what you did?
A. No.
Q. Do you think members of your family are now in danger because of what. you did?
(No response.)
Q. Is Mr. Fowler in danger because he is defending you?
(No response.)

Courtesy of:
https://aarclibrary.org/publib/jfk/wc/wr/pdf/WR_A17_PolygraphExamRuby.pdf

9. WC Counsel Burt Griffin and Leon Hubert Report regarding Adequacy of Ruby Investigation:

MEMORANDUM

May 14, 1964

To: J. Lee Rankin

From: Leon D. Hubert, Jr.
Burt W. Griffin

Subject: Adequacy of Ruby Investigation

1. Past Recommendations. In memoranda dated February 19, February 24, February 27, and March 11, we made various suggestions for extending the investigation initiated by the FBI in connection with the Oswald homicide. Shortly after March 11, 1964, we began preparation for the nearly 60 depositions taken in Dallas during the period March 21-April 2; after we returned from Dallas we took the deposition of C. L. Crafard (two days) and George Senator (two days), worked on editing the depositions taken in Dallas, and prepared for another series of 30 other depositions taken in Dallas during the period April 13-17. On our return from Dallas we continued the editing of the Dallas depositions, prepared the Dallas deposition exhibits for publication, and began working on a draft of the report in Area V. As a consequence of all of this activity during the period March 11-May 13, we did not press for the conferences and discussions referred to in the attached memoranda. The following represents our view at this time with respect to appropriate further investigation.

2. General Statement of Areas Not Adequately Investigated. In reporting on the murder of Lee Oswald by Jack Ruby, we must answer or at least advert to these questions:

a) Why did Ruby kill Oswald;

b) Was Ruby associated with the assassin of President Kennedy;

c) Did Ruby have any confederates in the murder of Oswald?

It is our belief that, although the evidence gathered so far does not show a conspiratorial link between Ruby and Oswald, or between Ruby and others, nevertheless evidence should be secured, if possible, to affirmatively exclude that:

a) Ruby was indirectly linked through others to Oswald;

b) Ruby killed Oswald, because of fear; or

c) Ruby killed Oswald at the suggestion of others.

3. **Summary of Evidence Suggesting Further Investigation.** The following facts suggest the necessity of further investigation:

a. Ruby had time to engage in substantial activities in addition to the management of his Clubs. Ruby's night club business usually occupied no more than five hours of a normal working day which began at about 10:00 a.m. and ended at 2:00 a.m. It was his practice to spend an average of only one hour a day at his Clubs between 10:00 a.m. and 9:00 p.m. Our depositions were confined primarily to persons familiar with Ruby's Club activities. The FBI has thoroughly investigated Ruby's night club operations but does not seem to have pinned down his other business or social activities. The basic materials do make reference to such other activities (see p. 27 of our report of February 18), but these are casual and collateral and were not explored to determine whether they involved any underlying sinister purpose. Nor were they probed in such a manner as to permit a determination as to how much of Ruby's time they occupied.

b. Ruby has always been a person who looked for money-making "sidelines." In the two months prior to November 22, Ruby supposedly spent considerable time promoting an exercise device known as a "twist board." The "twist board" was purportedly manufactured by Plastellite Engineering, a Fort Worth manufacturer of oil field equipment which has poor credit references and was the subject of an FBI investigation in 1952. We know of no sales of this item by Ruby, nor do we know if any "twist boards" were manufactured for sale. The possibility remains that the "twist board" was a front for some other illegal enterprise.

c. Ruby has long been close to persons pursuing illegal activities. Although Ruby had no known ideological or political interests (see p. 35 of our report of February 18), there is much evidence that he was interested in Cuban matters. In early 1959, Ruby inquired concerning the smuggling of persons out of Cuba. He has admitted that, at that time, he negotiated for the sale of jeeps to Castro. In September 1959, Ruby visited Havana at the invitation of Las Vegas racketeer, Louis J. McWillie, who paid Ruby's expenses for the trip and who was later expelled from Cuba by Castro. McWillie is described by Ralph Paul, Ruby's business partner, as one of Ruby's closest friends. Ruby mailed a gun to McWillie in early 1963. In 1961, it is reported that Ruby attended three meetings in Dallas in connection with the sale of arms to Cubans and the smuggling out of refugees. The informant identifies an Ed Brunner as Ruby's associate in this endeavor. Shortly after his arrest on November 24, Ruby named Fred Brunner as one of his expected attorneys. Brunner did not represent Ruby, however. Insufficient investigation has been conducted to confirm or deny the report about meetings in 1961. When Henry Wade announced to the Press on November 22, 1963 that Oswald was a member of the Free Cuba Committee, Ruby corrected Wade by stating "Not the Free Cuba Committee; The Fair Play for Cuba Committee. There is a difference." The Free Cuba Committee is an existing anti-Castro organization. Earl Ruby, brother of Jack Ruby, sent an unexplained telegram to Havana in April 1962. We believe that a reasonable possibility exists that Ruby has maintained a close interest in Cuban affairs to the extent necessary to participate in gun sales or smuggling.

4. Bits of evidence link Ruby to others who may have been interested in Cuban affairs. When Ruby's car was seized on November 24, it contained various right-wing radio scripts issued by H. L. Hunt and a copy of the Wall Street Journal bearing the mailing address of a man who has not yet been identified. In May 1963, Earl Ruby, operator of a dry cleaning business, is known to have telephoned the Welch Candy Company (owned by the founder of John Birch Society). The purpose of the call is unknown. Jack Ruby's personal notebook contained the Massachusetts telephone number and address of Thomas Hill, former Dallas resident, working at the Boston headquarters of the John Birch Society. Although it is most likely that all of those bits of circumstantial evidence have innocent explanations, none has yet been explained.

e. Although Ruby did not witness the motorcade through Dallas, he may have had a prior interest in the President's visit. A November 20 edition of the Fort Worth Telegram showing the President's proposed route through Fort Worth, and the November 20 edition of the Dallas Morning News showing the President's route through Dallas, were found in Ruby's car on November 24.

f. On November 16 Jack Ruby met at the Carousel Club with Bertha Cheek, sister of Mrs. Earlene Roberts, manager of Lee Oswald's rooming house. Mrs. Cheek said that she and Ruby discussed her lending Ruby money to open a new night club.

Ruby was not questioned about this matter. On November 20, 1963, a woman, who may be identical to Earlene Roberts, was reported to be in San Antonio at the time of President Kennedy's visit. The possible identification of Mrs. Roberts in San Antonio has not been checked out. In addition, the link formed by Mrs. Roberts between Oswald and Ruby is buttressed in some measure by the fact that one of Ruby's strippers dated a tenant of the Beckley Street rooming house during the tenancy of Lee Oswald. We have previously suggested the theory that Ruby and Mrs. Cheek could have been involved in Cuban arms sales of which Oswald gained knowledge through his efforts to infiltrate the anti-Castro Cubans. Our doubts concerning the real interest of Mrs. Cheek in Jack Ruby stem from the fact that one of her four husbands was a convicted felon and one of her friends was a police officer who married one of Ruby's strip-tease dancers. We have suggested that Ruby might have killed Oswald out of fear that Oswald might implicate Ruby and his friends falsely or not in an effort to save his own life. ~~Worthwhile thus, neither Oswald's Cuban interests in Dallas nor Ruby's Cuban activities have been adequately explored.~~

g. Ruby made or attempted to make contacts on November 22 and 23 with persons, known and unknown, who could have been co-conspirators. Ruby was visited in Dallas from November 21 to November 24, 1963 by Lawrence Meyers of Chicago. Meyers had visited Ruby two weeks previously. Ruby also made a long distance call shortly after the President's death to Alex Gruber in Los Angeles. Gruber had visited Ruby about the same time as Meyers in early November. Both Gruber and Meyers give innocent explanations. Meyers claims he was in Dallas enjoying life with a "dumb but accommodating broad." Gruber claims Ruby called to say he would not mail a dog that day, as he had promised to do. Finally between 11:35 p.m. and 12 midnight, Saturday, November 23, Ruby made a series of brief long distance phone calls culminating with a call to entertainer Breck Wall at a friend's house in Galveston. Wall claims Ruby called to compliment him for calling off his (Wall's) act at the Adolphus Hotel in Dallas. Background checks have not been made on these persons.

h. ~~Dominant, we believe that the possibility exists based on evidence already available, that Oswald was involved in dealings with elements who might have had connections abroad.~~ The existence of such dealings can only be surmised since the present investigation has not focused on that area.

3. We suggest that these matters cannot be left "hanging in the air." They must either be explored further or a firm decision must be made not to do so supported by stated reasons for the decision. As a general matter, we think the investigation deficient in these respects:

    (1) Substantial time-segments in Ruby's daily routine from September 26 to November 22 have not been accounted for.

    (2) About 46 persons who saw Ruby from November 22 to November 24 have not been questioned by staff members, although there are FBI reports of interviews with all these people.

    (3) <u>Persons who have been interviewed because of known associations with Ruby generally have not been investigated themselves so that their truthfulness can be evaluated.</u> The FBI reports specifically do not attempt evaluation. The exception has been that where the FBI has been given incriminating evidence against Ruby, it has made further investigation to determine whether others might also be implicated with Ruby. In every case where there was some evidence implicating others, those other persons were interviewed and denied the incriminating allegations. Further investigation has not been undertaken to resolve the conflicts.

    (4) Much of our knowledge of Ruby comes from his friends Andrew Armstrong, Ralph Paul, George Senator, and Larry Crafard. Investigations have not been undertaken to corroborate their claims.

4. Specific Investigative Recommendations

    a. We should obtain photos of all property found on Ruby's person, in his car, or at his home or clubs, now in possession of the Dallas District Attorney. We already have photos of Ruby's address books, but no other items have been photographed or delivered to the Commission. These items include the H. L. Hunt literature and newspapers mentioned in paragraphs 3d and 3e.

b. We should conduct staff interviews or take depositions with respect to Ruby's Cuban activities of the following persons:

1. Robert Ray McKeown. Ruby contacted McKeown in 1959 in connection with the sale of jeeps to Cuba. The objective of an interview or deposition of McKeown would be to obtain information on possible contacts Ruby would have made after 1959 if his interest in armament sales continued.

ii. Nancy Perrin. Perrin claims she met with Ruby three times in 1961 concerning refugee smuggling and arms sales. She says she can identify the house in Dallas where meetings took place. Perrin now lives in Boston. Ruby admits he was once interested in the sale of jeeps, at least, to Cuba.

c. [redacted] We should obtain reports from the CIA concerning Ruby's associations. The CIA has been requested to provide a report based on a memorandum delivered to them March 12, 1964 concerning Ruby's background, including his possible Cuban activities during July and August or September 1963.

d. We should obtain reports from the FBI based on requested investigation of allegations suggesting that Earlene Roberts was in San Antonio on November 21.

e. The Commission should take the testimony of the following persons for the reasons stated:

i. Hyman Rubenstein

Eva Grant

Earl Ruby

All are siblings of Jack Ruby. Hyman is the oldest child and presumably will be the best witness as to family history. He talked to Jack on November 22, reportedly visited Jack the week before the assassination, and participated in Ruby's twist board venture. Eva lived with Jack for 3 years in California prior to World War II, induced Jack to come to Dallas in 1947, and managed the Vegas Club for Jack in Dallas from 1959 to 1963. Earl was a travelling salesman with Jack from 1941-1943; a business partner 1946-1947, and made phone calls before November 22, 1963 and afterwards which require explanations.

ii. Henry Wade. This person can testify to the development of the testimony by Sgt. Dean and Det. Archer against Ruby and of seeing Ruby on November 22 in the Police Department building.

iii. Jack Ruby

f. We should take the depositions of the following persons for the reasons stated:

i. Tom Howard. This person is one of Ruby's original attorneys, and is reported to have been in the police basement a few minutes before Oswald was shot and to have inquired if Oswald had been moved. He filed a writ of habeas corpus for Ruby about one hour after the shooting of Oswald. He could explain these activities and possibly tell us about the Ruby trial. We should have these explanations.

ii. FBI Agent Hall. This person interviewed Ruby for 2½ hours on November 24 beginning at approximately 12 noon. His report is contradictory to Sgt. Dean's trial testimony. He also interviewed Ruby on December 21, 1963.

iii. Seth Kantor. This person was interviewed twice by the FBI and persists in his claim that he saw Ruby at Parkland Hospital shortly before or after the President's death was announced. Ruby denies that he was ever at Parkland Hospital. We must decide who is telling the truth, for there would be considerable significance if it were concluded that Ruby is lying. Should we make an evaluation without seeing Kantor ourselves?

iv. Bill DeMar. This person claims to have seen Oswald at the Carousel Club prior to November 22, and this rumor perhaps more than any other has been given wide circulation. Should we evaluate DeMar's credibility solely on the basis of FBI reports?

g. The FBI should re-interview the following persons for the purposes stated:

i. **Max Gruber.** To obtain personal history to establish original meeting and subsequent contacts with Ruby; to obtain details of visit to Dallas in November 1963, including where he stayed, how long, who saw him, etc. The FBI should also check its own files on Gruber.

ii. **Lawrence Meyers** (Same as Gruber)

iii. **Ken Dowe.** (KLIF reporter) To ascertain how he happened to first contact Ruby on November 22 or 23; (Ruby provided information to KLIF concerning the location of Chief Curry), and whether KLIF gave any inducements to Ruby to work for it on the weekend of November 22-24.

iv. **Rabbi Silverman.** To establish when Silverman saw Ruby at the Synagogue and obtain names of other persons who may have seen Ruby at the Synagogue on November 22 and 23. Silverman states that he saw Ruby at the 8 p.m. service on November 22 and at the 9 a.m. service on November 23; but both of these services lasted at least two hours and we do not know whether Ruby was present for the entire services. Silverman (and others) could "place" Ruby, or fail to do so, during critical hours.

v. **Mickey Ryan** (Same as Gruber plus employment in Dallas.)

vi. **Breck Wall.** This person was an entertainer at the Adolphus Hotel, Dallas, at the time of President Kennedy's assassination. Ruby called him in Galveston at 11:47 p.m. Saturday, November 23, 1963. He also visited Ruby at the County Jail. A background check should be conducted as to this person.

vii. **Andrew Armstrong, Bruce Carlin, Karen Bennett Carlin, Curtis Laverne Craford, Ralph Paul, George Senator.**

These six persons were deposed at length because of their friendship with Ruby, familiarity with Ruby's personal and business life, and contacts with Ruby on November 22, 23, and 24. In general, each has professed to have had no knowledge of Ruby's activities during those three days.

Andrew Armstrong was very active in the operation of the Carousel and worked closely with Ruby for 18 months. His deposition covers Ruby's activities and emotional state generally and particularly several hours on November 22 and 23. A background check should be conducted as to this person and selected parts of his testimony should be checked out to test his veracity.

Karen and Bruce Carlin were the recipients of a $25 money order bought by Ruby approximately 5 minutes before Ruby shot Oswald. Marguerite Oswald testified that she believed she knew Karen Carlin. Background checks should be conducted on the Carlins.

Crafard fled Dallas unexpectedly on Saturday morning November 23. Although we tend to believe his explanation, we believe a background check on him plus verification of some of his activities on November 23 are warranted.

Paul is Ruby's business partner. A background check should be conducted as to him and his telephone calls during November should be checked out.

George Senator, Ruby's roommate, alleged by Crafard to be a homosexual, claims not to have seen Ruby except at their apartment Sunday morning and for a few hours early Saturday morning. Senator's background and own admitted activities on November 22, 23, and 24 should be verified.

5. Other areas of Ruby Investigation which are not complete:

   a. [redacted]

   [redacted]

   [redacted]

iii. After the depositions of Nancy Perrin, Robert McKeown, and Sylvia Odio have been taken, further investigation may be necessary with respect to ~~Ruby's Cuban associations.~~

b. Ruby's notebooks contain numerous names, addresses, and telephone numbers. Many of these persons have either not been located or deny knowing Ruby. We believe further investigation is appropriate in some instances; however, we have not yet evaluated the reports now on hand.

c. We have no expert evidence as to Ruby's mental condition; however, we will obtain transcripts of the psychiatric testimony at the Ruby trial.

6. Other Investigative Suggestions. ~~We have suggested that [illegible] evidentiary material have been utilized elsewhere.~~

~~Radio tapes, movie film, recordings.~~ Two Dallas radio stations tape recorded every minute of air time on November 22, 23, and 24. We have obtained these radio tapes for all except a portion of November 24, and the tapes include a number of interviews with key witnesses in the Oswald area. In addition, the tapes shed considerable light on the manner in which Dallas public officials and federal agents conducted the investigation and performed in public view. We believe that similar video tapes and movie films should be obtained from ABC, CBS, NBC, UPI, and Movietone News, and relevant portions should be reviewed by staff members. Wherever witnesses appear on these films who have been considered by the Commission in preparing its report, a copy of such witnesses' appearance should be made a part of the Commission records by introducing them in evidence. If one person were directed to superintend and organize this effort, we believe it could be done without unreasonable expenditures of Commission time and money.

~~Hotel and motel registrations, airline passenger manifests, and emigration-immigration records.~~

Copies of Dallas hotel and motel registrations and airline manifests to and from Dallas should be obtained for the period September 29 to December 1, 1963. Similarly, Emigration and Immigration records should be obtained for the period October 1, 1963 to January 1, 1964. We believe that these records may provide a useful tool as new evidence develops after the Commission submits its report. We do not suggest that these records necessarily be examined by the Commission staff at the present time. But, for example, it is likely that in the future, persons will come forward who will claim to have been in Dallas during the critical period and who will claim to have important information. These records may serve to confirm or refute their claims.

LEHubert/smh
cc: Mr. Hubert

10. HSCA Layout of Dallas City Hall Basement

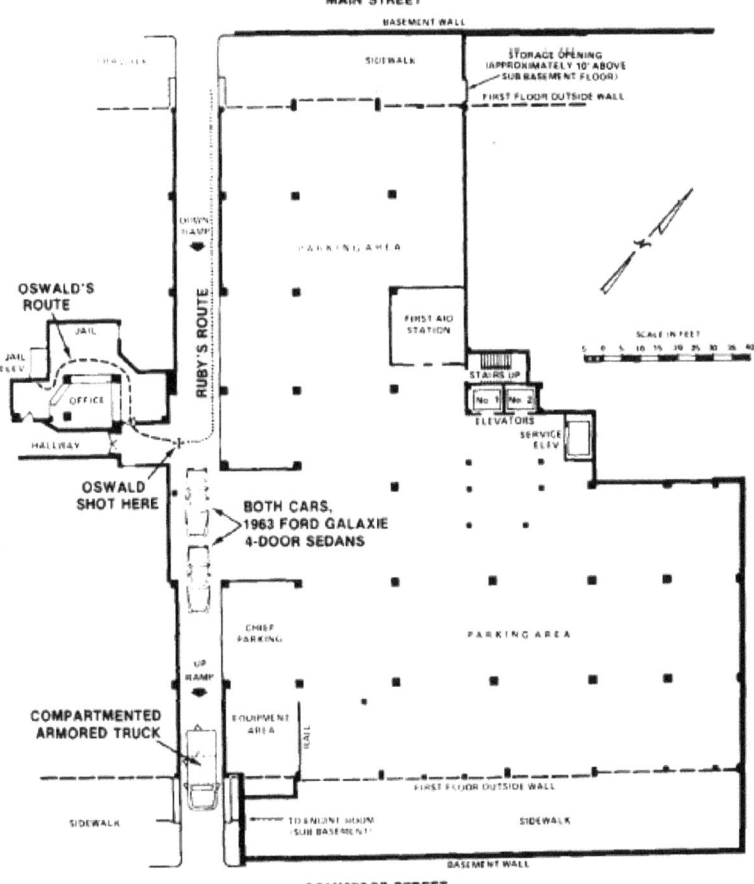

INDEX

, Ruth, 96
Adams, Robert, 12
Alexander, Steven, 57 - 58, 111, 138, 153, 154, 157, 194
Anderson, Kenneth K., 159
'Angel', 25, 36
Applin, George, 240 - 241
Archer, Don Ray, 163, 187, 191, 193, 201, 206, 220 - 221, 223, 225 - 228, 230 - 231, 233, 236, 288, 290, 315, 324, 335
Armstrong, Andrew, 241, 247
Armstrong, John, 26, 300, 317 - 319, 331, 338
Arnett, Charles Oliver, 64 - 65, 70, 150, 157, 163, 172 - 174, 202, 283
Arnold, Carolyn, 29
Aynesworth, Hugh, 149
Baker, Marrion, 32, 299 - 300
Banister, Guy, 24 - 25
Barnes, Gene, 111, 134 - 135
Bartes, Frank, 25
Batchelor, Charles, 89, 152 - 153, 163, 174 - 175, 186, 221, 283
Beaty, Buford, 105, 163, 190
Beavers, William R., 273
Beck, E.R., 185, 260 - 261
Beckham, Thomas, 25
Beers, Jack, 53, 58, 110 - 111, 127, 137 - 138, 185, 189 - 193, 195 - 196, 204, 329
Belin, David, 42
Belli, Melvin, 264, 289
Benton, Nelson, 111, 121, 144, 175
Biden, Joe, 44

Bieberdorf, Fred, 95, 176, 207 - 214, 216 - 218, 232, 236 - 237, 287, 307, 314
Blake, Gene, 111, 134, 141 - 142
Bleau, Paul 26
Bleckman, Isadore 'Izzy', 56 - 58, 111, 121, 137, 185, 191, 195, 329
Bledsoe, Mary, 32 - 33, 300
Boggs, Hale, 75
Brantley, D.G., 125 - 126, 163,
Bringuier, Carlos, 25
Brock, Alvis R., 65, 96 - 97, 154, 156 - 157, 159, 171 - 174, 207, 255, 283, 285, 306
Brockway, James D., 65, 158, 163
Brown, Charles W., 160, 185, 188, 260 - 261
Brown, Joe B., 266
Brown, Walt, 76
Brunner, Fred, 265
Burgess, D.L., 125, 163, 218
Burroughs, Butch, 39
Burton, T.R., 159, 173
Butler, George, 140, 174, 291, 317, 319
Cabell, Earle, 61, 223
Campbell, Vernon C., 163
Campisi, Joseph, 265
Capps, Arthur W., 65, 158
Carlin, Bruce, 248, 309
Carlin, Karen, 67, 248 - 251, 285, 295, 308
Carroll, Maurice, 110 - 111, 113, 115 - 124, 127, 131, 138, 147, 185, 190, 295, 329
Cason, Frances, 95, 216

Castro, Fidel, 23 - 24, 29, 35
Chabot, Tom: or Colbert, Tom, 176
Chambers, W.E., 125, 163, 202
Clardy, Barnard S., 163, 206, 221, 224, 226 - 231, 288, 290, 324, 335
Coleman, Kay, 245
Coleman, Kirk, 31
Combest, Billy S., 163, 189 - 190, 192 - 194, 201 - 203, 215, 287, 291
Connally, John B., 2, 4 - 6, 28, 35, 41, 53
Connally, Nellie, 4, 115
Cooper, Roy, 33
Cornwall, F.I., 62
Costner, Kevin, 298
Cox, Bill, 241, 327
Cox, Roland A., 65, 158
Crafard, Larry, 241, 245
Craig, A.B., 65, 163
Craig, Roger, 34, 300, 302
Crenshaw, Charles, 54, 218
Croy, Kenneth, 65, 158, 163, 182, 190, 195, 202, 291, 312 - 313, 318 - 319, 331
Crull, Elgin, 61
Crump, R.L., 151
Curry, Jesse, 50, 60 - 61, 64, 73, 80 - 81, 83 - 85, 89 - 90, 107 - 109, 112 - 113, 120, 124, 133, 152 - 153, 158, 175, 186, 222, 225, 246 - 247, 250, 261, 282 - 284, 286, 289, 292, 297, 305 - 306, 311, 316 - 317, 322, 324, 333
Cutchshaw, Wilbur J., 70, 125, 163, 166 - 167, 169, 188, 203, 208, 215, 292
Dane, Stan, 31
Daniels, Napoleon, 95, 106, 177 - 181, 321
Darnell, James, 31 - 32

Davidson, James, 55, 101, 111, 119, 127, 187, 206, 220, 315, 329
Davis, Robert T., 65, 157
Dawson, Harold, 163
de Mohrenschildt, George, 20
Dean, Patrick T., 70, 153, 155 - 157, 159, 171, 173 - 176, 183, 222 - 223, 225 - 230, 233, 235, 252 - 254, 265, 283, 286, 288, 291, 293, 306 - 307, 311, 315 - 317, 319, 321 - 324, 335
Decker, Bill, 81 - 83, 86 - 90, 152, 257 - 258, 261 - 262, 267, 283, 289
DeLaune, Gary, 111, 138, 194, 196
Dement, Nolan, 95, 105 - 106
Dhority, Charles N., 57, 128, 131, 139 -140, 160, 163, 185, 187 - 188, 196 - 199, 201, 205, 216 - 217, 224, 259 - 260, 287, 313
Dietrich, Edward C., 152
DiEugenio, James, 26
Douglass, James, 40
Doyle, Greg, 223
Droby, C.A., 278
Dulles, Allen, 5, 12, 20, 75, 320
Duncan, Lowell 'Jay', 111, 139
Duncan, William 'Glen', 111, 139, 244
Edwards, Geoff, 111, 113, 144
Eisenhower, Dwight D., 17
Ekdahl, John, 13
English, J.B., 56, 111, 127, 195
Erwin, D.K., 159
Espinosa, Melba, 105
Fenley, Bob, 111, 127, 196
Ferguson, Warren, 55, 111, 127
Ferrie, David, 25, 302
Ferris, M.E., 159
Fleming, Harold J., 152
Flusche, Don, 178 - 179, 323
Fonda, Henry, 118 - 119

Ford, Gerald, 42, 269 - 270
Foreman, Percy, 264
Forrest, Helen, 34
Fowler, Clayton, 273
Fox, L.L., 159
Frazier, Buell, 12, 29
Frazier, William, 83 - 84, 86, 88 - 89, 282, 296
Fritz, J.W., 34, 51 - 52, 55, 61, 65 - 67, 80 - 82, 89, 109, 116, 119 - 120, 128, 135, 140 - 141, 160, 163, 185 - 188, 191, 217, 222, 225, 231 - 233, 235, 242, 246 - 247, 257 - 259, 282, 285 - 286, 288, 292, 294, 305, 311, 313, 317, 324 - 325
Fuqua, Harold, 95 - 96, 98 - 102, 153 - 154, 168, 178, 207, 211, 251 - 252, 284, 307, 311
Gans, Curtis, 111, 177
Garrison, Jim, 25, 43, 149, 238 - 239
Goin, Don, 152, 174
Goldstein, Rubin, 223 - 224
Goldwater, Barry, 1
Golz, Earl, 240 - 241
Goolsby, C., 163, 165 - 167
Grammer, Billy, 83 - 86, 316
Grant, Eva, 239 - 240
Graves, L.C., 51 - 52, 55, 120, 160, 163, 186 - 187, 189, 191, 196 - 197, 201, 203 - 204, 213 - 218, 235, 258, 260, 286 - 287, 292
Greeson, C.A., 163
Gregory, Thomas R., 159
Griffin, Burt, 165 - 166, 186, 252 - 254, 321 - 322, 335
Haake, K.H., 223, 226
Haddad, Ed, 111, 134, 142
Haire, Bernard, 40
Hall, C. Ray, 230 - 231, 236
Hall, Loran, 25
Hall, Marvin 'Bert', 152, 174

Hankal, Robert L., 111, 127, 144, 190, 213, 216
Hardin, Michael, 95, 215 - 216
Harkness, D.V., 7
Harrison, Oliver W., 65, 158
Harrison, William J. 'Blackie', 56, 146, 161, 163 - 169, 175, 185, 193 - 194, 196, 199, 203 - 204, 206, 220, 235, 284, 294, 307 - 309, 312 - 313, 316, 319 - 321, 323 - 324, 335
Hart, Gary, 42
Hart, H.M., 62
Hatley, H.L., 159
Herndon, Bell, 273 - 275
Hibbs, Warren E., 159
Hill, Gladwin, 111, 133, 141 - 142
Holly, Harold J., 65, 158, 172, 295
Holmes, E.L., 273
Hoover, J. Edgar, 83, 109, 335
Hopkins, J.R., 65, 157
Howard, Tom, 102 -106, 230 - 231, 235, 263 - 264, 278 - 279, 294, 310, 315
Hubert, Leon, 73 - 74, 88, 100 - 101, 178, 209, 211, 224, 257 - 261, 335
Huffaker, Robert, 111, 127, 138, 154 - 155, 174 - 175, 196
Hughes, David, 111, 229, 288, 315 - 316
Hunt, J.C., 65, 157, 159
Hunter, Bill, 278 - 279
Hutchinson, J.D., 163
Inbau, Fred E., 274
Jackson, Bob, 52, 58, 110 - 111, 127, 137 - 138, 161, 194, 196, 199, 201, 329
Jez, Leonard E., 158
Joannides, George, 43
Johnson, Lyndon B., 2, 5, 75, 267 - 268, 270, 334

Johnston, Frank B., 57, 111, 127, 191, 193 - 194, 197, 200
Johnston, James P., 40
Jones, Orville A., 62, 70, 161, 163, 188, 233
Jones, Wilford, 95, 106
Kaiser, Richard Wood, 121
Kamp, Bart, 31, 46, 66, 80, 299,
Kantor, Seth, 111, 127, 193 - 94, 197, 240, 250, 317, 335
Kasten, Jerome, 65, 157
Kaufman, Ferd, 241
Kaufman, Stanley, 263 - 264
Kelley, Thomas J., 222
Kelly, Edward, 95, 154, 207, 254
Kennedy Jr. John F., 246
Kennedy, Caroline, 224, 246, 276
Kennedy, Jacqueline, 2 - 3, 224, 277
Kennedy, John F., 1 - 7, 11, 13, 20 - 31, 33, 35 - 38, 40 - 44, 46, 53, 59, 61, 80, 88, 110, 148 - 150, 159, 221 - 222, 224, 229, 232, 237, 239, 241, 244, 246, 249, 264, 266 - 267, 269 - 270, 277, 279, 281 - 282, 289, 298 - 299, 301 - 303, 317, 325, 327, 332 - 334, 337
Kennedy, Robert F., 41, 330, 337
Kerr, Jim, 109
Khrushchev, Nikita, 17, 35
Kilduff, Malcolm, 7, 240
King Jr., Martin Luther, 41, 43, 337
King, Glen, 125, 163, 206, 220
King, Otis H. 'Karl', 111, 132 - 133
Knox, Earl, 179
Koethe, Jim, 278 - 279
Kriss, Harry M., 65, 158, 163, 197
Labro, Philippe, 246
Lane, Doyle, 95, 249, 285, 311
Lane, Mark, 75, 149

Leavelle, James R., 51 - 52, 55, 70, 120, 138, 160, 163, 187, 189, 193, 196 - 197, 201 - 203, 215 - 216, 256 - 261, 286 - 287, 315
LeDoux, Ed, 31
'Leopoldo', 25, 36 - 37
Levine, Ken, 144
Lewis, Carroll G., 163, 171, 176
Lord, Bill, 111, 133
Lowery, Roy Lee, 125, 163, 167 - 168, 203
Lumpkin, George, 102, 153, 163
Lunday, R.H., 159
Machariella, Hank, 111, 144
Mailer, Norman, 11
Manchester, William, 2, 60
Mann, Tedd, 111, 134 - 135
Marks, J.E., 151
Martin, Frank M., 167
Martin, Jim H., 278 - 279, 296, 310
Maxey, Billy Joe, 176, 180, 286
Mayo, Logan W., 65, 158
McBride, Joseph, 9
McCain, J.C., 65, 157
McCloy, John J., 5
McCoy, Ben, 65, 151, 157, 172 - 174
McCoy, C.C., 82 - 83, 86 - 88, 296
McDonald, D.J., 65, 157
McGaghren, P.G., 62
McGarry, Terence, 111, 130, 132
McGee, Homer Lee, 103 - 104, 125 - 126, 163
McKinzie, Louis, 95, 97 - 99, 254
McKnight, Gerald, 76
McMillon, Thomas D., 163, 188 - 189, 192, 194, 203 - 204, 206, 220 - 221, 223, 225 - 231, 233, 288, 290, 324, 335
McWatters, Cecil, 32 - 33
Meagher, Sylvia, 75 - 76
Mellen, Joan, 26
Mercer, Bill, 80, 302

Mercer, Julia Anne, 237 - 238, 302
Merrell, Barney, 65, 151, 158, 163, 182, 291
Miller, Johnny, 166
Miller, Louis D., 163, 165 - 166, 168 - 169, 203, 205, 284, 294, 315 - 316, 319, 323 - 324, 336,
Milton-Jones, Roy, 33
Molina, Ben, 111, 144
Mondale, Walter, 42
Montgomery, FNU 65,157
Montgomery, Lesley D., 51, 55, 120, 157, 160, 163, 187, 203, 258, 260, 286
Moore, Elmer, 269
Morley, Jefferson, 43,
Muller, O.S., 151
Murphy, Sean, 31
Nagell, Richard Case, 25, 36
Nelson, Ronald C., 156, 163, 283
Newman, William J., 65, 157, 172, 174, 182 - 184, 295
Newnam, John, 239 - 240, 296
Newsom, Milt, 82 - 83, 86 - 89
Newton, Johnny F., 95, 105
O'Leary, Jeremiah 'Jerry', 111 - 113, 115 - 123, 130 - 131, 199, 295
Oakes, Oliver, 111, 177
Odio, Silvia, 36 - 37
Odum, Bardwell, 120
Olsen, Harry, 244 - 245, 295, 327 - 328
Oswald, June, 19, 26
Oswald, 'Leon', 36 - 37
Oswald, Marguerite, 13, 279
Oswald, Marina, 11, 18 - 19, 21 - 22, 26, 29, 37, 149, 279
Oswald, Robert, 14
Oswald Sr., Robert Edward Lee, 13
Paine, Ruth, 11 - 12, 20, 302
Pappas, Ike, 109, 111, 115 - 124, 127, 131, 137, 140, 145, 161,

185, 189 - 191, 194, 197, 199, 243, 295, 329
Pasczalek, Gene, 111, 144, 174
Pate, D.L., 158
Paterni, Paul, 222
Patterson, Bobby G., 156, 283
Payne, Darwin, 111
Pelou, Francois, 111, 127, 197
Pena, Orestes, 25
Pennington, James, 34
Perry, Malcolm, 6 - 7, 269
Pettit, Tom, 109 - 111, 127, 144 - 145, 147, 161, 175, 190, 198, 329
Phenix, George, 56, 58, 111, 127, 174, 191, 198
Pic, John Edward, 13
Pic, Margaret, 13
Pierce, Edward, 93, 95 - 96, 98, 254
Pierce, Rio S., 153, 155, 175 - 176, 179 - 181, 184 - 186, 228, 256, 286, 323
Pitts, Elnora, 248
Powers, Gary, 17 - 18
Prusakov, Marina Nikolayevna. *See* Marina Oswald
Putnam, James A., 69 - 70, 84, 153, 156, 171, 176, 180, 188, 253, 254
Rabun, Henry, 111, 137, 154 - 155
Ramsey, James K., 163, 214 - 215, 218, 292
Randle, Linnie Mae, 12
Rankin, J. Lee, 269, 321
Raz, Jerry, 159
Reid, John E., 274
Revill, Jack, 62, 248, 320
Reynolds, H. Baron, 104, 163, 193
Rheinstein, Fred, 111, 138, 245 - 247
Rhinehart, Bert, 111, 144
Richey, Warren, 111, 248, 309

Riggs, Alfreadia, 95, 98 - 102, 153 - 154, 168, 178, 207, 211, 251 - 252, 284, 307, 311
Ripley, Anthony 'Tony', 111, 121, 140 - 141
Roberts, Earlene, 38
Robertson Jr., Vic, 242
Robinson, Marvin, 33
Rubenstein, Hyman, 242
Ruby, Earl, 264
Ruby, Jack, 53, 55 – 59, 61 - 62, 64, 66 – 69, 71–75, 77, 84 – 86, 94, 99, 103 – 4, 113, 117, 122 - 123, 125 – 26, 130 - 133, 135, 139, 141, 43, 144 – 46, 148, 161, 166, 172, 176, 179, 181– 82, 184 – 85, 191 – 206, 208 – 9, 212– 16, 219 - 231, 233, 235 – 51, 255 – 275, 277 - 279, 282, 285, 287 - 296, 298, 301–304, 307 – 313, 315 – 17, 319 - 329, 333, 335, 337
Rushing, Ray, 248
Russell, Dick, 26
Russell, Richard, 75
Schweiker, Richard, 42
Senator, George, 245, 248, 278 - 279, 299, 308 - 310
Servance, John, 95, 254
Seymour, Billy, 25
Shaw, Clay, 25
Shelley, Bill, 31
Siegel, Evelyn, 14
Simpson, Peggy, 111, 130 - 133, 175
Sims, Richard M., 242
Sisco, Paul, 111, 142 - 143, 177 - 178, 247
Slack, Willie, 163
Slocum, Jerry D., 95, 105
Smith, David F., 111, 127, 145
Smith, Joe M., 7
Smith, Johnnie, 111, 248

Solomon, James M., 151
Sorrels, Forrest, 186, 221 - 227, 233, 235, 263, 288, 321
Sosin, Milt, 111, 144
Spears, George Riley, 134 - 135
Specter, Arlen, 269, 273
Springer, G.K. 176
Standard, James N., 111, 143
Steele, Don Francis, 160
Stephens, Ivan R., 163, 215
Stevenson, Adlai, 3
Stevenson, M.W., 62, 93, 152 - 153, 163, 166, 175, 186, 286
Stone, Oliver, 43, 147, 239,
Suits, Donald, 65, 157, 163, 182
Sullivan, Coley, 103
Summers, Anthony, 26
Swatalin, Richard E., 51, 55, 120, 163, 187 - 188, 198, 286
Tague, James, 5, 35
Talbert, Cecil, 89, 128, 153, 155, 173, 282
Tankersley, John, 111, 121, 124 - 127, 175
Tasker, Harry T., 142 - 143, 178 - 180
Taylor, L.C., 158
Thomas, Albert, 2
Thornton, Robert, 111, 127, 139, 177, 198
Timmons, David, 111, 121, 124 - 127, 175
Tippit, J.D., 5, 8 - 9, 13, 28, 38 - 39, 41, 59, 65, 80, 148, 229, 281, 298, 301, 303, 318 - 319, 327 - 328
Tolbert, Gerald L., 159
Tonahill, Joe, 264, 272 - 273, 275, 277, 327
Tropolis, George, 150
Truly, Roy, 12, 65, 300
Trump, Donald, 44, 333

Turner, Jimmie, 56, 73 - 75, 111, 121, 125 - 127, 182, 256
Van Cleave, I.F., 163
Vanderslice, Robert Murray, 239
Vaughn, Roy, 99, 102, 156, 158, 176 - 181, 229, 283, 286, 320 - 321, 323
Venso, Homer, 56, 111, 127, 198
Wade, Henry, 107, 243 - 244, 247, 322
Wagner, R.C., 163
Waldo, Thayer, 108 - 109, 111, 139 - 141, 247, 291, 317
Walker, Edwin A., 21 - 22
Walker, Ira N., 111, 248
Wall, Breck, 248
Warren, Earl, 5, 266 - 273
Watkins, Richard.A., 158, 176
Watson, James C., 163
Webster, Robert, 18 - 19
Weisberg, Harold, 75
Westbrook, William R. 62, 151, 317 - 320, 331
Whaley, William, 33
White, T.F., 20
Wiegman, Dave, 31, 299
Wiggins, Woodrow, 161, 163, 187, 215
Wise, Marvin L. 159
Wise, Wes, 111, 246 - 247
Wolfe, Harold, 216
Woodfield, William Read, 221
Woods, James, 273
Worley, Gano E. 65, 156 - 157, 171 - 174, 207, 254, 283, 285, 306
Worthington, Peter, 111, 135 - 136, 190, 198
X, Malcolm, 41, 337
Yarborough, Ralph, 2
Zoppi, Tony, 111

www.ingramcontent.com/pod-product-compliance
Lightning Source LLC
Chambersburg PA
CBHW041302240426
43661CB00010B/990